Enjoy God's wondrous handiwork
Alaska, where they assisted missio⊥
ning errands, and cleaning had new meanings for volunteers and career
missionaries alike. As the eyes of your heart are opened, you just may realize God is calling you, too. What will you say?

> —Mary Hiebert, Mission Service Corps Association Volunteerism Director
> LifeCall Missions Advocate, Baptist General Convention of Texas

Yes, this grandma went as an itinerant missionary—serving in a wide variety of ministries and locations. She is somewhat typical (with distinctive
differences, as you will see) of many Mission Service Corps missionaries—serving when and where the Lord called them. It's a great narrative of
the Lord and a missionary combining to "tell the story" to many who
never have heard. May He call forth many more grandmas like this one.

> —Sam Pearis, Retired Director, Mission Service Corps
> Baptist General Convention of Texas

For the ultimate road trip on the North American continent without pur-
chasing one gallon of gas, travel with "Grandma" from Texas to Alaska!
Places and experiences are vividly described, all in the context of sensing
the wonders of God's creative work. Having traveled some of this route, I
was able to relive my own adventures.

> —Robert Raus, consultant, Resort and Leisure Ministries,
> Baptist General Convention of Texas
> Coordinator of Direct Ministries, Campers on Mission of Texas

Finding and following God's will is a challenge for many in our day.
Grandma's Ultimate Road Trip will help you find God's hand at work in
the life of one pilgrim on life's journey. Dr. Carol Weishampel guides you
along life's road discovering and experiencing God's direction in a beautiful narrative of her journey to fulfill a life goal. *Road Trip* is a must-read
for those who feel that God's call on their lives has somehow been negated
because of choices or circumstances.

> —Cecil Deadman, Missions Specialist
> LifeCall Missions, Baptist General Convention of Texas

Grandma's Ultimate Road Trip is a testimony to God's faithfulness (Jer.
29:11). Carol shares that no matter someone's age or experience, God has
a plan for every person's life. He desires to use and will use anyone who
obeys His leadership. This book reminds that whenever and however God
leads, He will provide.

> —Michael R. Procter, Director of State Missions and Men's Ministries
> Alaska Baptist Convention

Published by
Hannibal Books
PO Box 461592
Garland, Texas 75046-1592
Copyright Carol Weishampel 2006
All Rights Reserved
Printed by in the United States of America
by Lightning Source
Cover design by Greg Crull
Except where otherwise indicated, all Scripture taken from the Holy Bible,
New International Version, copyright 1973, 1978, 1984
by International Bible Society
ISBN 0-929292-41-3
Library of Congress Control Number: 2006926037

TO ORDER ADDITIONAL COPIES, SEE PAGE 233

GRANDMA'S
ULTIMATE
ROAD TRIP

Retired, Rejuvenated
and Raring to Go From
TEXAS to **ALASKA**

Carol Weishampel

CAROL V. WEISHAMPEL, ED.D

✝HANNIBAL BOOKS
www.hannibalbooks.com

Contents

Dedicated
to

volunteers with Campers on Mission,
a national fellowship of Christian campers
who "share Christ as we go"

and

volunteers with Mission Service Corps,
who follow "wherever He leads"

Acknowledgments

A special thank you to—

Sam Pearis, retired director of missions, Mission Service Corps, Baptist General Convention of Texas, who introduced me to volunteer opportunities in Alaska

Wintford and Martha Haynes, Campers on Mission coordinators, North American Mission Board, Southern Baptist Convention

Foreword

As an Alaskan professional who, in my work with children, has seen the benefits of involving caring volunteers, I highly encourage people to read this book. Carol Weishampel's personal journey of volunteering at a youth recreation camp an hour north of Anchorage, AK, not only is heartwarming, it is inspiring and real! I know it's real, because many times I have been to the camp she describes. Year after year my clients have been blessed by the many helping hands of Campers on Mission—the very real people described in Carol's story. Alaska is as beautiful as she tells it—and made even more so by volunteers!

Patricia Cochran, Director of Prevention and Intervention Services
Volunteers of America, AK, Inc.

Preface

In Pursuit of a Dream

Early-morning sun glinted blindingly off of the side mirrors of my 27-foot motor home. Today was a superb spring morning for traveling. Behind me Houston's triple-layered overpasses, multi-storied skyscrapers, and bumper-to-bumper traffic were a vague memory. I now was free from the constraints of mini-malls, auto dealerships, and congestion.

The gently rolling, wildflower-sprinkled landscape was brilliant with sunshine. Through my open window a fresh, sweet, spring breeze and an exhilarating sense of freedom greeted me. I relaxed my grip on the wheel and set the cruise control. Interstate 10. Due West. Then "Way up North" to ALASKA!

On this trip of a lifetime, would over-planning detract from spontaneity? A rush of adrenaline caught my breath. Had I balanced hopes and dreams with reality and ignorance? Would this trip be all I had envisioned? Would planning and preparations keep us out of trouble? This road trip would be a challenge of facing the unpre-dictable.

In amazement I laughed out loud. After imagining it for so many years, this trip actually was happening!

As I remembered, I chuckled. A year ago, my feisty, 83-year-old mother *again* sweetly stated, "You're not still thinking of driving to Alaska, are you." This was not a question.

"Yes, I am," I had asserted as defiantly as I dared. "I'm not just thinking about it. I'm planning, praying, and pinching pennies."

"Just you and Chris," she had commented, with a hint of a question.

"And my dogs." I added. "You're still invited to go with us."

"I'll let you know," she answered, as she tried to mask her lack of enthusiasm.

I was well aware of her purpose for considering accompanying us. If she could not talk me out of going, she wanted to keep an eye on me and keep me out of trouble.

Chapter 1

Planning, Praying, and Pinching Pennies

The boring expanse of straight freeway put my mind on cruise control. I began to reminisce. The year 2002 had been my target date for "The Trip." In 2002 the famous AlCan Highway, built during World War II, and I both would celebrate our 60th birthdays. What better way to change lanes on the highway of my life than to celebrate in a big way? I'd go "over-the-hill" in senior style.

Planning had consumed much time and energy, many waking hours, and even dreams at night. Long before I retired from teaching in 1998, my collection of wall maps, road atlases, travel guides, and new travel websites had excited my Gypsy gene.

I had been slow getting on the Internet information highway, but then, as I practiced, it had become no more intimidating than a Houston freeway was. I pulled up a book titles by subject, jotted down the call number, and then cruised the stacks for related titles. Good titles I checked out. Great books I bought on the Internet for greatly reduced prices.

Online I found this quote by Mark Twain: "The person who does not read has absolutely no advantage over those who can not read."

For a dime each I bought old copies of *National Geographic, Motor Home, Trailer Life*, and *Texas Highways* magazines; clipped articles; and sorted these goodies into files. I added all the free stuff that state tourist bureaus sent me. I accumulated an itinerary of places to explore and then used a road atlas to plan a route.

As my dreams became more specific, I learned that on May 1 the rates for the Alaska State Ferry on the Inside Passage increased from off-season to tourist rates. If we could leave Houston by mid-April, allowing at least two weeks to travel to Bellingham, WA, we could make the ferry before the rates went up.

Advertising photos of the ferry showed a boat that looked as though it were a cruise ship—nothing like our local ferry. Photos of icebergs, whales surfacing alongside the ferry, and glacial mountains gave me shivers of excitement. We could spend four days and three nights on board with port calls along the way from Bellingham, WA, to Skagway, AK, the northernmost port on the Inside Passage. In July I phoned with questions. The motor home would be charged according to length. As driver, I traveled free. Chris, my 12-year-old grandson, would be charged adult fare. My two Shetland Sheep dogs would travel for an additional $25 each. In September I would order tickets.

I planned to drive through the Southwest and visit the Grand Canyon and then on to Seattle. We'd take the ferry to Skagway and drive to Anchorage. Denali National Park and Fairbanks would complete our trip North. We could explore the AlCan from Fairbanks back to Dawson Creek. In Canada we'd visit the Tyrell Museum of Paleontology in Drumheller, then on to Yellowstone National Park, Dinosaur Monument, and Mesa Verde in Colorado, then back to Texas. I estimated that we'd be away from home for about three months.

I struggled to justify the expenses of such a long road trip. What a memorable way to celebrate my birthday and deny becoming a "Senior Citizen"!

Several years before I retired, I had become a volunteer with Campers on Mission, an organization sponsored by the Southern Baptist North American Mission Board. Most volunteers were retired couples who, on weeks-long projects, did construction work at churches and church camps. Chris and I were not available to be of much help, but we enjoyed what we could do.

In the summer of 2000 my brother, Alan, a Baptist pastor, began planning a mission trip into the interior of Mexico for Thanksgiving week. I asked to be allowed to go, too. The primary purpose of the trip was to construct a mission station. I doubted that we'd be much help with building. We also would take part in street evangelism through clowning. Alan was hesitant to take Chris, since he would be the only child on the trip. I felt led for both of us to participate in this experience.

Our group traveled in a car caravan through a blustery cold, wet, winter storm. The Mexican village was cold and dusty. While the men worked on construction, we women cooked and cleaned. We dressed as clowns, made balloon animals, and walked the dirt streets to attract children and adults to outdoor worship. Since he attracted kids like a magnet, Chris proved to be a valuable asset.

I had heard that participating in a mission trip would change a person's life. This trip changed the direction of mine. I realized that in order to witness, I didn't have to be a preacher. Volunteering as a servant behind the scenes was vital to the success of missions. I thanked the Lord for this opportunity to volunteer and learn.

The next April, Chris and I returned to Mexico with the group. Our Mexican friends warmly greeted us. Although we still struggled with language, we felt at home. The men continued working on the building as they sweated in the sweltering, blustery wind. We repeated street witnessing and clowning. Of course the cooking and cleaning jobs were never ending. Many nationals accepted Christ as their Savior.

The Lord was leading me to become more active as a volunteer. I contacted the Mission Service Corps directors of our local Baptist association, who suggested that I attend a four-day orientation. While at the training, I was encouraged to become an itinerant missionary, which simply means "do what you can, when you can."

During the training I expressed my desire to visit Alaska and received the name and address of the director of missions in Anchorage. I wrote immediately. I was surprised by his quick reply, which was dated the day he received my letter. We were invited to volunteer in Alaska! He asked for my resumé. He would forward my letter and resumé to the directors of two youth camps. We could volunteer at the camps and not be tourists. We could stay longer, see more, and really get a feel for Alaska. God had provided a purpose for my dream trip!

In August 2001 my brother led a commissioning service at our church and officially made me a Missions Service Corps volunteer. My daughter, Cora, sang a song titled "Go Light Your World" by Kathy Troccoli. The song is an encouragement to take your talents, trust God, and go wherever He sends.

After I retired from public school, I had taken on the job of administrator (also teacher, custodian, and bus driver) for a small Christian school. Although the weather still was hot and humid, summer officially was over in August when school started. My travels had been curtailed for a while as we prepared for classes, so I asked my friend, Brett, to check out the motor home's oil and transmission fluid.

He popped the inside hood latch, walked to the front, and reached for the front latch. I heard him curse.

"Brett! You know better!" I admonished.

"If you saw what I just saw, you'd say that, too!" he replied. "Get over here and look."

I never knew what this joker was up to, so apprehensively, I walked closer to the front end. "I don't trust you. I'm not getting any closer."

"Give me that long stick. I'm going to open the hood all the way." Up creaked the hood. A huge snakeskin stretched from one side to the other across the top of the radiator.

I jumped back, as I yelled, "Oh, brother!"

"The snakeskin goes into the breather," he explained. "Sure hope its owner's not in there some place."

"Me, too!" I agreed. "I'm so glad you're the mechanic and I'm not!"

"Get me a screwdriver and another stick. I'm goin' to take this air cleaner off." He carefully loosened several screws and with his stick pried the top off the air cleaner.

"Do you see it?"

I jumped back. "Is a snake really in there?"

"You bet it is! It's curled up under the filter. Look!"

"No way. I'll take your word for it. Now what? Start the engine and make snakeburgers?"

"I don't think so. You'd really have a mess. Get me a couple more long sticks. Really long."

Brett gingerly removed more screws while he held the air-cleaner cover down with a stick wedged over it. With his feet far back, he leaned over the grill and was ready to jump back.

I grabbed his camera from his truck and told him to pose. He didn't think I was at all funny.

"Look out!" he warned, as he lifted the cover and filter. Nothing. The snake had retreated into the air intake. With the sticks at arms' length Brett lifted the intake and shook the snake out onto the grass. It struck at the sticks and began to slither away. With one of the sticks Brett pinned its head down. To my horror he picked it up behind the head and then grabbed its tail and stretched it out. From a safe distance I took pictures.

He had captured a five-foot-long chicken snake. In the air cleaner we found leaves and dry grass. A mouse appeared to have nested in there; the snake was going after its dinner. I refused to let Chris keep it as a pet. Brett threw the irate snake over the fence and into the woods.

During meetings with my students and parents I explained my calling to volunteer in Alaska. With their agreement we scheduled a school calendar that eliminated some holidays and condensed the school year without being detrimental to the students' academics. I confirmed the last day of school to be April 11, 2002. The next morning Chris and I would be packed and ready to leave. We would allow three weeks to explore the Southwest, the Grand Canyon, and to visit a cousin in Seattle.

On September 10, 2001, I telephoned Bellingham, WA, to the Alaska Ferry System to order tickets for April 2002. I wanted the last winter ferry to Skagway, before the rates went up. I reached a phone recording. Tickets for spring travel would not go on sale until after October 15. Assured that they would not be sold out, I was content to wait.

On September 11, 2001, I was teaching in the Christian school. My daughter phoned me with news she had heard on her car radio about an explosion at the World Trade Center. I went to another room and turned on the TV. I watched, as did millions of Americans and many in foreign countries. I first was in shock and then watched in horror and fear for United States citizens and for our government. The TV image of the first attack on the twin towers was replayed. I called my high-school students in to watch with me. I thought the whole thing had been an accident.

In confusion we watched live broadcasts as the second plane hit the second tower. Smoke was discovered rising from the Pentagon. Then we saw the collapse of the towers. I prayed aloud.

I told the other teachers what little we knew. They brought the older students and joined us. In silent disbelief our students reacted as we did. Soon they had seen enough. I took them back to class. The aftershock and fear created such great tension that I could not pray aloud for my students and our country. We held hands. The kids began praying on their own. I sobbed silently. Questions. *Where is God? Is this the end of the world?* How could I answer them?

Parents began to call. I released the students whose parents wanted to retrieve them. The next day they were allowed to stay home. By Thursday most of my students had returned to class. We held small-group sessions to discuss their reactions to America in crisis and mourning. On Friday the entire school participated in President Bush's declared National Day of Prayer.

The next week we joined in the national "See You at the Pole" day, an annual event in which Christians rally around their school's flagpole to pray. Then numbness set in. I hesitated to watch the news but was more hesitant not to do so. Prayer was constant in my heart. Prayer always has been a part of my life: private, public, and collective. Now our country openly had declared the value of prayer.

What was I to do about Alaska? A third mission trip to Mexico, scheduled for October, was canceled. I felt a sense of relief that I had not committed money to the Alaska ferry. Never had I felt so uncertain about tomorrow. Living here by the Houston Ship Channel, between oil refineries to the south and chemical plants to the north, I knew we were vulnerable. *Why do we seem to pray only when we are in trouble?*

KSBJ Christian Radio, a local station, conducted talk shows, played music, and led in public prayer to address the issues in the news. The next week I drove home with KSBJ Christian music playing on my car radio. I listened intently to the announcer as he discussed Christians' reactions to the terrorist attacks.

He said, "While we play the next song, let the Lord speak to your heart about what you should do in your life."

As the music and words, "Carry your candle, run to the darkness . . ." filled the air, I choked up and tears welled. The song, titled "Go Light Your World", was the song that my daughter, Cora, had sung at my commissioning service for Mission Service Corps. Tears flowed as the song ended with the words, "Take your candle, and go light your world."

Wow! God is good! Here was the answer to my prayers. Without a doubt I knew that I was to continue to plan to go to Alaska. The volunteer assignment still was vague, but I knew He wanted us to go.

Within days I received an email from the director of missions in Anchorage. The email encouraged us to come. He invited us to stay for five months! I ordered the ferry tickets for Friday, April 26, 2002, to leave from Bellingham, WA.

By Christmas our world almost was back to normal; my plans were materializing. I added sweatsuits and warm clothing to our Christmas-gift lists. For fun I purchased a large, wooden box of games and addressed the gift to "Gus", my secret pet name for our Gulfstream motor home. The tagged package went under the tree. Chris agonized over the identity of "Gus" until I let him open the present. My mom reluctantly gave her blessing and knitted each of us a toboggan cap.

As New Year 2002 and my birthday rapidly approached, I became obsessed with plans. An email from Anchorage gave me the names of Larry and Sharon, the directors of the LaVerne Griffin Youth Camp in Wasilla.

On a huge Alaska wall map I circled the tiny town of Wasilla, 40 miles north of Anchorage. I immediately sent a letter that asked dozens of questions about our volunteer assignments. I had a nagging concern that we'd reach Alaska cold (pun intended) and have no contacts there.

My "to-do" list for January included getting rabies shots for our two Shelties—Sam and Lady. For years the dogs had traveled with me, but this would be their first time out of the country. The Alaska ferry required a health certificate that was dated no earlier than 30 days before departure, so after a through checkup, the vet arranged a return visit in April for their certificates.

Most state and national parks allow pets on leashes. Some ask for proof of vaccinations. Private parks in which we have stayed have allowed pets. Picking up after the dogs always has been in the best interest of campers and the environment, so I collected a large supply of small, plastic grocery sacks. Chris purchased new fishing equipment and a supply of hand-held electronic games.

On a warm spring day in late February, I answered the school's phone to hear, "This is Larry, LaVerne Griffin Camp."

He had received my letter, resumé, and recommendations from Anchorage. "Get on up here," he encouraged.

We would have plenty of work to do. Chris and I would be expected to work about 25 hours a week with two days off. We would be provided with RV hookups and meals on the days we worked. I knew that volunteers paid all their own transportation and living expenses except when they actually were working, so financial planning—along with prayer—had been my top priority. Larry explained that work teams would be arriving from the Lower Forty-eight in May to help with construction and pre-camp maintenance. Weekend camps were scheduled. Weeklong camps would begin in June. We would be doing a lot of cooking, housekeeping, and grounds maintenance.

Larry was friendly and informative as he answered my questions about Chris, my dogs, and the weather. He said that several feet of snow were on the ground. The 150-acre lake was solid with ice 32-inches thick. Chris would enjoy fishing when the lake thawed. I would have time to do some touring.

Larry startled me when he stated, "I'm afraid I'm not going to get to meet you when you get here."

For five years he and his wife had been directors of the camp. On the first of April they and their children were leaving to return to their original home in Florida. New directors had not been hired. Larry would leave all my information so that the new directors could contact me. I hung up the phone elated that I had talked to someone from the camp. I was apprehensive, too. *Who would be there to meet us? What if the new directors didn't need us or want us to be there?*

March roared in with winds and warmer temperatures. I stopped the newspaper to wean myself from my morning-paper habit. Much to Chris's dismay, I canceled the cable TV. We would be out of touch with electronics, so he'd better get used to no TV.

By mid-March I had our passports, medical records, the dogs' shot records, prescription medication, and "to-do" lists ready for a final checkoff. I bought film for a 35-mm camera, videotapes for a video camera, and audiotapes for a small tape recorder. I packed a used notebook computer and a small printer. I was determined to make great journal entries. Reference books filled a small overhead shelf in the RV. Maps and brochures were filed in a box.

Houston's winter was over. I packed winter clothes into plastic under-the-bed storage totes to stack in the motor home's basement. I made lists of groceries, clipped coupons, and stocked up on non-perishables. I was too excited to leave anything for the last minute. I still had no definite conformation from the camp.

In advance I paid those recurring bills that had a set payment. My friend, Wanda, would receive my mail and pay bills, such as electricity, that could fluctuate. As soon as I had an address she would forward anything important. Wanda's husband, Brett, agreed to check on my house, feed our cats, and mow the grass.

April. What a busy month. Final exams were given and graded, report cards and permanent records were completed. Graduation exercises had to be planned.

As I was completing the final packing of clothes, camping gear, and groceries, I got an email from the camp. Anna explained that she and her husband, Mickey, had been hired as the new directors. They both were Alaskans, although they had had spent the previous year in the Lower Forty-Eight. Their two children were close to Chris's age. The family had two dogs and recently lost a Sheltie to old age. We connected immediately. She concluded, "Let us know when you get to Wasilla."

I emailed back that I expected to arrive around May 1 or 2. She urged me, if I could, to bring Chris's bike. Her kids loved to ride bikes once the snow melted. They were as eager to meet us as we were to get to know them.

One last trip to the vets' office for the dogs' health certificates. Atlas and maps were packed; groceries, cash, credit cards, and all the lists were taken care of—I hoped. School was out.

We were off!

Chapter 2

On the Road at Last

Friday, April 12, 2002. Early in the morning Brett arrived to turn off the gas, turn off water to toilets and sinks, check locks and the alarm system, and to see us off.

Yes! We finally were on the road. My mom, my older kids, and friends had our tentative itinerary. I had a general idea of where we were headed and the places we'd like to visit.

Chris had not been overly excited about our trip, although he was a seasoned traveler. As long as he had hand-held games and access to food, he was reasonably happy. He had refused to get excited by my enthusiasm for our Alaskan adventure. I'd tried to get him interested in visiting the Grand Canyon and Yellowstone National Park. Not even anticipation of the ferry ride shook him out of his 12-year-old apathy. He finally admitted that he wanted to see bears and whales and to catch a salmon. And he'd like to see snow. But otherwise, "Ho hum."

I made an agreement with him. If he would not complain about seeing the things I wanted to see, I would take him to places I knew he would enjoy, such as dinosaur museums. Good behavior would guarantee him at least a dollar a day spending money besides his meager savings. Obnoxious behavior would cause money and/or electronic games to disappear. He was reminded that he was out of school in April, while his friends in public school had another six weeks before vacation.

Chris settled on the bed and was disinterested in the scenery west of Houston. The dogs found their favorite places. Lady hid under the table. Sam planted his front feet on my armrest and nuzzled my ear before he responded to "No, Sam. Down" and curled up between the front seats.

Mile after mile of eight lanes of traffic congestion bordered by mile after mile of businesses would have bored me, too, except that I was too excited about beginning "The Trip."

Small thuds and soft thunks announced things settling down. The bathroom door stayed shut, as did the overhead cabinets. I'd made sure that nothing in the cab-over would fall on my head. As we crossed the Brazos River, the traffic thinned, as did evidence of commercialism. I became contemplative. What if this trip turned out to be a disaster? Was I crazy to attempt a 10,000-mile trip in a 10-year-old motor home with a kid and two dogs? Adventures, surprises, and facing the unknown are only some of the reasons for this trip. I liked having a sense of self-reliance, with a strong dependence on faith. Unlike true pioneers of bygone days, our day-to-day survival would be in comfort. Roughing it would be boondocking—camping without hookups.

In planning this trip finances had been a very important consideration. I had a debit card, credit cards, and a stash of cash. Would we find ourselves in an emergency that I couldn't cover? Would we return to overdrafts at the bank? What about Canada? Chris called Mexican money "funny money." What kind of "funny money" would we find in Canada? At least in Mexico we had had friends on which to rely and were there for only one week at a time.

I was prepared to record our adventures with cameras, a travel-log, and a small tape recorder that I kept handy. I laughed to myself as I thought about the highway of life. As I grew up, top highway speed was 60 mph; 60 years was old. The speed limits have been raised to 65, 70, and 75 mph; so has life expectancy. *Did better roads indicate better health? Or were things the other way around?*

We approached the outskirts of Austin. Our first stop was to be an educational one for Chris, but of course I didn't tell him that. In both *Texas Parks and Wildlife* and the *Houston Chronicle's Texas* magazine I had read about the new Bob Bullock Museum of Texas History The museum, open for less than a year, presented great displays of Texas' diversity.

I was disappointed that the museum was situated near downtown, with no parking for large vehicles anywhere in the vicinity.

As I drove around and around, I finally found two adjacent, metered spaces along a side street. Chris fed quarters into two parking meters. In the hot sun we walked to the museum. Chris was interested in the displays of early Texana, so our first stop was successful.

I had planned to camp our first night at Pedernales Falls State Park. I wanted to stop early so that before dark we could explore the park. When we arrived, the parking lot was full. The tiny office was elbow-to-elbow with potential campers. All campsites had been taken by reservation only. No overflow parking was available. Astonished that this park, so far from Austin, already was booked, we continued on to Johnson City.

There, Wildflower RV Park welcomed us and presented my dogs with doggie biscuits and a note:

"Here's a little treat
For our four-legged campers
And a gentle reminder
They're not wearing Pampers."

The campground fronted a stream dammed to form a small lake. Chris happily tried his luck fishing. The dogs and I walked through the rustling grass of a meadow and listened to the evening calls of larks. Although we had no fresh fish for dinner, we cooked over an open fire while we watched the glow of the sunset change from pinks and golds to aqua and royal blue. The aroma of wood smoke was a welcome change from auto exhaust.

Saturday, April 13. My dogs have made me a morning person. They are better than an alarm clock. At 6 a.m. Sam begins, "Yip. Yip." If I try to ignore him, I get a cold nose or a furry paw on my face. I put on my trifocal glasses, tied the dogs outside, and went inside to dress. To my dismay I found one of my contact lenses broken in half in its case.

Fortunately I had brought an extra pair. I wear glasses for reading over the contacts, but without the aid of both I'm as blind as that proverbial "bat." When I have the contacts off, I use trifocal glasses. I also carry a lighted magnifying glass for fine print on maps. When I found the broken contact lens, I said to myself, *Good thing I don't believe in "bad omens."*

That first morning on the road established a routine. The dogs took me for an early walk. I disconnected the electric-cord shoreline, checked maps, and was on the road as the sun rose. Early in the morning the road was quiet and peaceful. Mockingbirds chirped and dove onto the early worm. Chris slept. Not until later would either of us be hungry enough for breakfast. To record my thoughts I took a small tape recorder from the pocket of my seat bag.

Traveling from Johnson City, birthplace of President Lyndon B. Johnson, I marveled at the vast stretches of brilliant wildflowers along the highway and in the fields. Bluebonnets predominated with orange-red Indian Paintbrush and patches of smaller varieties of flowers. The floral display was the result of a mild winter and adequate spring rain. Nearing LBJ Ranch longhorn cattle, buffalo, and whitetail deer enjoyed the spring growth.

I woke Chris for us to have a quick breakfast. After a visit to the Johnson museum, we walked to the Johnson homestead. Farm animals greeted us. Cows and goats hung over the fence for petting or to receive a treat. Chickens, ducks, turkeys scrambled out from under our feet.

Delicious smells wafted from the small, clapboard farmhouse. We followed the aroma to the kitchen door. Two women dressed in late 1800s period clothing were serving a farmer in overalls. His breakfast of salt-back, eggs, and homemade biscuits made our mouths water. The cooks explained that in a Dutch oven they were starting a venison stew. For lunch they also would cook corn bread in a skillet in the wood stove and would cook sweet potatoes, turnip greens, and field peas.

I mentioned seeing a Fifth Wheel RV trailer under nearby oak trees. The pioneers admitted that they were volunteers who enjoyed re-enactment. They would stay all summer living the life of homesteaders for visitors to experience. What fun, I thought as we walked back to the RV.

I drove west toward Fredricksburg. I was intrigued by a sign, "Wildseed Farms Market Center." Chris protested that he didn't want to see "any ole flowers." I promised him a snack when we stopped and reminded him of our agreement to try to enjoy each other's interests. The farm gate was open, but the visitors' center still was closed.

A distant rumble broke the morning stillness. Chris's attention suddenly was riveted by the arrival of several Corvettes. He jumped outside and watched in admiration as antique and brand-new Corvettes arrived to park around the perimeter of the huge parking lot. I coaxed him to go and talk to one of the drivers to find out what was happening. Suddenly shy, he balked. I announced that I was going to inquire about the cars. He could go with me or not. Chris timidly followed me to the nearest cool car—a candy-apple red convertible. The driver was happy to have an excuse to show off his toy. He explained that a Corvette club was having a driving rally through Fredricksburg. It wouldn't start until 11, so we had plenty of time to see the flowers before we saw the cars drive off.

Chris and I walked the gardens and were amazed at the color varieties of Texas lupine, called Bluebonnets, that the farm had developed. It had white "bluebonnets" and also pink, red, and a maroon variety in honor of Texas A&M University, whose school colors were maroon and white. The multicolored "blue"bonnets, Indian Paintbrush, and many other varieties of local wildflowers were a kaleidoscope of bloom in fields where they were being grown to be harvested for their seeds.

Passing through a gift shop that featured seeds, plants, and a large range of flower-related souvenir gifts, we smelled wood smoke. Our noses led us to a large corner of the gardens, where several Dutch ovens were being heated over beds of coals. Hot biscuits, just turned out from the ovens, tempted us to try samples of honey and jellies made and sold at the farm. With urging from the cooks, Chris and I enjoyed a delicious second breakfast and bought a jar of local honey.

I started a conversation with one of the cooks dressed in Western garb topped with a white chef's apron. He was browning meat for a stew. It would be ready for the lunch crowd to sample. He explained that he and the other cooks were members of a Dutch-oven society. Every Saturday in good weather they gave demonstrations. We compared notes on Boy Scout cobbler and agreed that making a bad one is impossible.

The Corvettes, antique and new, queued and paraded from the parking lot down the highway. We followed them toward our next stop. Several years ago we had stopped at the Admiral Nimitz Museum in Fredericksburg. I had promised Chris to stop again. We learned that the museum had expanded into the National Museum of the Pacific War with updated displays, an outdoor memorial, a Memorial Wall and, according to Chris, fewer weapons.

A few blocks away a new area was under construction. The George Bush Pacific Combat Zone was open to visitors, even though a few of the exhibits were not. A guide led our group through outdoor displays that simulated a beach assault and landing and combat zones complete with landing craft, tanks, and planes. Sound effects of aircraft screeching overhead, air-raid sirens, and bombs being detonated added to the reality. We went through buildings that represented submarine bases, officers' and enlisted men's quarters, and a medic's clinic. I was less impressed with "war stuff" than Chris was, but the interactive museum made me more knowledgeable of this period of U.S. history.

Fredericksburg is a German town, with names like *der Linderhausen* on board signs mounted on stone and clapboard buildings. Antique furniture and collectibles were piled onto boardwalks and porches of two-storied shops. Overhanging porches with railings of wood and iron protect shopping tourists from the sun. Flowers provide a profusion of color.

West of Fredericksburg, the northern hills were spiked with three-bladed windmills. The rolling hills of central Texas dried considerably as the terrain became hills of limestone rubble-flecked with scrub cedar. Sections of the highway had been blasted through the limestone to expose layers of multi-colored strata in the cuts and passes.

As we passed through the limestone outcropping, the Texas landscape changed again. The terrain became flatter and more dry. We passed bicyclists, singly and in groups of two or three. Some riders were in expensive cycling clothes with hydration systems on their backs, with tubing leading to their mouths. They rode multiple-speed racing bikes. Other riders wore shorts and T-shirts and were riding touring bikes. No one wore a numbered tag. This must have been a bike rally and not a race.

American geographers insist that the West begins at the 100th meridian. In Texas I'd call this demarcation "Near West" between East (east of Austin) and Far West (west of El Paso). West Texas is a vast, rolling prairie that was beginning its short burst of spring growth. Hovering above the distant, southern horizon, thunderheads began to build. Lightning flashed. To the north were heavy clouds. I checked my maps.

I had read about Balmorhea State Park and planned to camp there. The encroaching storms darkened the sky as we turned off the Interstate toward the park. Here was an attempted co-existence between prairie wilderness and civilization. The small ranger station was closed, but the gates were open. A sign, "Campground Full", was posted on the door. The storms rapidly approached from several directions. A chilly wind blew dust and tumbleweeds. Lightning flashed overhead. I smelled ozone and rain. I was 60 miles past Fort Stockton and 70 miles from Van Horn. My maps did not indicate another park or even a large town in the vicinity.

I drove through the campground and searched for a park ranger or a campground host. Finding neither, I pulled into an overflow parking area to boondock. We ate a cold supper and waited for the rain.

Not a drop of rain fell. Within an hour the heavy storm clouds passed over. The setting sun brightened the sky. Chris wanted to see the spring-fed pool that I had read about, so we walked toward a long, low stone building housing changing rooms. Beyond was a grassy picnic area dotted with live oaks. Sidewalks led to a large "L"-shaped pool. The sides of the pool were cemented, but the bottom was natural gravel and sand. A sign explained that a natural spring fed the pool from a deep fissure at the apex of the "L." The water was a constant 74 to 76 degrees. As the sun set, Chris, dressed in shorts and a T-shirt, insisted on swimming with the fish.

I preferred to sit and think about our trip rather than walk back to Gus (the motor home) to change into a swimsuit. We had no hookups. No electricity. So were we roughing it? Not really. I liked the feeling of being self-reliant, but our day-to-day survival would be in comfort. I wanted to do things on a whim, be spontaneous, be adventurous, to face the unknown and be surprised. But I didn't want to put either Chris or me in danger. Again I recognized that I was God-reliant. He was directing our travels.

Chapter 3

New Mexico

Over the next few days I lost track of the calendar. We passed through El Paso and into New Mexico. Near Deming we located Rockhound State Park. This is the only park in which visitors are encouraged to take rocks. Most parks have a sign that reads;

"Take only pictures.
Leave only footprints."

Rockhound State Park is situated at the base of the western slope of the dry, gravely Florida, NM, mountains. The campground was a short hike from the base of the ascending slopes. Immediately we began hiking. Chris wanted to look for geodes, agate, and quartz. I looked out for snakes, scorpions, and tarantulas so he wouldn't try to catch them. The afternoon heat quickly dissipated as the sun began to set. The mountains cast their cool shadows to warn us that time for dinner almost had arrived.

Chris collected two small geodes and an assortment of rocks that we wedged into our pockets for the hike back down. As we neared our campsite, we stopped to talk to a "young" woman (about my age) who wore heavy leather gloves and worked in a rock-walled flower bed—not really flower bed because it had no flowers blooming. Just a large collection of prickly, stickery, dagger-leafed desert natives were planted there.

The New Mexico Parks Department had hired the gardener, a retired botanist, to set up plantings of native vegetation. She readily showed off her rock and cactus gardens and educated us on plant names and their idiosyncrasies. Her job was to gather the thorny plants from the mountainside and to transplant them into gardens.

She was an amateur geologist, too. She pointed out minerals and rough specimens of common opal, jasper, and thunder eggs (geodes.) She encouraged Chris to become a rock hound.

When I shared our itinerary with her, she insisted that we must stop at the City of Rocks State Park. She had designed rock gardens at the visitors center and "just knew" we'd like this unusual park. She asked Chris whether he liked to hike and then recommended that we also stop at the Catwalks north of Silver City.

In the morning we passed through the high hills of the Chihuahuan Desert and turned toward City of Rocks. Rounding an outcropping, we descended onto a broad, dry plain. Piercing the skyline in the distance rose a group of huge, stone monoliths. The towering vertical rocks rising abruptly from the flat plains indeed did look as though they were a city of skyscrapers. A "city of rocks."

We parked at the visitors' center to learn that the hard rocks were remnants of volcanic extrusions. Volcanic eruptions had covered the area with ash, lava, and pumice. Heat "welded" the material into tuff rock. "Tuff" is a geological term that means rock composed of volcanic debris. Vertical cracks developed as it cooled. These geologic towers were sculpted by erosion from rain and wind. Freezing and thawing widened cracks. Continued erosion had stripped away the softer rock. The resulting rock columns, oddly shaped, free-form sculptures, were smooth, house-sized, and up to 40-feet tall.

Chris climbed everything climbable. He inched his way into small caves and openings. Some of the slick rock columns and pinnacles reached from the dust around our feet high over our heads into the azure sky. We worked our way around and through the vertical maze of formations. Lanes or paths separated the monumental granite towers. We felt as if we were in the twisting alleys and narrow streets of an ancient city.

I had planned to visit the Gila Cliff Dwellings north of Silver City. However I learned that the highway department did not recommend taking an RV the size of mine on the narrow, serpentine road. Disappointed, I vowed to visit Gila some other time.

The visitors' center at the Catwalks was closed, but returning hikers directed us in the right direction with praises of the scenery. A sign informed us that the hike was only 1.1 miles. *Easy*, I thought, as we started along a level trail that followed the wide Whitewater creek under huge cottonwood trees, sycamore, and scrub oaks. Canyon wrens flitted through the branches.

The trail began to climb—first with well-defined stone steps and then up and over rocks. The stream below us became more turbulent. The higher we climbed, the more narrow and steep the river's gorge became. In places the trail was slippery gravel. Then, catwalks. The trail with no rock ledges to follow along the walls of slick rock became "catwalks." Narrow bridges of expanded metal flooring with pipe handrails and fencing enticed us to continue over the gorge and around the rock walls.

The walks were suspended from the slick, rock walls of the narrow chasm. As I looked far down into the rocky bed of Whitewater Canyon, I prayed that the catwalks were well-anchored!

The walkway became so narrow that two-way traffic was difficult, so we clung to the rail to let others pass. The bridges climbed a series of stairs that were broken by landings. Below us the rushing torrent appeared closer as we climbed toward its source. Returning hikers told us that the catwalk's trail followed an old mule trail that 19th-century silver miners had used to get equipment to a mine that now was played out and abandoned. As I looked through the flooring, I couldn't see anything on which a mule could have walked.

Chris pointed out two men fly-fishing in rock-dammed pools. I vetoed his demands to climb back down to the motor home (and up again) to get his fishing pole. I compromised and let him carry a horned toad that he caught with my admonition that "No. It can't go to Alaska. It would freeze."

A reminder of "take nothing but pictures" is tough on young boys. He eventually let it go.

I was hot, very tired, and almost out of water. Hearing the gurgling of water falls echoing through the canyon kept me going. I tried to keep up with Chris as he scampered along the catwalks and out of sight around protruding boulders. We rested at the falls with the wind sending spray from the falls over us. I marveled at the tropical vegetation of ferns and other plants high in this canyon watered by the spray and the cascading river.

After we were rejuvenated and cooled off, our descent was much easier and faster. We felt good to have completed the climb and to be able to encourage new hikers. As we neared the cottonwoods, we met a ranger repairing the trail. Recalling how I had slipped on the gravel, I asked him whether accidents had occurred on the trail. He replied that since he'd been working at the park, he knew of no serious accidents.

On the plains above the canyon had been a horseback accident. He'd been part of the rescue team. Not needing to be prompted for details, he recounted that a group of riders from a ranch had been on a trail ride on the rim. A horse had spooked and had thrown its rider—a young woman. The horse then fell on her and injured her spine. The only way to get her out was for the rangers to climb the catwalks and then climb another trail to the rim of the canyon. They had secured her to a backboard and stretcher and then used ropes to lower her back down the canyon to the catwalks. They lowered her down the steps and carried her to the parking lot to a waiting helicopter. After several weeks in the hospital she recovered. She got back on a horse.

We continued our hike to the motor home and were surprised that the 1.1-mile hike had taken two hours. *Maybe that sign was for one-way only. Or was I just out of shape?*

As the highway climbed into the forested mountains toward the Continental Divide and Arizona, signs warned of dangerous curves, 25 mph, and steep assents. We crept upward. I warned Chris to go play on the bed in the back of the motor home and leave me alone to deal with the steep, twisting, narrow highway. His excitement over the roller-coaster ride got on my nerves.

What was that? The engine bucked. For a second it sort-of hesitated and then raced. It was similar to how my previous motor home, a 24-foot, 1988 Tioga had acted in the Smokey Mountains of North Carolina. I was scared then, too. A few miles further on it bucked again. And again. Climbing a particularly steep grade, Gus hesitated and bucked once more. In my un-mechanical mind I felt as though if the transmission was slipping. I certainly didn't know the consequences of that prognosis. I prayed fervently to get out of the mountains. *What about Alaskan mountains? Could we make that journey? Was I foolish to try?*

Gingerly negotiating a sharp descent, alternately braking hard, and coasting so as to not overheat the brakes, I prayed, "Oh, God, please don't let us break down here in the middle of this wilderness with no shoulder on which to pull over and no traffic to flag down for help."

We must have passed over the Continental Divide. The highway led down a steep decline with switchbacks marked 15 mph. If I didn't cause the brakes to overheat as I crept down, I'd make it. In the valley below I caught a glimpse of civilization. Then as the highway finally leveled out, God answered my prayers with an auto-repair shop on the edge of a small town.

"I'm not a mechanic," I said as I approached a real mechanic dressed in grease-stained coveralls, "but as I went through the mountains something funny was going on. I think it might have been the transmission. Would you mind checking the fluid?"

He obliged and pulled the dipstick. The fluid level and color were fine. As well as I could, I described the bucking. He asked whether the overdrive was off. I admitted my incompetence. I didn't know whether I had overdrive. As an excuse I explained that I was from Houston where the land was flat. The only "mountains" were Interstate overpasses.

I was shown the overdrive "off" button on the end of the gearshift. With Chris's reminders to turn it off after stops, we had no more bucking transmission. I sighed a "Thank You, God" that I had not yielded to the temptation to try the climb to Gila National Park.

Chapter 4

Arizona

We continued northwest. Forested mountains leveled to dry plains in Arizona. The distant hills, back-lighted by the sunset, contrasted with the evening sky, which now was a wash of grays with only a hint of blue near the western horizon. Although a cold wind began to blow, the promise of rain to this parched land didn't materialize. We found a campsite at Lake Lyman. Its deep shoreline and low water level were a testimony to drought.

Approaching the Petrified Forest from the south, mini strip-mall advertising enticed us from both sides of the highway. "Petrified Wood, Rock Shops, Souvenirs, Cactus, T-Shirts, Snacks, Gas." We stopped for gas and to "just look." Porch pillars and the outer walls of the store were constructed of polished, petrified wood and other beautifully colored rocks. Huge piles of rocks, sorted by mineral content, attracted Chris. I stopped to admire the cactus gardens and desert plants potted for sale. How could travelers transport these specimens of "touch-me-nots"?

Rubber snakes, tomahawks, and T-shirts jumbled the counters. Thin, translucent, and transparent slabs of agate, jasper, and crystal hung as mobiles glitted in front of the windows. I leaned on a dusty glass case packed with Native American jewelry. Turquoise and blood coral, my favorite, set in cast silver called out to my credit card. Some pieces were contemporary and newly made. I was especially tempted by several pieces of old pawn but kept the credit card in my pocket for gas. Geode halves with sparkling crystals, polished, petrified wood, and bins of every imaginable rock, mineral, and semi-precious stones enticed Chris to touch. Limited by my budget Chris selected a small cut geode with violet crystals and several postcards.

At the entrance to Petrified Forest National Park, I purchased a National Parks Pass. For $50 the pass allowed us one year free access to all the National Parks and gave discounts for camping. With the pass sticker on my windshield, like a badge of honor, we made several stops to see the giant fossilized logs that lie scattered across the desert landscape.

The huge, petrified conifer logs, often broken into sections, appeared to be oriented in the same general direction. They were scattered across the desert as if left behind by a tremendous flood that had rafted them along as it tore off branches, roots, and bark. Brush and smaller trees were washed away and destroyed. Noah's Flood?

These giant tree trunks floated along and got heavier with absorbed water to be beached or stranded as the floodwaters subsided. Volcanic ash and sediment rapidly covered the logs and caused fossilization, called *silification* from the silica in the volcanic ash. The wood-turned-to-stone was tinted in multicolored rainbows of semi-precious gems and given the names of quartz, amethyst, and agate.

How tempting to gather up some of the beautiful fragments, but recalling the history of the military, gem-collectors, and fortune hunters who had hauled off tons of rock, we took only pictures. I walked out on an overlook to explore the Anasazi petroglyphs on Newspaper Rock in Utah. I was disappointed that, although I used binoculars, I could see very little of the markings that I'd read about.

The Petrified Forest Park road passed under Interstate 40 and looped through the Painted Desert. Here we marveled at the amazing cliffs, tinted variegated colors of the rainbow. Noah's Flood would have left the mineral deposits and volcanic ash, which colored the strata.

The towns of Holbrook and Winslow, now bypassed by Interstate 40, jogged my memory of the famous U.S. Route 66. This highway, which John Steinbeck in *The Grapes of Wrath* called the Mother Road, was designated in 1926 as the only through route from Chicago to Los Angles. Two-hundred-thousand displaced,

Dust Bowl migrants were drawn to the West—to the setting sun, to the rich farmland of California. In the 1950s, the 2,500-mile roadway shifted from a passage to becoming an icon as tourists traveled west. A song, "Get Your Kicks On Route 66" by Bob Troup, led to a TV series, "Route 66", that followed adventure-seekers to discover Western America.

I recalled a trip I took with my family when I was very young. We had a wooden-sided station wagon, with an air-cooler cylinder hanging from the window. A heavy canvas, olive-drab water bag hung from the radiator cap. A heavier, olive-drab canvas tent was strapped to the roof. We traveled mostly at night to avoid the heat. Carlsbad Caverns and the Grand Canyon were our destinations. I-40 still was Route 66.

Chris had studied about meteors and craters. We stopped at Meteor Crater east of Flagstaff. In the late 1800s scientists denied that rock from space could hit the earth. Yet, later, the main fragment of a meteor was found buried beneath more than 1,000 feet of sediment in the crater. Scientists now agree that the prehistoric impact and explosion of a meteor, 80 to 100 feet in diameter, formed the 4,200-foot -wide, 570-foot-deep crater.

As we stood on the observation decks, we could see the three-mile, up-turned rim and the gigantic depression in the earth. Perhaps this meteor and others rained on the earth during the upheaval of Noah's Flood.

Near Flagstaff I was surprised to reenter forest. We traveled north on a high plateau toward the Grand Canyon. I was glad that our arrival was in the middle of the week, for I knew that this national park is very popular and crowded, even in early spring. I resisted stopping at a private campground and hoped that we would arrive before Mather Campground near Grand Canyon Village was full. Fortunately a few more dry sites were available, so we registered for two nights.

The ranger explained that the South Rim was closed to automobiles. Free shuttle-bus service to all points along the rim was available from the bus stop near the campground entrance. We had a National Parks map, so we could plan our exploration. After a cookout, Chris and I walked the dogs and noted the different languages that we heard. To our amazement several Germans set up a small tent across from us, began to change clothes, and were oblivious to the 34-degree temperature and to us. We bundled up, built up the fire, and watched the stars appear in the darkening sky.

By morning the temperature had dropped. The weather was windy and brisk as we donned our daypacks with water bottles and snacks, put on hats and gloves, and hiked to the bus stop. During the night I had lain awake in anticipation of seeing God's handiwork in the Grand Canyon. I also had been worried that this trip was not in His Will. We were having a great time, but I was concerned that having a good time was not be the purpose of the trip. Did God really plan for us to go to Alaska to work?

A couple joined us to wait at the bus stop in the cold, crisp air. We spoke briefly about the weather and then boarded a bus to take us to a transfer station. When we all got off to wait for another bus to Hermits Rest, we picked up our brief conversation.

"Where are you from?" I asked.

"We're from Alaska." The gentleman answered. "And you?"

"We're from Houston. We are on our way to Alaska." I replied Unexpectedly he asked, "What's your name?"

I had noticed that travelers were very friendly and started conversations easily, but they didn't usually ask for introductions. I answered anyway, "I'm Carol. This is Chris."

He reached over to shake my hand, "Larry. Glad to meet you."

"Larry?" I stammered. "From the camp? You've got to be kidding!" My mouth dropped open, "How did you . . .?"

"I heard you talk to Chris and wondered if you could be the same person I had talked to on the phone. When you said *Houston*, everything fit together. I just took a guess. This is my wife, Sharon."

I couldn't contain my amazement. I stammered. I was flabbergasted. We shook hands.

"It's a God-thing, " I said. "No other way could we have met."

The couple had left the camp in Alaska about the time we had left Houston. They traveled the Casiar Highway to Washington

State, and followed the coast south to northern California. After they visited relatives, they had turned east through Nevada and stopped here at the Grand Canyon on their way to Florida.

This was the answer. I thanked God for verifying my dreams to go to Alaska. This meeting in no way could have been accidental or by coincidence. The possibility, the statistical probability, of us meeting at that bus stop on a cold, off-season morning was astronomical. Mind-boggling. We all agreed that an Amazing God had brought us together.

We all boarded the bus to Hermits Rest and sat together so we could visit. I bombarded them with questions about the camp. They shared experiences of rearing their kids in Alaska. Larry told Chris how much fun he would have, especially fishing in the lake. Larry assured Chris that snow still would be on the ground when we arrived. Originally from Florida, with their kids now grown, they felt called to return south.

The bus stopped for us to enjoy from several overlooks the awesome beauty of the canyons. Arriving at Hermits Rest, we discussed how Noah's Flood had deposited mountains of sediments and then caused erosion as the waters receded.

I had had difficulty believing that water during Noah's Flood could have covered the earth. That was until the 2001 flood in Houston. In one area alone, where my daughter lived, 36 inches of rain had been recorded in just 12 hours. That's six FEET of water falling, not accumulated, in just 24 hours. What if that much rain fell over 40 days? And that was just rain. No volcanoes had erupted and forced underground water to the surface.

After this tiny, local flood, we saw much evidence of erosion damage to highway overpasses caused by the torrents of receding waters. How could anyone experiencing or seeing the devastation of this flood on TV doubt that God could cause a worldwide flood of a magnitude to lay down sediment thousands of feet thick? Rushing, receding floodwaters gouged through the soft sediment layers and carried debris that scoured the forming canyon.

I never will forget my first glimpse, when I was a child, of the canyon. The awe and grandeur, the vast magnificence, the strangeness of the canyon is not dispelled by a second or third visit. Walking above the rim the plateau is relatively flat and forested, civilized with concessions, parking areas, people, and sidewalks. Then, the dizzying drop from the rim. My mind tried to grasp this spectacle of stone sculpture in a color spectrum like no other. The scale—the sheer magnitude of the canyon and its cliffs dwarfs me into insignificance. The main canyon cut by the Colorado River stretches 277 miles. The river, a mile below the rim, appears to be a length of embroidery floss sewn between towering spires and pinnacles called "temples." Within the main canyon, which is four- to 18-miles wide, are other canyons, chasms, buttes, gorges, and ravines. Striations, uplifts, and faults exposing vast wedding-cake layering of sediments treated me to an artist's rainbow palette.

Our new friends returned to the campground on an early shuttle from Hermit's Rest. We were not able to visit with them again. As I sat waiting for Chris to explore the gift shop, the abrupt, unexpected drop into the canyon, the vast expanse of colored cliffs and the deep gorges mesmerized me. My thoughts were a jumble. How could God, who is so powerful, care about insignificant me so much that He arranged a meeting with Larry and Sharon to verify that making this trip was His Will?

How could anyone not see God's power here? His hand and mind had to be behind the creation of this majestic wonder that attracts hundreds of thousands of visitors every year. Since this was not the time of a school holiday, few children were here. In the short time we had been here, I had heard languages from many foreign countries: German, French, Swiss, Spanish, and Asian. The park was crowded with visitors. I wondered what these others visitors thought. *Did they know God?*

While at Hermits Rest I noticed an old wooden sign on one of the support pillars. It read:

"Sing to God
Sing Praises to His Name
Lift up a song to Him
Who rides upon

The clouds:
His name is the Lord
Exult before Him"

Credit for the poem was illegible. It sounded like the psalms. (I later found that it was a paraphrase of Ps. 68:4.) I made a note to look it up and wondered whether other visitors stopped to read it.

Catching the shuttle back to Grand Canyon Village, at noon we stopped at the trailhead for the Bright Angel Trail. I was tempted to hike a little way down even though we weren't prepared with water. Chris was too hungry to hike down the enticing trail and vetoed a hike. I enviously watched day-hikers and backpackers buried under enormous packs as they descended into Douglas firs.

We ate a picnic and then visited Lookout Studio, a stone building that literally clung onto the side of the canyon. It was perched on a promontory like a pile of surreal stone with flowers and weeds growing from its roof. This helped to blend the building into the boulders. Inside, an impressive collection of watercolor, oil, and acrylic paintings greeted us from several multistoried galleries. The art works were the previous year's entries in the Arts for the Parks annual contest. They were magnificent. Most were realistic interpretations of scenery; some were of wildlife, and a few featured people. I was inspired to get out my paints and begin painting again. Meanwhile I thanked God for my limited talent and for the ability to appreciate other artists' work.

We returned for a rest at the motor home and to check the dogs. The sun still was high when we caught a shuttle for Yaki Point off the East Rim Drive. Instead we got off at the trailhead for the South Kaibab Trail. I stopped to read the park service's cautionary signs that warned hikers to carry plenty of water, have a permit for overnight camping at the river, and to take out the trash.

Chris rounded an outcropping of rock. He discovered the trail that cut to our left following the cliff wall below us. Without a "Mother, may I" he started down the steep grade. I called after him to no avail. Although we were unprepared to hike, Chris insisted that we go down. I reluctantly agreed to go down a little ways.

At the first switchback I was not happy. The trail clung to the cliffs to the left and dropped abruptly to the right. It was very steep and narrow with hairpin switchbacks, so that now the wall was to my right and the dropoff to infinity was to the left.

A little way down was a sign that warned:

"When mules pass
stand quietly and
follow mule guide's
instructions"

If mules could negotiate this trail, then I possibly could. Would it have room for mules and hikers? I didn't want to find out. I was getting more and more nervous about this venture. I tried not to complain, but I was scared. The switchbacks became steeper, the trail narrower, and the dropoff side of the trail more vertical. Mule riders far below were mere specks. The view, more than a mile straight-down, gave me vertigo.

The afternoon sun glaring off the rock was blinding. Areas of the trail shaded by overhanging cliffs offered some relief. The wind began blowing dust and reminders of the mules.

Chris forged ahead. He was too close to the outer edge of the trail. I clung to the inner side by the cliff face. The breeze became a dust storm. It whipped dust into my eyes and coated my contact lenses with boulder-sized grit. Blinded by dust and tears, I called it quits. I hiked close to the wall; I trailed it with my fingers and inched down as I called to Chris to stop. As I wimped out, he got braver and was determined to hike to the Colorado River that was seven trail miles and 7,000 feet below. I refused to budge from a protected spot by the wall. He rounded an outcropping out of sight. I panicked. Motherhood overruled fear. I called "Chris, Chris, wait!" and crept along the trail as I dragged my hand along the cliff.

Chris stood with his back to me and surveyed the trail that zig-zagged to a thin thread far below. I pleaded that I couldn't see and that we didn't have water. I recklessly promised that we'd return someday. Demanding to ascend, I threatened to leave him. Grit under my contact lens was causing my eyes to burn and water. Being blinded on the side of a mountain was not my idea of fun.

My eyes teared. My nose ran. I begged Chris to go back up. He argued that he was having fun and that I was a coward. He was right. Then the wind blasted us into the wall. Fortunately it was the wall to which I clung and not the outer edge of the trail, which had no railing or curbing—just DOWN.

Two ascending hikers stopped to inform us that a rockfall had just missed them. I adamantly insisted that we hike back up to the rim. I made a rash promise to hike the Bright Angel Trail the next time we were there. It was less steep and less scary. Chris complained about turning back without seeing the rockfall but reluctantly agreed.

As we reached the rim, I cleaned my contacts and thanked God for getting us out of there. We stopped by corrals to pet some of the resting mules. I would have liked to have ridden a mule to the bottom, but the park service has a strict weight limit of 200 pounds. My "little" boy at five-foot-10 would be overweight. After experiencing our limited hike, I wasn't sure I'd be brave enough to ride a mule on that trail.

We caught a bus back to the campground for a short rest, dinner, and to re-energize. Another shuttle ride and short hike took us to Yavapai Point to photograph the sunset. The chirping of birds became hushed. The buzz of excited tourists settled onto benches or along the rim's handrails. In awed silence we watched as the peaks, gorges, and craggy cliffs changed from one lavender-tinted rainbow hue to another. The sun descended lower and lower. The last rays of the sun disappeared beyond the almost-level western horizon. The temperature pummeled.

Other photographers and their families, cold but exuberant, boarded the shuttle with us. Muted voices in many foreign languages whispered about their overloaded sensations.

Hot chocolate by a crackling fire, a myriad of brilliant stars in a velvety black sky, and a warm sleeping bag were the perfect ending to a fantastically exciting day.

Before dawn lightened the blue-black sky, my alarm-clock dogs woke me. I took them for a short, very brisk walk in the frosty air. Chris refused to budge as I started up the engine. I determined to watch the sunrise over the canyon, since I was up anyway.

Traveling east I pulled over several times and took photos of the mists and slowly brightening palette of colors on the distant western rim. In the distance through the mist, I saw what appeared to be a rock tower rising from the edge of a sharp cliff. It appeared to be made by human hands, as though it were a castle turret. Chris, now in the navigator's seat, insisted we go check this out. I agreed. A sign announced "Desert View Watchtower."

We walked up a stone path to the tower and were amazed at how the stone of the foundation blended seamlessly into the boulders of the cliff face. Native plants further anchored the tower. Squirrels scampered as they chased each other in to the brush.

Inside, a small gift shop filled a circular room with a low ceiling of huge logs. A climb up a narrow, twisting staircase to the top of the 70-foot hollow tower cost a quarter. Our coins opened the revolving turnstile that led us up to a fantasy world. On the interior walls and ceiling were painted strutting birds, slithering snakes, and figures depicting Hopi legends. The Havasupai, "People of the blue-green water" (Hopi predecessors), had lived in these canyons.

A 360-degree view from the top of the tower was breathtaking. Here was another view of layer-cake geology. Ravens squawked and soared on the morning thermals. The aqua-blue Colorado River snaked through the canyon far below. To the east the stratified walls dropped steeply from the plains toward the Painted Desert.

Returning to the gift shop I learned that the architect, Mary Colter, in the early 1900's designed the Watchtower, Lookout Studio, Hermits Rest, and other buildings. A genius, she constructed her buildings to blend into the surrounding scenery and even hand-picked the stones used in the tower. This building and the others compliment one of the earth's most beautiful spots.

On a plaque I read an old saying about the canyon, "What God hath put asunder, let no man join together." Except for a two-lane road across the Glen Canyon Dam at the narrow, northern gorge at

Page, Utah, the northern and southern plateau rims of the canyon can only be joined by flight or a two-day hike.

In one of the shops I had read what Theodore Roosevelt wrote after his visit to the canyon: "Do nothing to mar its grandeur for the ages have been at work upon it and man cannot improve it. Keep it for your children, your children's children and all who come after you."

Chapter 5

Utah

Vowing to return to the Grand Canyon, Lord willing, I continued on to Page, UT. We crossed high over the Colorado River on the top of the Glen Canyon Dam. To our right was beautiful Lake Powell.

I enjoy exploring caves, so when I saw Moqui Cave on the map, I planned a stop. As it passed through the town of Kana, the highway followed a small river that twisted and wound through a fertile valley. Irrigated farms and pretty, well-maintained homesteads were quite a contrast to the dry, rocky hills and distant mountains. I wondered if this were a Mormon settlement.

The sign announcing Moqui Cave, topped by a dancing, Native American maiden, and the stonework replica of Native American cliff dwellings tempted me to pass by what appeared to be a commercial tourist trap. We stopped anyway.

Outside the rubble, rock entrance we were met by a tall, thin, young man in faded jeans, scuffed Western boots, worn "cowboy" shirt, and felt Stetson hat. He was sweeping leaves and sand from the stone path. He welcomed us and led us inside.

The shallow cave had been an Native American shelter. It had no formations at all. The cave housed a treasury of Native American artifacts, slabs of limestone bearing three-toed dinosaur tracks, and a huge collection of gorgeously glowing fluorescent minerals.

We were the only visitors. The young man told us the story of the cave. It first belonged to his grandfather, who had used it as a barn. An aging panoramic photograph showed his grandfather, a Mormon, his six wives and most of his 52 children. The owner's father had used the cave as a tavern and for collecting artifacts and minerals. As a child the present owner began collecting and had helped his father turn the cave into a museum. After his father's death, the young man bought out his brothers, who had no interest in the venture. I did not learn whether this man was a practicing Mormon, but I did discover that the beautifully tended farms in the valley did indeed belong to Mormon families.

The road began to climb and twist again. My books jolted loose from the shelf and tumbled onto the table, the bench, and on top of the startled dogs. Chris took some of the books to the rear bed. I chuckled. What a good way to get him to read! Bombard him.

I had planned to explore Utah's Zion National Park and the Grand Staircase. Checking the map, I decided that US 89 North would be scenic enough for this trip. I wondered, *Do other travelers lay out an itinerary and stick to it?* As the miles and mountains slipped past, I became philosophical about life. *Do many people set life goals and actually reach them?* I know of very few people who have set major goals and met them. The rest of us seem to have many small goals—often one after another—for which we strive.

I changed lanes to pass a slow-moving truck. My life has had many lane changes, detours, and side trips. I am a single parent who reared 35 foster kids and nine adopted kids and my grandson as well as my two biological daughters. My life as a single parent has been full of detours: illnesses and family problems, as well as milestones. *Do we stop and ask for help in life or fumble along the way?* I've often asked others for advice. *Can we always trust the person giving us directions?* When I've trusted God, He always provided the best answers, even though I may not have agreed at the time.

As I entered a small town, I slowed down because of traffic congestion. At times I was made to slow down to see things more clearly, not in a speedy blur. This trip is one of those times.

South of Provo we began to see snow high in the crevasses of the surrounding mountains. Clouds hovered and lowered; they obscured the peaks. The sky above us was clear. The sun shone through breaks in the heavy cumulus clouds. This caused streaks of sunlight that I wished I could photograph, but the road had no pull-outs. I watched clouds pile onto the mountains and wondered whether they contained more snow. For the night I chose a Kamp

Grounds of America (KOA) private campground, because the state parks still were under winter restrictions or closed

I planned to sleep late, but at the first hint of daybreak, regardless of clock-time, Sam and Lady emitted a few pitiful, tentative whimpers. I didn't move. I tried to control my breathing and carefully snuggled into the sleeping bag. They knew I was awake and yipped louder.

I grabbed their leashes and admonished them to be considerate of our neighboring campers while I fumbled into shoes, zipped a jacket over my sweats, and searched for my trifocal glasses. I had no time to put on contacts or brush my hair; a hat would have to do.

Leaving Chris snuggled in his sleeping bag, the dogs and I took a brisk, 30-minute walk to welcome the day. An inch of fresh snow frosted the picnic tables. Very little sprinkled the dry grass. Satisfied, the dogs led me back to the motor home. The promise of snow didn't entice Chris out of his sleeping bag.

South of Salt Lake City, sleet pelted the roof and the windshield. This awakened Chris. He wrapped his sleeping bag around himself and joined me up front. He was excited to see his first snowfall, even if it actually was sleet. Sleet blanketed the windshield as fast as the wipers cleared it. Sleet fell so heavily that I pulled off the freeway into a parking lot. Chris hopped outside and slid on the pellets. Passing drivers shook their heads in amusement, as they saws his delight when sleet hit his out stretched arms. I laughed at the sight of the tiny, white balls of ice ricocheting off his black sweatshirt and black hair.

Chris finally admitted to being cold and got back inside. The sleet subsided. Farther north, wet snow began to fall. It obscured my vision. Traffic became congested. My nerves began to tingle. Chris saw a sign for the North American Museum of Ancient Life. We circled back through hard-driving snow and into the parking lot. He pelted me with wet snowballs that were scooped from the pavement. Fingers and toes freezing, I called a stop to the play. The snowfall was subsiding, but the parking lot and highway were slushy. This was one of those wonderful, unexpected detours. We decided to investigate the museum. For several enjoyable hours we explored the dinosaur exhibits and hands-on displays while we waited out the freak, late snowstorm.

Surprisingly the snow had stopped and the sky was clearing when we left the museum to walk the dogs and to have lunch. Closer to the center of Salt Lake City, snow began falling again. I decided against trying to navigate to Antelope Island through the increasingly slow traffic, so I turned west on I-80.

I stopped at the visitor center west of town to ask about the weather. The storm system carrying snow was predicted to be moving slowly northeast away from us. The wind would continue to be very strong. The weather still could be messy.

I pulled into the parking area of Bonniville Salt Flats so we could explore the phenomenon. Chris followed other footprints out onto the hard, crusty, white salt. I walked the dogs but kept them off the salt. I did not know if it would irritate their feet. We read information signs about the Bonniville Salt Flats Speedway and how the flats are used as a testing raceway for high-performance cars. How we wished we could have watched the races!

Chapter 6

Nevada and Idaho

Continuing west we entered Nevada, just to say we'd been in the state. Then we turned north into Idaho. Passing Twin Falls, we stopped briefly at Hagerman Fossil Beds National Monument and then hurried on to spend the night at Three Island Crossing State Park at Glenns Ferry. We arrived early enough to explore an excellent pioneer museum which is part of Hagerman National Monument. It honors the rugged Oregon Trail pioneers who challenged the Snake River by floating their covered wagons across at this location. A successful crossing from island to island through the unpredictable river would mean a shorter route to the Pacific. In the spring, the museum hosts a re-enactment of the crossing with mule- or ox-drawn wagons and riders wearing period costume.

Attracted to the river, Chris asked whether he could fish. He was young enough that he didn't need a fishing license. He gathered up a rod and tackle box. I got the dogs and their long rope so they could get more exercise. Off we hiked. Chris tried fishing at several locations along the high bank of the brush-lined river, but he had no luck. As I was trying to convince him to reel in and go back, he hooked a big one. He tried to reel it in. The fish hung up in a tangle of small willow trees and bushes at the bottom of the embankment. He tugged. He sawed his pole back and forth. The line got more tangled. Afraid that his fish was gone, he insisted on sliding down the bank to check his hook rather than to cut the line.

I hated to see him lose the fish, but the fast-flowing water was turbulent and swift. I was afraid I'd lose him. I had an idea. I tied one end of the dogs' sturdy rope around his waist and held tightly to the other end. Down the embankment he slid. Fortunately his feet, stopped by the brush, did not get too wet. If he had fallen in, I doubted that I would have had the strength to pull him up, but at least he would not have gotten washed away.

To our surprise the fish still was on the hook. Chris untangled a large bass and handed the slippery fish up to me. I grabbed it with one hand and tossed it up on the bank, then pulled on the rope to help him regain the top. Chris yelled at the dogs to leave his fish alone, caught the bass under the gills, and proudly strutted off down the path. His shoes squished muddy water.

Reaching our campsite, Chris insisted on doing everything to prepare his fish while I cooked supper over a fire. He spread out a plastic bag to catch the scales and gutted his fish. I didn't have any flour or cornmeal to bread it, nor did I have the right seasonings. He fried it in hot oil over the fire. He said that he really liked the taste of the first side of the fish but then then grew tired of it. I helped finish it off. Neither of us really liked the taste without breading or tartar sauce but didn't want to admit it. Just catching the fish was quite an accomplishment!

Chapter 7

Oregon

Crossing the Snake River we entered Oregon. I calculated enough time to leave the Interstate to travel west to the John Day Fossil Beds National Monument. The John Day River road was a beautiful, scenic byway, but it was tiring. As we at last reached the Interpretive Center, we were disappointed that the 1,000-square miles of fossil beds was not open to the public. A small museum housed locally found fossils. The curator was friendly and informative. Only paleontologists their students and volunteers were allowed into certain areas to explore. Seeing our disappointment, the curator suggested that we stop at the town of Fossil. She showed us some plant imprints from that area. We could find plant fossils in the shale behind the high school.

In the town of Fossil, I followed Main Street a few blocks past wooden storefronts to the base of a hill. A narrow road climbed the hill to a single-story, cinder-block building housing the high school. I parked at the bottom of the hill. A faded sign described the plant fossils that had been found here. We had been given directions to walk up the driveway and then to go behind the school to the back of the baseball diamond.

This late in the afternoon no one was around to ask questions. We walked up the drive and past the side of the building to the rear. Another hill rose behind the leveled baseball field. We followed the third-base line to the backstop and around the rusting chain-link fencing to a small set of wooden bleachers.

Chris and I questioned each other. *Now what?* Chris scrambled up the shale hillside. Falling to his hands and knees he scooped up shale shards and began to throw them. I gave him a stern warning. I picked up and turned over small, reddish-tan wafers of rock. I encouraged Chris to do the same. I found one! The partial imprint of a leaf was darker than was the rock. Somewhat disappointed in its size, I showed it to Chris. The hunt was on. We were hooked. Climbing, digging, and sorting rocks revealed several more "finds."

As the sun sank lower, Chris, tired of turning over small slabs of rock, began again to see how far he could throw the rocks. I turned my back on him and sat on the bleachers to ignore him. I wondered how many generations of teens had poked around here, either fascinated with their finds or in boredom had thrown what might have been museum-quality treasures.

I checked the time of the remaining daylight. By holding my hand at arms' length, fingers parallel to me, toward the setting sun and closing one eye, I could figure how much time remained until the sun went down past the horizon. If four fingers were between the bottom of the sun and the horizon, the sun would set in an hour. Each finger represented about 15 minutes. Only two fingers were now between the sun's bottom rim and the horizon. We had about 30 minutes to gather up our fossils, walk back to the motor home, and find a campground.

On our way from the highway into town I had noticed a small fairgrounds with a few trailers in a field. I turned in at the gate. No one was at the guardhouse. I saw no notice about paying a camping fee. I drove over to where a small trailer was parked. A worker, returning to the trailer, said staying one night without paying would be fine if I didn't use any utilities. The restrooms were closed and locked. Boondocking was fine with me.

Leaving Fossil early in the morning, I turned on my tape recorder to catch up on my notes. I thought about all the maps, campground literature, postcards, rolls of exposed film, and other junk I had collected and thrown into a tote box. Funny how a map will give you all kinds of information except to tell you how to fold it up again! I wrote a note to myself on a page of a sticky-note pad to find time to file the accumulated stuff in the plastic file box I had brought for that purpose. I stuck the note on my visor. In Seattle I hoped to find a one-hour photo developing place so we could mount our pictures in an album before they got lost.

Before I left home, I had been in email contact with a cousin in Seattle. Although we never had met, he and his family invited us to visit for a few days on our way to the ferry terminal in Bellingham. Perhaps while we were stopped there I'd have time to organize into files my collection of papers and postcards.

State Highway 19 abruptly ended at an intersection with a major freeway. Interstate 84 West followed the famous Columbia River that Lewis and Clark investigated. The six-lane freeway clung to the base of the mountains to my left. The right shoulder dropped to the wide-flowing river below. At intervals several dams held back the rushing river. Debris in the trees below and along the canyon shore was evidence of flooding. The Interstate had limited access to a few side roads. Some crossed bridges to the north; others disappeared into the forested mountains to the south. I worriedly watched the fuel gauge.

A service station ahead was on the left, which meant maneuvering over several lanes and crossing traffic. I didn't want to get into Portland and have to get off the freeway for gas and possibly get lost, so I exited.

To my surprise an attendant emerged to pump my gas. *Where was self-service?* Accustomed to doing it myself, I wondered how much extra in tips I'd have to pay for this service. The pump displayed $1.70 per gallon for regular—the highest price I'd paid on this trip. The tank was too empty to try for another, cheaper station. I asked the attendant about price and was told that all Oregon stations were full-service and the prices were about the same throughout the state. Washington, he'd heard, was cheaper. I asked him to stop the pump at 10 gallons and hoped we'd make it into the state of Washington.

Chapter 8

Washington

As I crossed a congested bridge over the Columbia River into Vancouver, WA, I did find the gas prices much cheaper and filled up my 55-gallon tank. Since Chris had seen Meteor Crater, I wanted him to see the crater of Mt. St. Helens, the volcano that suddenly erupted in 1980.

A secondary road leading to Spirit Lake wound up the forested, western approach to the mountain. We stopped at the Mt. St. Helens National Volcanic Monument Visitor Center, a beautifully constructed memorial to the 36 known people who lost their lives and the 21 people missing in the destruction of the volcano's eruption. Here we learned that the 5.1 earthquake triggered the largest landslide ever recorded. The slide reached 150 mph in just 10 minutes, raced 15 miles, and covered 25 square miles in debris that averaged 150-feet deep. A second blast ripped through the sliding debris at 670 mph and impacted 230 square miles. Clouds of ash rose 70,000 feet into the air. The summit of Mt. St. Helens now was a crater blasted 1,314 feet lower than the original summit.

The devastated remains of a vast fir forest on the north slope littered lower slopes with stripped tree trunks radiating out from the blast. Where Spirit Lake once stood at the base of the mountain, huge boulders rested on dried mud hundreds of feet from the original shore. I wondered whether a volcanic eruption in a similar manner had killed, stripped, and oriented the trees that we saw in the Petrified Forest. I pondered the results of this type of destruction on a worldwide basis during Noah's Flood.

The museum docent recommended that we stop at the half-house. As we continued our climb through pine and spruce forests to the crater, we watched for an A-frame house and gift shop. A huge, 20-foot tall cement Sasquatch on the right was difficult to miss. Getting out in the parking lot, Chris commented that the weather suddenly was colder. I noticed that the sky had become

the count-

us

St.

e

road. They saw newscasts debris flowing into the lower floor of the house and then the second level.

Several days later, when they were able to return, they surv the damage and realized that their home was unsalvageable. Thei household possessions were buried under 10 feet of debris. For se\ eral years the family stayed in the area and tried to make the best of things by building the small gift shop and information center on their property. As the man's children grew up, they left him, as did his wife. The gentleman invited us to carefully look around the remains of his home: the half-house.

We walked around the exterior of the house, which now was only a roof. We could see through broken windows at the front and back of the gable. Down inside the fenced-off interior still contained furniture, appliances, and fixtures that ash sediment probably had "fossilized." Water from recent snows puddled the area.

We returned to the gift shop. I commented to the owner that he had a good attitude toward the destruction of his home. He said his Christian faith got him through. I bought a small Nativity set cast from the volcanic ash. I asked him about driving up to the crater. He gave directions for finding an overlook that would not be closed by the recent snows. He invited us to boondock on his parking lot that evening. Thanking him, we continued driving north up the mountainside.

Snow began falling. The higher we climbed, the heavier the snow fell. Signs warned that the highest overlook was closed. We parked at the last open overlook, grabbed jackets and hats, and got out long enough to see in the distance the barren, scooped-out top of the mountain. The rugged crater almost was obscured by falling snow.

Returning down the mountain, the snow decreased and then stopped. Boondocking in the parking lot presented a new challenge, because no grill or fire ring was there for cooking outdoors. We wanted a hot meal. I solved the problem by pulling out a large, foil roasting pan to contain the charcoal and set it on the gravel of the parking lot. I decided to do an experiment.

I had been using a homemade charcoal chimney made from a #10 can, with holes punched along the bottom for air ventilation. Chicken wire was stuffed in the bottom of the can to hold paper and charcoal. Earlier in our trip I had bought a commercially made charcoal chimney in Wal-Mart but had not used it. The new one was larger, better designed, and had a handle on the side. I'd see which one worked best.

I set both containers in the foil pan and put loosely wadded paper towels and some clothes-dryer lint and a few self-starting charcoal briquettes in each chimney. I lit each with a single match. Both caught quickly and began to burn. To each container I added a handful of regular charcoal. Both sets of charcoal heated nicely. I poured one container of white-hot charcoal into the foil pan.

I emptied into my Dutch oven two cans of chili with beans. Corn bread batter prepared from a mix topped the chili. Grated cheese went on top of the corn bread. I put on the lid. I set the Dutch oven over the coals in the foil pan and poured the remaining coals on the lid. The two chimneys had worked equally well.

For about 30 minutes we walked the dogs, until the aroma of baked corn bread drew us back. Mexican chili pie warmed us as the sun set behind heavy clouds.

The next morning, grateful for a free, safe place to overnight, we headed down the mountain and north to Seattle. Cousin Tom had emailed his phone number and address to me with instructions to "call me when you get here." He and his wife both worked outside the home. Their kids were in school. I planned to arrive in the late afternoon when they should be home. His address was in an older,

general direction of Tom's neighborhood. I'm willing to ask for directions, but the next service station attendant wasn't any help, either. The streets became more narrow and winding and began to climb and descend hills. Well-maintained, older commercial buildings climbed close to both sides of the streets. Sightseeing would have been fun if I hadn't been driving a 27-foot monster through impatient mini-sedans.

To our left Chris noticed a garage with large service doors. I negotiated around a block that was far from square and pulled into a small business lot next door to the garage.

An uniformed service man greeted me. He said the driveway into the garage bay was too narrow and the turn too tight for me to get in. He was unwilling to change the oil on the ground in his neighbor's parking lot. I couldn't blame him. He offered no alternatives, so I consulted my maps and decided to try to find Tom's house.

The further north I crept on the city streets, the steeper the hills became. Climbing from a stoplight put a strain on poor Gus. Braking for stoplights put a strain on me. Impatient drivers wanted me to get out of the way. Shops and older, quaint apartment buildings nudged sidewalks that hugged the streets. Beautiful plantings amid rock retaining walls filled spaces between the walks and buildings.

I turned onto Tom's narrow street to find a beautifully restored residential area. As I tried to find the correct house number, I zigzagged around small sedans and mini-vans parked along the curb. Many of the addresses were painted on the curb or on the mailboxes and were blocked by cars. I couldn't find a place to park along the crowded street near his address, so I explored residential streets for several blocks. I chose ones with less-steep grades. At last I found a vacant curb long enough to park Gus and pulled over.

From my cell phone I called Tom's number and got no answer. Perhaps he and his wife weren't home from work yet. I watched people watching me. I'm sure the neighbors were curious as to why I was parked here. I phoned again. No answer. I checked my notes. I'd been calling the wrong number.

Tom's wife, Donna, answered the phone and said that she had just returned home from work. She gave me directions to their home, which was on a corner lot. She guaranteed that I could fit Gus into their driveway. Donna was waiting on the front sidewalk to hold back traffic so I could maneuver Gus in a wide turn and climb the short driveway. Even with Gus' nose almost touching the gate to the backyard, our bikes on the bumper rack were over the front sidewalk. Banks of colorful flowers surrounded my cousin's beautiful, two-story, older home. To the left of Gus and the driveway, a rocky ledge held a mixture of spring flowers that cascaded to a sidewalk below.

We introduced ourselves. My cousins' kids arrived home from school at the same time Tom arrived from work. Introductions were made again. Chris was happy to talk to a boy cousin about his age. He especially was glad to discover the family cat. A delicious pasta and clam dish and salad for dinner encouraged family talks. After dinner, Donna invited me to take the dogs for an evening stroll. She led us down brick stairs to a lower street level, then past charming, turn-of-the-century brick buildings that had been renovated into condos and small shops.

People jogged, walked dogs, or pushed baby strollers along the brick walks lined with flowering cherry trees and rock gardens. Commercial buildings and apartments blended in well with the hills. They were anchored by extensive plantings and many ancient trees.

From a broad boulevard centered with spruce and other evergreens high above the harbor of Elliott Bay, we could see cruise liners at the docks far below. Views of the city stretched in layers beneath us. Far to the west, beyond Puget Sound, the sun began to descend behind the Olympic Mountains.

Donna explained that Seattle, like Rome, was built on seven hills. Over the years, as Seattle grew, the city encompassed more hills. Queen Anne Hill, the site of their home, at high tide is 400-feet above sea level. I hadn't thought about climbing back up those hills. My calves ached. Donna was in great shape. She walked almost every evening that rain wasn't falling. Donna said that winters were mild with weeks of rain or very cloudy weather. In the summer they had less rain. She said that Seattle averaged 50 clear days and 315 cloudy, rainy, misty, or foggy days a year. I was grateful that we were experiencing clear weather. She explained that Seattle seldom freezes and is not unbearably hot in August, so the rain was just something to complain about. Besides, the mild, moist weather was responsible for the lush, flowering plants and trees that made Seattle so beautiful.

Returning home, Donna and Tom explained their work and the kids' school schedules. They recommended that while they were gone, Chris and I visit the Pacific Science Center in the Seattle Center. I was given a bus schedule with a city map. That night I appreciated being able to sleep in my own bed in the RV and not to have to impose on relatives.

After a quick breakfast, Chris and I got out of the family's way by putting on hats and gloves to ward off the chill and walked south, downhill. I admired more neat, clean, inner-city neighborhoods of classic frame houses and brownstone-style apartments mixed with small shops.

Chris counted the cross streets to make sure we returned to the right corner. High above the trees and buildings we spotted the tip of a thin metal tower. Through another opening I recognized the revolving restaurant and observation deck of the 600-foot tall Space

map showed the Space Needle to be on the east side of
/ Center. As long as we walked in the general direction of
e Needle, we wouldn't get lost.

walked past parking lots lined with shrubs, trees, and tulip
Signs pointed the way through the 74-acre center. Built in
ʌ as the site of Century 21 World's Fair, it is a recreational,
.ertainment and cultural combination of architecture, grass, trees
and gardens, fountains, and public art. We passed between theaters
and by the coliseum. A huge, shallow fountain/pool centered with a
very large metallic dome attracted Chris. Like the petals of a flower
pebbled paving radiated from the center to a low wall. Following
signs, we passed the Flag Plaza Pavilion and reached the Pacific
Science Center.

The ticket booth had not yet opened. We walked around admir-
ing the futuristic sculptural arches and shallow pools bordered with
containers of brilliant flowers.

"Stay in line. Hands to your self. Hold your partner's hand."

Lines of school children accompanied by their teachers and
chaperones filed up to the ticket areas. I commented to Chris that I
felt as though I was playing hooky. Kids of all ages began to con-
verge. Little ones in matching field-trip T-shirts and teens in jeans
and logo sweatshirts carrying backpacks tried to ignore teachers. I
was glad to be retired and no longer responsible for other peoples'
children. Homeschooling Chris meant that we could take a three-
months' field trip.

Watching the kids, I was confused to see many faces that
seemed to be South Pacific Islanders. They resembled our Tongan
and Samoan friends at home. Many had Oriental/Asian features;
some Hispanics and many blacks were there. I heard languages that
I couldn't identify. Anglos seemed to be a minority. The kids got
along well. They didn't gang up in ethnic groups but interacted
interracially.

We bought our tickets and crossed a bridge over a shallow pool
where life-sized triceratops and stegosaur models waded. I followed
Chris into a special traveling exhibit featuring animated dinosaurs
and hands-on discovery exhibits. Throughout the morning I fol-

lowed him through five huge buildings as he explored many aspects of science through child-oriented activities. The buildings had computers, games, spacecraft, levers and gears, and of course, a gift shop.

My favorite exhibit was a butterfly center, with many exotic, brightly colored butterflies flitting among the equally exotic flowers. Butterflies landed on our clothing and in our hair. We were not allowed to touch them, but we could encourage them to land. Before leaving the greenhouse area, we had to be inspected for "hitchhikers"—butterflies that had landed on us and might be carried outside.

Outdoors, water blasters and water play toys lined the perimeter of the shallow pools for kids to explore the properties of water pressure. While Chris shot streams of water at suspended pinwheel targets, I sat down to rest and to watch the kids at play. School groups converged on the tables and benches to eat their sack lunches. A little boy put his paper sack near the edge of a pool and turned his back on it to watch the play.

Several sea gulls swooped down to land on the water. They were hoping for handouts. One of the gulls glided just above the water's surface and snatched the boy's lunch sack. Paddling backward the gull dragged the sack out into the water, where he shook it until it tore open. The boy's soda can, banana, and bag of chips floated away. The gull pecked at a wrapped sandwich until he got it out of the wrapper. Chris and a crowd of kids gathered to watch as more gulls gathered to squabble over the soggy sandwich. The banana sank. The soda floated toward the pool edge; the gulls played keep-away with an employee who tried to rescue the surviving lunch.

Walking back through the Seattle Center I invited Chris to ride the elevator to the restaurant at the 500-foot level of the Space Needle. Chris declined, so we watched from the ground as the outer ring of the restaurant made a 360-degree revolution. I was glad he wasn't interested in going up there. I was happy down here, too.

We heard music and followed it to the domed fountain. The center of the fountain now was spurting and spraying water in a pattern that changed with the music. The water made shallow puddles in the pool in which children waded. Despite the cold, Chris pulled off his shoes and ran into the shallow fountain to dodge the sprays of water. What a popular place this would be in the summer!

While I waited for his feet to get cold, I wandered over to a sign that described the International Fountain as being electronically operated. The spray was synchronized to change patterns according to the accompanying music. At night the fountain and water sprays were lighted. I would like to see it.

The 13-block walk back to Tom's certainly was not a stroll but was an uphill hike. When we were not near a bus stop, a couple of city buses passed us, so we kept on trudging. By the time we reached to top of the hills and climbed the stairway to Tom's street, my calves and shins burned. A rest and another great dinner revived me but not enough to join Donna on her evening walk.

Chris and his cousin rode bikes, while we relaxed on the back deck and watched the sun set. I learned about Pike Place Market and the waterfront, the Woodland Park Zoo, and Pioneer Square. We regretted leaving our newly located relatives in the morning to catch the ferry, but we planned to visit again.

Chapter 9

Alaskan Ferry

Thursday we left at mid-morning and hoped to avoid the "going-to-work" traffic. The route led through sections of older, three-storied, narrow-fronted, wood-framed houses that crowded each other on both sides of the road. Wooden railings enclosed front gallery porches on all three levels of the houses. The unity of architectural design, once evident of a fine home, now was broken by diverse clutter. Each floor had been converted into an apartment.

We climbed the irregular hillsides. Tall, narrow buildings elbowed one another for space on which to cling. The town appeared toy-like. The houses diminished in size as they receded up and into the hills.

Back on Interstate 5, I drove 100 miles due north to Bellingham and the ferry terminal. I stopped at Larrabee State Park and made a reservation for the night. I thought the park might fill up with RV's whose drivers planned to catch the last winter ferry to avoid higher summer rates.

We drove a short distance from the park to the ferry terminal. Very few vehicles were on the parking lot. After familiarizing myself with the area, I drove back a few blocks to explore a tiny, quaint village. The old wooden buildings housed antique and souvenir shops designed to attract ferry passengers. Chris pulled me into a canine cuisine shop that sold only high-class, very expensive pet supplies and dog treats. A glass-fronted bakery counter held an assortment of freshly baked gingerbread mail carriers, sugar-cookie fire hydrants, and for the weight-conscious pooches, all-grain doggie bones. Sam and Lady had been left in the motor home, so they didn't know what they were missing.

Made hungry by the tempting doggie treats, we found a caboose diner that, at small tables on an outdoor deck, served fresh clam chowder and fried clams. I knew that Chris liked seafood from the Gulf Coast and Louisiana crawfish, but I was surprised at how much he liked clams, too.

Exploring completed, we returned to the state park. Tomorrow would be the big day. I looked forward to experiencing four days and three nights on the ferry as it made its way north. My "Milepost" Plan-A-Trip map marked the Inside Passage along the coast of British Columbia, Canada, and the southeast finger of Alaska. We would be cruising between mountainous barrier islands.

I made sure that I had the tickets and reviewed the confirmation papers the Alaska Marine Highway System sent me. Vehicle staging was to begin at noon. I checked our passports and the dogs' rabies and health certificates and then put all the papers together in my belt bag. On the car deck I would have limited access to the RV. In the motor home we neither could eat nor sleep. However we would have times in which we could go below to walk the dogs.

Friday morning dawned misty and cold, with a heavy cloud cover. Rather than stay at the campground until noon, at 9 a.m. we drove to the ferry terminal and parked by a sign that directed us to vehicle loading. The gates were closed. I was restless. The weather was too cold and damp to walk the dogs for more than a few minutes. However we had to brave the wind to take the bikes off the bike rack, store them inside, and remove the bike rack. We battled cabin fever by playing games, reading, snacking, and looking at my watch.

Around 1 p.m. the gates opened. I was instructed to follow other vehicles into a larger parking area with numbered lanes. I then was directed to leave the line of cars and to park near some delivery trucks and 18-wheelers. I read my papers again to find that although staging, which I assumed meant lining up, began at noon, vehicle check-in time wasn't until 3 p.m., with departure at 6 p.m.

Steady drizzle blurred the hard edges of the modern terminal building. With hours to wait, we put on jackets and walked in the misty rain to the terminal for lunch and to explore the gift shop. I saw only one vessel—a very large cruise ship. Showing my ignorance, I inquired about the whereabouts of the ferry and was surprised to learn that the huge ship *was* the ferry.

The weather was too chilly and wet to walk into town, so I wrote postcards, read, and people-watched while Chris napped. A diesel truck pulling a long horse trailer parked near us. A large dog kennel was mounted over the tongue of the trailer. I curiously watched as bags of ice were poured through an opening in the top of the kennel. The crate door was opened and a massive, furry, Alaskan Malamute dog was allowed to jump to the ground. I guessed that ice was put into his kennel to keep him from getting too hot in the ferry.

We waited and watched while other vehicles joined one line or another. RV's began to congregate behind and alongside me. Other pet owners walked their dogs. Two men with clipboards and a measuring tape checked some of the vehicles' length, bumper to bumper. I was glad we had put the bikes inside. I didn't want to have to pay an extra charge for the added length.

Three o'clock passed, but no one moved forward. Around 4 p.m. autos began to creep toward the ferry. Small trucks, vehicles with trailers, and us "big guys" had coded stickers slapped on the windshield so we could move.

Inching forward and crossing a ramp, we stopped near the gaping entrance to the cavernous car deck. I presented all my papers and officially was allowed to board. When I questioned the hour's delay, I was told, "We're on Alaska time."

Gus was jammed bumper-to-bumper between two trucks. We were so close to the vehicles on either side that we didn't have enough space to squeeze out of the passenger-side door. We carried our backpacks, sleeping bags, jackets, and a small duffel bag as we threaded our way through the narrow passage between the vehicles. We followed others toward the bow of the ship and hoped they knew where they were going. Passengers entered a narrow door into a central gangway that climbed up several flights of stairs.

I had read that passengers could set up a small, self-supporting tent on the open part of the observation deck. We had planned to set up Chris's tent. We reached Deck 6 and stepped outside on the passageway. It was so cold, wet, and rainy that we opted for the recliner lounge. Here were airliner-style reclining seats, large windows, and small restrooms. Many other passengers already had staked out their territory, so we couldn't get seats by the windows.

Following the lead of others, we left our backpacks, loaded with snack food, to claim our seats. Chris and I took a look around outside. The wind and mist quickly forced us back inside. Dark was falling and we couldn't see much outside, anyway. Taking stock of our accommodations, I decided that we were in as good a place as any. I was glad we had not carried the tent in with us. More experienced passengers were shaking out sleeping bags, so we did too.

About 8 p.m. the purser announced we were about to be under way. The ship began to shudder and move ponderously like an elephant tip-toeing through a tulip field. As soon as we had cleared the port, the ship would have a car-deck call. We were admonished to spend only 15 minutes below deck. At the signal Chris and I left our jackets and other belongings on the seats and scurried down the inside stairway to check on the dogs.

The dogs barked. They were happy to see us. With a pocket full of plastic trash bags and a roll of paper towels for cleanup we took them on leashes onto the car deck. We squeezed between vehicles and dodged other dogs and owners amid a lot of barking.

All of us dog owners were looking for a dog walk. The ship didn't have a designated area. Any place on the deck was acceptable, as long as it got cleaned up. My dogs didn't understand. They just sniffed and scampered around until the warning call that the car deck was closing. The dogs weren't interested in doing their business. We returned them to the RV, fed them, and joined other pet owners to climb the stairs.

I wanted one more peek outside. I put on my jacket, hat, and gloves and braved the cold to go out on the deck. I couldn't see down the length of the gangway or past the railing into the choppy water far below. The mist and freezing wind drove me back inside.

Chris already had laid back his chair and was getting comfortable and hungry. We had agreed to carry tuna, crackers, granola bars, trail mix, and fruit on which to snack so we wouldn't be too tempted to eat expensive cafeteria food. People around us set up housekeeping on the floor with their gear and laid out their sleeping bags. Since this seemed to be the acceptable norm, we stretched out our sleeping bags in the aisle between the seats, too. The experienced travelers had the right idea; the floor was more comfortable than the seats. During the night when I had to make a trip to the "head" (the restroom), I had to step over and around people cocooned in sleeping bags in the corridors.

I must have been on Texas time, because I woke before 5 a.m. just as the sky was beginning to brighten. I grabbed my jacket, hat and gloves, and camera. I braced myself to go outside. The sky was clearing. The rising sun caused the remaining mist to glow. In the lee of a lifeboat I took shelter from the wind. All too soon the piercing cold sent shivers down my spine from ears and nose to fingers and toes. I'd wait a while inside.

Around 7 a.m. someone made an announcement that a pod of Orcas was spotted on the starboard (right-hand side facing forward, for us landlubbers). I woke Chris, coaxed him into his jacket, grabbed cameras, and rushed to join other passengers on the deck outside.

The whales merely were tiny, dark, moving dots between the ship and the far islands. Someone on the intercom explained Orca facts. Orcas are also called killer whales because they are supreme hunters. Unlike most other whales that have baleen, these whales have many interlocking, blunt teeth. They prey on fish as well as on large marine mammals including seals, sea otters, and even other whales.

As the ship approached, we could see individual black whales surfacing to blow and breathe through the blowholes on the top of their heads. They were communicating with whistles, clicks, and a pulsating call. A few whales soared into the air and slammed onto the water. We were close enough to see the white belly, chin, and eye patches on some of whales. Others rose above the surface like a black island and then submerged with their tall dorsal fin straight up like a periscope.

The speaker informed us that this pod of 10 to 15 mammals was resident to the area. The males could reach 32-feet long and weigh nine to 10 tons. The females are slightly smaller. Males live 30 to 50 years, while females can live up to 70 years. They can swim at speeds of 25 to 30 mph. The whales were so familiar with the ferry that, as we passed them, they went about their business of feeding.

An announcement was made that we were navigating the passage through Queen Charlotte Sound. On Sunday morning, 36 hours after departure, we would make our first port call at Ketchikan. A car-deck call allowed us to go below to check on the dogs and to restock on snacks.

On the car deck a woman was having trouble getting into her car because her cat was loose. The cat had been in a carrier, but she had let it out to use the litter box. Now the poor cat was so upset that he was scratching the window to get her to let him out of the car. An understanding pet owner wiggled his fingers on the window on the opposite side, called the cat, and distracted it so the owner could get in to feed it. He had to distract the cat again so she could get out without the cat escaping.

Sam and Lady jumped up on the passenger seats as soon as they heard our voices. Sam jumped out the open passenger door. Chris took his leash and began to walk him. I helped fat Lady down. We followed Chris. A young man with a bird dog called to Chris. "Has your dog 'gone' yet?"

Chris replied, "Huh?"

"I thought that if your dog has used it, then maybe mine would smell it and would get the idea that it's OK."

Smart thinking. Hopefully my dogs would get the scent. They didn't. They were bashful. Better get the idea next time.

Bundled up again against the cold we explored the open gangways. I saw our passage marked on a marine chart, but it was very confusing with numerous large islands and winding waterways. The islands really were small mountains covered with spruce and other evergreens, with rocky shores and snow on the top. Mist hung in the valleys. The now-cloudless sky was azure. Blinding sun glinted off the wind-ruffled sea.

We climbed to an upper deck. Here a jungle-gym of rigging clung to the superstructure. Chris wandered while I stared at the swells and noted color changes and lacy foam. A red life preserver lashed to the railing near lifeboats had "Matanuska" stenciled on it. What a funny name for a ship! I wondered what it meant.

The observation deck was swarming with young people who had duct-taped their domed tents to the open deck. Others slept on chaise lounge chairs in the semi-enclosed, sheltered part of the rear deck. Sleeping bags, backpacks, boots, and assorted stuff littered the area. For some reason the ones who were not cocooned in their sleeping bags didn't seem to mind the cold.

At 10:30 a.m. the announcer recommended that passengers return to the lounge areas because the ferry would be "experiencing ocean motion." He was right. I felt a metallic tremble. The ship's skin shuttered. The ship began to roll and pitch from side to side. I had a tough time keeping my balance. I lay back on the seat, tried not to think about being seasick, and tried to sleep.

After what seemed to be hours, the seas became calmer. Once again barrier islands protected us from the ungraspable breadth of the Pacific Ocean. An announcement was made that soon we would hear a "car-di-ac" call so we could check our vehicles for shifting. I hoped this gave the crew enough time to check for properly set brakes before we went below.

Another announcement instructed all of us in the recliner lounge to assemble in the dining room for a safety meeting. We were shown how to put on life jackets, told where the lifeboats were, and given other safety instructions. The galley cooks were preparing lunch. Delicious aromas distracted us from the safety class. I agreed with Chris that we should try the cafeteria for lunch. While waiting we visited the gift shop and bought pocket guides to reference Alaskan mammals and birds. We visited with some of the crew in crisp, white uniforms with epaulets and tie, just like on a cruise ship. The baked salmon was great and reasonably priced.

In the forward cocktail lounge an Alaska Parks Service ranger presented a talk. He spoke about marine animals and passed around pelts for us to feel. He talked about summer jobs in Alaska and about his previous job as log salvager. We were invited back for another talk that afternoon to be presented by a couple who had spent seven years traveling around the world in a sailboat. I thought I was adventurous on a four-day ferry.

Chris discovered a video game room, begged a handful of quarters from me, and left me to gaze through the large bow windows. The sea was a cold green-blue. Jagged atolls and islands were coated in deep, emerald green spruce that were punctuated by cascades of ice-blue glaciers and waterfalls. I walked back to the stern observation deck to people-watch. Brave, young sunseekers had stripped to shorts, tank tops and sandals. A few young men were shirtless. They sat in the sun on the aft deck. The cabin sheltered them from the wind. The temperature was in the 50s. Even though I wore a heavy jacket, gloves, and hats, I still was freezing in the wind.

I overheard snatches of conversation between the long-haired and bearded young men about going to Alaska for summer jobs. Some were planning to fish or be hunting guides. Others would take any job they could find. Few seemed already to have a job lined up. Many single young women were on the deck, too. They talked of looking for restaurant-server or sales jobs. They seemed too young to be so independent. I watched while they warmed up by playing hacky-sack and Frisbee on the deck.

A gray-haired woman about my age sat by herself knitting. Another really big "mama" dozed with her crocheting dropped in her lap. They seemed out of place with all the 20-somethings. Few middle-aged people and very few children were there.

Walking to the forward lounge I stopped to talk to a group of older folks whose fashion statement was quite opposite that of the young. An Elder Hostel group was traveling together to Haines on a tour. They wore earmuffs, mufflers, and expensive insulated jackets with their pressed jeans. I met a couple from Rockport, TX, who told me that others were from Silsbee, Fort Worth, Tyler, and Austin. Texas was well-represented.

I couldn't help noticing a bleached-blond "society lady" with heavy makeup. She wore a low-cut, tube top beneath her open leather jacket and over skintight jeans. A much younger man sporting a long, dark ponytail trailed her. I never saw them speak to each other as she paraded the decks with him close behind.

Back in the recliner lounge to warm up, I met Ingrid, a grandmother who in the winter lived in Seattle and in the summer worked on a steam train from Anchorage to Fairbanks. She, too, slept in the recliner lounge. Her car was below. She would get off in Haines and drive to Anchorage.

I met a young mother with her 4-year-old son, Angelo. They were walk-on passengers. She had shared a cabin with a friend, but they returned to the lounge because the tiny cabin with double berths was too confining for Angelo. They would sleep on the floor with us until they reached Ketchikan, where they would take another, smaller ferry to Prince Rupert, her home.

I explored the small shower room, now crowded with passengers, and decided to get "dry-cleaned" with baby wipes. As I read and dozed in my seat, I kept thinking about jobs. *What would teaching in Alaska be like? How would the winters be? Would I have the nerve to travel that far without a job already secured?* I thanked God for this fascinating trip and for the opportunity to volunteer at the camp without having to worry about wages.

During the next car-deck call we descended a different set of stairs and emerged on the crowded deck further aft. Passing the huge horse trailer that we recognized from Bellingham, I spoke to a man walking the Malute. The trailer was hauling Clydesdale horses to Ketchikan to pull carriages for the summer tourist season. They would return to Seattle for the winter.

A horse poked his muzzle out the window of a single horse trailer and begged Chris to pet him. Chris was glad we wouldn't have the job of cleaning those horse trailers. I agreed. I couldn't imagine that hauling the horses back and forth on the ferry was more cost-effective rather than was importing feed north to care for them over the winter.

As he returned to our lounge, Chris was pleased to find a movie on the large-screen TV. I dozed until it was over. We reclaimed our spots on the floor, spread out sleeping bags, and settled for our second night.

Sunday dawned clear and cold. The ship had no church services, so we spent time on deck watching a pod of porpoise. Approaching Ketchikan we saw eagles soaring high overhead. Some swooped down to the surface of the water, while others perched in the spruce trees. Eagles rode the thermals. Gulls rode the wind and waves as they dove, squabbled, and whirled away in a follow-the-leader flock.

Near the docks, the announcer pointed out sea otters. These adorable, furry creatures appeared to be playing as they rolled, dove, and splashed. Some floated on their backs with their kitten-like faces, front paws, and back flippers above the water line. The announcer explained that sea otters were making a comeback after almost becoming extinct. The high value of their luxurious, dense fur resulted in extensive hunting fueled by the fur trade of a century ago. He pointed out a large female floating on her back with a baby pup resting on her chest. Other otters dove to pluck mussels or crabs from the coastal waters, surfaced, and rolled on their backs. The otters brought up rocks, too, and rested them on their chests. They hit the mussels against the rocks to crack them open.

Docking in Ketchikan, we were allowed to take the dogs off the ferry and to walk them while we were in port. The weather was clear. The air didn't seem as cold. Was I acclimating? I wanted to explore the town and see the totem poles I had read about. Town was a long walk from the ferry terminal. We walked for a while and then returned the dogs to the motor home. We resumed walking toward town. Chris griped. I wished I could have left him with the dogs.

We found a small shopping center with a Burger King that featured large windows overlooking a seawall far below. Here we ate lunch while we watched kayakers braving the cold wind. Out of the protection of the shore, the fragile craft hit the face of approaching waves with an explosive, white flash of powdery foam. Wind-blown waves crashed on the seawall and sent spray to glitter in the sun on our window. Sea gulls, eagles, and other birds filled the air. At a small market we picked up some groceries before we returned to the ferry.

The ferry got under way. Passengers settled into their seats or stood in small groups along the railing. The sunseekers called our attention to another pod of Orcas feeding on krill and zooplankton. As we approached port in Wrangell, we heard the announcement that 150 high-school students would be joining us in the recliner lounge. We were asked to make room for them. This addition would put the ferry at its capacity of 450 passengers. Before walking the dogs during the Wrangell port call, we made sure our seats were reserved with our belongings and took extra stuff to the RV.

Returning to "our" lounge, I felt my space being invaded. Teens and their belongings were everywhere. I became very territorial—mama bear protecting her cub. I was defensive of our space and spread our sleeping bags on the floor to make sure we had a place to sleep. Even though the time was 9 p.m., daylight still was outside. The students were having a good time. Rap music on CD players became annoying. Despite a warning sign against smoking, two guys were flicking lighters. The teacher in me put authority in my voice as I asked them to put the lighters away. Amazingly they did. As darkness fell, the kids settled down to watch TV, play cards, read, do homework on the floor, and finally fall asleep.

I bundled up and went astern in the dark. The engines sent up boiling, dark swells topped with sparkling foam. The collapsing crests of foam, like white crocheted doilies or spider webs, trailed into braided streamers of phosphorescence. A myriad of sparkling stars echoed the foam. Blue-black sky and blue-black ocean met at an invisible horizon. The moaning wind and stinging salt spray chased me inside.

At 3 a.m., we made a port call in Petersburg, called "Little Norway." Few of us stirred through the jolts, groans, creaks, and bangs of docking and unloading.

Monday morning some of the students no longer were with us. When I overheard the conversations of some of the other students, I forgave the teens for their intrusion. I began to talk to them. They were from different towns along the ferry route and were returning home from a fine-arts festival in Ketchikan. They had been in competition in vocal and instrumental music and drama.

A video of the competition was shown on the large-screened TV. It featured classical violin solos, vocal solos and ensembles, one-act plays, and instrumental solos and ensembles. I was amazed at the talent and that teachers were willing to work with such small groups. A girl going home to Skagway told me that only 34 students were in her high school.

An older girl on her way to Skagway to look for work began talking to a student. She had met a girl, Sara, in Hawaii who was from Skagway. "Do you know her?" The reply was "No, but my grandmother probably does. She knows everybody." Must be a really small town.

I took a photo of a girl wearing a T-shirt reading: "Big Bang Theory; you've got to be kidding, God." I would like to have a shirt like that.

High cirrus clouds and warmer winds greeted us at our port call in Juneau. The capital of Alaska is hidden beyond the docks. While I walked the dogs, I met a women with two boys who were boarding in Juneau. I learned that no road—only ships and planes—existed from the "outside" to the capital. Juneau citizens are divided over a plan to develop an 800-mile road to Anchorage. Environmentalists say that the proposed road would harm wildlife and the Tongass National Forest. No one wanted the capital moved to Anchorage. The expense of such a project has held it at bay since the capital was founded in 1906.

She said that spring weather usually was misty and damp but that this spring had been unusually dry. A fresh-water shortage existed. As we pulled away from the dock, she pointed out the massive Mendenhall Glacier hanging between mountain peaks. We had seen other pockets of ice in the high, mountainous valleys, but this was our first real glacier. It was overwhelmingly huge and glistened white with deep turquoise shadows.

Before we reached Haines, we saw another pod of whales— probably humpbacks, many high valley glaciers, and adorable sea otters. The ferry made port. I walked the dogs through the parking area to the base of a mountain cliff. Here was an icefall—a frozen water fall, with melt water beginning to flow through and around the ice. High racing clouds like beaten egg whites dotted the bright, blue sky.

Skagway, our destination, only was another hour away. I gathered belongings and got ready for the next leg of our adventure.

Chapter 10

Alaska at Last

Skagway! We made it! Although Skagway is the northernmost town on the ferry system and not in the main body of Alaska, I felt as if I now truly was in Alaska. A "Welcome to Skagway" sign led to a narrow road and a very small, old-fashioned village backed by snow-encrusted mountains and Sitka spruce.

Leaving the familiarity and comfort of the ferry, we were one of few vehicles to exit across a gangway. A sign for "Pullen Creek RV Park, Gateway to the Klondike" directed me to a very small, deserted campground near the port that was within walking distance of the town. Snows had melted and left dry, rocky sites dotted with small, bare trees.

I located the camp manager and his dogs in a tiny office-cabin where he was cooking chili over a hot plate. He gave us our choice of the sites, all of which were vacant. He warned that the water and sewer lines still were frozen to all of the sites and bathhouse.

Following the only road from the campground, we crossed railroad tracks and passed the White Horse steam engine. We walked into town. A signboard with a map of Skagway at the ferry landing showed four north/south streets with several short cross streets. The road from the ferry terminal became State Street through the north end of town, where it split. The northern route led to Canada. The other branch trailed to Dyea, a ghost town where in 1896, 30,000 gold prospectors attempted to cross the mountains on the Chilkoot Trail to reach the Klondike gold fields.

Boarded-up, wooden, false-fronted buildings lined both sides of the narrow street. We felt as though we had had walked onto the abandoned set of a Gold Rush movie. The small frontier town consisted of more than 100 restored, historic structures dating back to the 1880s. We walked on wooden boardwalks past closed, Old West-style buildings. The town appeared deserted. No cars passed. No people could be seen.

Further down State Street, we passed the White Pass and Yukon Route Rail Road Depot, now the Parks Department Visitors Center, which was closed. The Red Onion Saloon, one of many bars, leaned into The Arctic Brotherhood Hall, a two-storied building faced with river driftwood in intricate patterns. The Golden North Hotel topped by a gold Russian style dome appeared out of character.

Crossing a side street, the sound of hammering drew us toward several young men working on the facade of another wooden building. Even though the time now was 7 p.m., workers were painting and repairing in a spring fix-up frenzy. On May 1, in just two days, the first cruise ship would arrive. The ghost town would spring alive with tourists.

The Mascot Saloon was the only open business with doors open to the evening breeze. A young woman was applying for a server job. She got it. Several other businesses, gift shops, saloons, jewelry stores, and small cafés had "Help Wanted" signs posted in their windows. Also displayed were Gold Rush artifacts: gold pans, knapsacks, hammers and chisels, old clothes, and boots.

Returning to the visitors center, we stopped at a window display depicting the stampeders on the Chilkoot Trail out of Dyea. A section of the trail, called the Golden Stairs, only was a quarter of a mile long but climbed 1,000 vertical feet. The Canadian government required each of the 30,000 prospectors to carry a year's supply or one "ton of goods" over the mountain summit into the Canadian wilderness. This required that each prospector, male or female, struggle on foot under enormous loads as they made 20 to 40 trips from Dyea to the summit. Three months often was required to carry a person's gear to the Canadian boarder.

An alternate but longer route, the White Pass Trail, later was named Dead Horse Trail because 3,000 horses died the first winter as gold-seekers tried to moved tons of supplies through the snows.

I noted a listing of what was required for a year's "outfit." Besides heavy outdoor clothing, a person needed a MacKinaw coat, heavy underwear, two pairs of rubber boots, two pairs of heavy shoes, hats and gloves, blankets, and a tent. Equipment included a stove, gold pan, buckets, pick, saw, hammers, chisels, hatchet, shovel, eating utensils, cups and plates, compass, and matches. Guns and ammunition were not listed. Besides all of that, each person had to carry a year's supply of food including but not limited to: 100 pounds of bacon, 400 pounds of flour, 100 pounds of dried fruit, 100 pounds of beans, 100 pounds of sugar, 40 pounds of corn meal, 40 pounds of rice, 10 pounds of tea, 10 pounds of salt, 25 pounds of coffee, 25 cans of butter, and assorted dried meats and vegetables.

This list of supplies easily could have added up to a ton. I shook my head and commented to Chris that we were spoiled with a motor home and all the conveniences we needed to live well. These brave people didn't have the advantage of up-to-date, lightweight backpacking and camping equipment.

I shuddered to think of climbing the Golden Stairs and, in freezing weather, making 40 round-trips with a 50-pound pack on my back. At twilight we returned to the comfort of the RV. I couldn't sleep. I could sense ghosts of the wild frontier. Gold-crazed, tough, daring individuals who didn't realize the hardships. The promise of adventure and quick wealth led many stalwart, tough women to follow gold-crazed husbands or strike out on their own. Most suffered the same fate as did the men. With claims already staked, they faced hunger, depression, and destitution. A few women, though, became entrepreneurs. They became small merchants, cooks, or took in laundry. Some worked in the saloons. They survived and made their fortune in the wild boomtowns and not in the gold fields.

I thought about how easy we have life compared to the newly arrived Pilgrims. They met Native Americans and followed their network of trails trampled into the East Coast forests. The Pilgrims, striving for religious freedom, carried their beliefs with them. Crowds of immigrant settlers walked, rode, and paddled westward. Land-hungry settlers conquered the wilderness in a single generation. Westward-drifting Americans reached the plains, then restlessly crossed the plains and reached the Pacific. As they settled the West, immigrants made sure that they took God with them.

When migrants thought they had no more frontier to explore, the Gold Rush beckoned to Alaska. I wondered whether Christian missionaries had accompanied the prospectors.

I contemplated how the gold prospectors felt as they climbed these glorious mountains on foot in deep snow with as much as half their body weight in monstrous backpacks. Before the Gold Rush Russian fur-trappers and hunters encroached on the native population. I learned that a few Russian Orthodox missionaries had arrived with early settlers to Christianize the natives. I pondered over their determination and courage to spread the Word of God in such perilous times when survival was doubtful.

Could I have done it? Would I have wanted to? Today we are so spoiled by easy living that we take everything, including eternity, for granted.

By 6:30 the next morning, the sun was high enough beyond the mountains to brighten the Skagway valley and waken the birds. Humming "On the Road Again" by Willie Nelson, I followed the only highway out of town. Quaint homes on small parcels of land were wedged into crevices of the valley. The narrow, two-lane wound northward and quickly left the outskirts of town.

We began a steep climb toward Dead Horse Pass used by the gold miners and named for the thousands of horses that died as they attempted the climb. Gus's transmission groaned. How much more so had the prospectors suffered making this climb! Numerous icefalls on the cliffs to my left enticed me to stop and take photos, but the road had no shoulder or turnouts—only a dropoff to my right.

Snow bordered the road and covered the rocky mountainsides. Earlier, infrequent traffic had melted the fresh snow into two tracks. Fortunately the road had not refrozen. I encountered no other vehicles.

Chapter 11

Canada, the Yukon

At the summit of the 3,000-foot pass, we crossed into British Columbia, Canada. The brilliant sun had thawed the almost-level summit free of ground snow. Railroad tracks appeared. I passed a deserted train station that bore the name "Fraser." To my left, a lonely border-patrol building occupied the side of this "wide spot in the road."

A young woman wearing a Canadian uniform and looking as though she were a female Sergeant Preston of the Yukon took our passports and the dogs' papers. Knowing we had arrived by the ferry, she just glanced at the dogs' papers. She spoke to Chris in the passenger seat.

"Who is this?"she asked, indicating me.

Confused, he hesitated and answered, "Carol."

"I mean, who is she to you?"

"My mom," he replied.

She was satisfied and didn't ask for proof of our relationship.

"You certainly are isolated," I said as I retrieved my papers.

She replied that she loved being out here. Things were quiet and peaceful. The unusually late snow had caught them off-guard.

Even though the altitude was higher, the brilliant, spring sun was warming the snow and ice so that small waterfalls were rushing down the mountainsides, alongside and through the still-frozen ice-falls. The narrow road continued twisting northward along the base of cliffs where snowpack avalanches had dumped snow, ice, rock, and gravel. In some places the avalanches were so recent that debris covered the road, which was marked by the tires of transport trucks.

South of Carcross, Yukon, in a long valley far below the road-way, a lake frozen from shore to shore glittered like fragmented crystals. Chris, too, seemed mesmerized by the beauty of the sunshine on snow. The cloudless sky was a watercolor wash of Payne's gray. Many times I had questioned my motives for this trip. Yes, we were going to do volunteer work, but we could have found it much closer to home. Deep in my heart I was being blessed deep by experiencing the grandeur of God's creation. I didn't deserve it.

Often on this trip I had congratulated myself on being self-reliant. Now I realized that being self-sufficient is a weakness. Only by depending on God do I have strength.

At last. The junction with the Alaskan Highway 1—the famed AlCan. I turned west toward Whitehorse and Alaska. Behind me, far to the east, was Dawson Creek, the official beginning of the AlCan. Begun in 1942, not long after my birth, the AlCan (Alaskan-Canadian) Highway was a joint U.S. and Canadian effort to connect Alaska to the Lower Forty-Eight in the event of a Japanese invasion of Alaska. The stories surrounding the construction of this highway have intrigued historians. Not being a historian, my interest still was because of history—*my* history.

I pulled onto a wide spot on the shoulder to look over my maps and the Milepost guide book. An incredible engineering feat conquered this vast rugged terrain. I knew that I'd learn a lot more by traveling this road than by consulting all the maps and travel guides I've packed. I'd live geography, too. How gratifying to experience life, rather than read about it.

On the outskirts of Whitehorse we stopped for gas and postcards. Continuing west I began mental games. The gasoline was priced at $.80 Canadian, per liter. I had used a debit card, which had been charged $80 for 100 liter of gas. So far, so good. *But what was my cost in American dollars?* One-hundred dollars American was equal to about $130 Canadian, and 3.8 liters equal one U.S. gallon, so if I paid $.80 per liter, that would almost be four times per gallon, or $3.20 Canadian per gallon, *but what would that be in American dollars?* That's expensive gasoline any way you figure it, so I'll let my bank take care of it.

I noticed some speed-limit signs in mph and some in kilometers. The speed limit was 80 KM; was I speeding at 60 mph? I posed the question of converting kilometers to miles to Chris. He figured it out quickly. I asked him to convert 50 KM to miles. He guessed 35 mph. I questioned him. He was certain he was right. So I asked how he figured it out so quickly. He laughed at me and pointed to the series of small numbers under the speedometer on the dash. Here speed was indicated in kilometers. By comparing the two sets of numbers, I even could figure out how far we were from a distant village.

The farther north we traveled, the smaller and more distant were the villages. Some only were a few service buildings by the roadside. All were closed. The roadway was gaining altitude while transversing a long broad valley floor. Mountain ranges appeared and receded in layers on the right, left, and ahead. Deep, green spruce forests were broken by groves of bare-branched aspens. Their spidery tracery was finely embroidered against a burnished silver sky.

I started watching for mile markers and was concerned that I wouldn't have any idea of where I was if I need help. I wondered whether the numbers were in kilometers or miles. At one of our infrequent rest and gas stops, I thumbed through the Milepost trying to pinpoint our location. I found an explanation. The numbers on the mileposts were "miles", the original or traditional miles from when the roadway first was laid out. Since the road has been straightened, the traditional mile markers may not be the actual miles (or kilometers). Then, too, the number on the post may not be in the Milepost.

I stopped playing mind games and slowed down. The highway deteriorated to gravel with parallel ridges, like corduroy, running across its width. A teeth-rattling vibration could not be stopped by slowing down or by speeding up. We crept along. Little dust was there because of the melting snow and lack of traffic. For at least 100 miles, as close as I could figure, we passed only a few abandoned road-construction vehicles. Bright, pink flags, marking major cracks caused by ice heaves from permafrost, were the only signs that humans had been here.

The original construction crews had blasted the roadway through virgin forest and rock. They had contended with mountains and mud, snow and sleet, equipment breakdown and backbreaking labor. Stories of the soldiers and civilian workers and their heroic efforts during a time of war were astounding. Fourteen-hundred miles of highway, from Dawson Creek, Yukon, to Delta Junction, Alaska, were completed in just nine months. Today this is the only highway for most of this distance and is constantly being repaired.

The sky was bright and clear. The sun glinted off snowbanks, waterfalls, and the snow-encrusted boughs of spruce trees. Brush and deadfall created a thick brocade of interlaced, bare branches silhouetted against the snowfall. It was a long day but not a boring one. I recalled hearing a quotation by Robert Service of his impression of Alaska,

"It's the beauty that fills me with wonder. It's the stillness that fills me with peace."

I pulled into the first service station in Haines Junction to fill up. The bored attendant was talkative. He advised me always to use a credit card, because I'd get a better rate of exchange. We were getting hungry and needed a break, so I asked the attendant to recommend a place to eat. He suggested the Cozy Café, which was north along the AlCan, to my left.

As we entered the tiny café, two men were drinking coffee. They paid and left. We took our choice of the empty tables. A young man wearing a white apron left the cash register to bring us menus. He excused himself to go into the kitchen. I had decided to splurge, because I had no idea where we'd spend the night. The menu prices seemed high until I thought about trucking food so far from a major town. Still mulling over the rate of exchange and worrying about my budget, I did some mental math and figured that my cost in American dollars would be about 3/4 of the Canadian price.

We ordered. I decided on a buffalo burger and fries. Chris wanted a burger, too. He ordered the house special—a Reinhart's burger. The waiter-cashier-cook highly recommended it to a growing boy with an appetite. To this day we talk about that burger. Between the oversized buns were a beef patty, ham, bacon, lettuce, tomato, grilled onions, mushrooms, cheese slices, pickles, and a fried egg! This was dressed with mayo and mustard and served with fried onion rings and potato salad. Chris loved it. I talked him into trading bites. Very tasty! I thought that meal should hold him for a while.

As we waited for our check, I wandered over to a currency-exchange chart on the wall by the register. I had been right, or at least close, with my figures. Our bill was about $25 Canadian and was equivalent to $18 American. I had figured $25 divided by 2 equals $12.50. Half of $12.50 is $6.25. Add $12.50 and $6.25; that equals $18.75. Pretty close to $18. Except that the cashier said that was not the way to it worked. Americans were not given a discount—just a rate of exchange. Oh, well—debit cards and the bank can figure it out.

Our new friend exchanged small talk with us. As I was paying, he asked Chris if he would like some Canadian coins. I gave him three American dollars and trusted him to do a fair exchange. He gave Chris a Loonie, a silver coin worth a Canadian dollar with Queen Elizabeth on one side and a loon on the other. He handed Chris another large coin with a silver center and a gold rim. This one was worth $2 Canadian. It was called a Toonie—two colors, $2. He also gave Chris a few lesser-denomination coins. Chris happily pocketed his "funny money."

On the road again I tried to remember the conversion formulas for temperature. I think Fahrenheit is equal to 9/7 times Celsius plus 32, and Celsius is equal to 7/9 times Fahrenheit minus 32. When I get to Alaska, I'm determined to find conversion charts to add to the end of this book.

We traveled only about 10 miles west of Haines Junction when we were confronted by another stretch of rough, bad, gravely, frost-heave cracked road. Was it under construction or being torn up for repairs? A certain relief happens with change, even if it's from bad to worse. We progressed about 15 miles at 10 mph. One-and-a-half-hours later we regained the two-lane, paved road.

To my right, the shore of a huge, ice-covered lake enticed us to stop. Amazingly, walking in the sun was not cold enough for a jacket. Chris and I walked the dogs to the shoreline. Sam walked out onto the ice and licked it. Chris tried to follow, but I was afraid the ice would crack up and he would fall through. I warned him repeatedly to get back to the shore.

An elderly couple traveling south parked their Class A motor home to walk their small dog. As all RV'ers do we exchanged "Hi"s. They warned that we had an additional 20 miles of bad road, then good road, and more bad. Traveling this stretch was like this last year, too. Hopes of having any good roads repaired before our return trip were shattered.

They asked if we had seen any bears, which we hadn't. They were excited about seeing a large bear on the frozen lake, just north of were we were parked. We jumped back in and got Gus going. Chris hung out the window watching the shore ice near the bank for the bear. He spotted it way out on the ice near the center of the lake. We stopped and pulled over to take videos.

With the zoom lens the bear's light-brown fur seemed close enough to touch. We watched it pad across the ice. Its large feet and lower legs were wet and a darker color of brown. Chris laughed at me for not wanting him to walk on the ice, when the bear could walk on it way out there.

I still didn't want him to take chances. Chris said the bear could walk on the ice because it had four feet to spread out its weight and he had only two feet. Good enough reasoning for a worried mama.

I had been driving now for 14 hours. Our average speed was less than 50 mph. How far had we traveled? Somewhere I had read that traveling by horse, a rider averaged 12 miles a day. How long would be required to make this trip by horseback?

The sun still was shining. The long, daylight hours belied the time. I was tired and ready to stop for the night, but all the provincial parks and private campgrounds still were closed for the winter. Few scattered settlements consisted of only a homestead and outbuildings.

Bored, Chris had climbed into my sleeping bag on the rear bed to snooze. Suddenly appeared a caribou that crossed from the hillside to my left to the hillside on the right. And another.

"Chris!" I yelled, "Caribou! Caribou! Caribou!"

Still in the zipped-up sleeping bag, he jumped up and hopped down the hallway as if he was in a toesack race. Laughing, I could see him in the rearview mirror as he bounced and stumbled forward. I counted caribou out loud. "That makes three, no, four of them! Get the camera!"

He grabbed the video camera and stumbled into the passenger's seat as I coasted to a stop. He aimed the camera at the line of caribou still crossing in front of us. Twelve of them caused a caribou traffic jam. I was the only vehicle in sight. What a day. First a bear, then caribou.

The weather began to deteriorate rapidly as we climbed higher into the mountains. Heavy clouds, looking as though they were white fog, obscured most of the landscape. Chris's sharp eyes saw dark, moving shapes on the snowbank. Two huge moose with awkwardly heavy racks made their way across the road and into the cold, swirling mist. I was driving on adrenaline. Gus was on fumes when I noticed a small gas station-motel-café that appeared to be open. Whether or not the place was open, I would park here at Ida's 24-Hour Café and Motel for the night.

We got out to stretch. With the setting sun the temperature had dropped. To our surprise a bearded man in a parka entered the darkened café doorway. He offered to pump gas for me while we went inside to warm up.

The wind swept us into the open, empty café. I had been driving for more than 16 hours through 400 miles of the most scenic, most awesome wilderness I ever had encountered. We had followed the shoreline of Kluane Lake for 30 miles. Glacial steams that fed this 50-mile-long lake gave the waters a turquoise color. We crept through Destruction Bay, a tiny village named for the many boats wrecked and lives lost here during the Klondike days.

After he filled Gus's tank, the attendant entered to warm up and talk. He invited us to park in front of the motel at no charge. I thanked him and paid for the gas and hot chocolate. We hurried through the damp cold to snuggle down in our sleeping bags.

My doggie alarm clocks woke me at daylight. They didn't care about the cold. They wanted out. I preferred to stay deep inside my sleeping bag, so I tried not to move. It didn't fool Sam. He pawed at my covered-up head and stuck his cold nose on my ear. Sam won. Gus had no heater. The night before, I had tried to set the thermostat on heat, but only frigid air blew from the vents. On previous trips I never had needed the RV's heater and had assumed it worked as well as did the air-conditioner. Before I left Texas, with highs in the 80s, I never thought to check out the system. I braved the frigid air and quickly pulled on a second sweatsuit over the one in which I slept and shrugged on a heavy jacket, knit cap, and gloves. The inside thermometer read 30 degrees.

Back in balmy Houston at a resale store, I had bought a pair of bright blue *mukluks*—tall Eskimo boots with rubber soles and waterproof uppers. They had a felt liner like an extra sock. Not taking off my gloves, I pulled them on over two pairs of socks while I tried to get Sam and Lady out of my way.

The dogs strained at their leashes and yapped to get outside. The wind slammed the door back. I stepped down into several inches of fresh snow while I struggled to close the door. They tried to pull me in opposite directions. Laughing at their excitement, I called them back to me so I could bang open the door and yell, "Snow, Chris! It's snowing a lot!"

Huge soft flakes swirled everywhere. The dogs went crazy scampering, sniffing, and pulling me. My hands were freezing. In spite of the gloves my ears and nose tingled. I had to share this fun with Chris, so I tied the dogs and climbed back inside to coax him out of his sleeping bag. Convinced that this was real snow, not just a few flakes like in Salt Lake City, he layered his clothes to join me to play in the fresh snow.

Chris found snowbanks that had frozen over. He tried to get Sam to play "King of the Mountain." I took some great photos of Chris sliding down the snowbanks without benefit of a sled. The dogs' dark fur speckled with flakes.

The sky brightened. Heavy, mottled, gray clouds hung low over the Sitka spruce. They intermittently dumped clouds of fluffy flakes that drifted and danced in the wind. Chris wanted to stay outside, but my Southern, senior bones were groaning. I wanted to warm up.

Chris cupped his hands against the frosted café window. The lights were on, he said, but it was empty. The attendant walked from the kitchen in back, recognized Chris at the window, and motioned him inside. Chris called to me.

I put the dogs back inside the RV. I didn't want to drive until trucks had melted ice on the roadbed. A set of dark tracks was evidence that only a few trucks had passed during the night. I'd wait for the weather to clear. I joined Chris at a window table where he was reading a breakfast menu.

Without his parka and heavy clothing, the only employee vaguely resembled the attendant from last night. A portly, middle-aged man with a trimmed, gray-flecked beard and a long graying ponytail called with familiarity from the entrance to the kitchen.

"I'm Grady, Ma'am. Can I get you coffee?"

I apologized for not being a coffee-drinker and ordered two hot chocolates instead.

Within minutes he carried to our table two steaming mugs of cocoa topped with whipped cream.

Chris asked, "What is the Yukoner's Breakfast Special "?

Our new friend replied, "Most truckers have a hard time finishing that. But I bet a boy like you can. It's a large stack of sourdough hotcakes, ham, sausage, bacon, two eggs, home fries, a biscuit, toast, and jelly. I'll bring an extra plate for your mom."

"That's a good idea. We'll order one Yukoner's Special with an extra plate."

Chris grumbled about the extra plate. He thought he could eat it all. I replied that he could try. We wiped the frosted window to watch black ravens swirling through the blowing snow. The sky gradually became brighter. The clouds were breaking up. Snowflakes glittering in the weak sun mesmerized us.

The aroma of bacon heralded the arrival of a huge platter piled high with the most awesome breakfast. Grady's eyes twinkled as he set it before Chris. Chris's eyes grew as large as the extra plate. He declared that he could eat it all. I smiled at him, returned Grady's smile, and sipped my cocoa.

No other customers entered. Our waiter/cook sat on a stool near the kitchen and watched Chris attack his breakfast. I told him that my thermometer inside the RV read 30 degrees. He said his read minus-1 degree centigrade. I had forgotten how to convert temperature. He didn't know how, either.

With conversational ice broken, I told him we were from Texas and making our first trip to Alaska. He said that he originally was from Nova Scotia. This was his second time to cook at Ida's. He'd been here several years before and then went to work in Wyoming. He didn't have a family and valued his freedom. I got the impression that he took odd jobs only whenever doing so was absolutely necessary.

I paid our breakfast bill, $17 CAN, $9.20 US by his chart. I left our host a Canadian tip.

By 9 a.m. the snowfall lessened. Heavy snow clouds admitted a few feeble rays of morning sun. The road, although covered with snow, had dark, parallel truck tracks to show me the way. Chris laughed as large, wet flakes splattered the windshield then slid down to accumulate on the wipers. Intermittent snow flurries, heart-stopping frost heaves, and snow-covered gravel construction led northwest into Alaska.

As I prepared for our adventure, I had repeated to myself, "Carry only what you can't do without." After months of planning and almost three weeks on the road, this was a good time to rethink that preparation. Thus far the only thing I regretted not having was a heater. Who would have expected a freak snowstorm on May first? I remembered something I had heard or read that adventure is putting into motion our ignorance.

Chapter 12

Tok, Alaska

The bright sky turned a flat, steel gray as we approached the border crossing into Alaska. I had expected a small village to mark the border, but I saw only a small building. An officer walked up to my window. He asked the usual questions, looked at our papers, then, indicating my belt bag asked, "Do you have a gun in there?"

I assured him that I carried only a concealed cell phone. We continued across the border. Kilometers returned to miles. The familiarity of mileage made me feel at home, even though the forested wilderness was a continuation of paper birch whose stark white branches stood out against the dark, emerald greens of the spruce. Somewhere the Alaska 1 highway had become Alaska 2. No way we could have gotten on the wrong road. No others were around.

Wind gusts battered Gus. Holding onto to the snow-covered road was difficult. Light snow began to fall as we entered the out-skirts of Tok. Small businesses scattered along the highway frontage were a welcome sight.

I pulled into an open service station with large bays and doors that were closed against the weather. I had not gotten an oil change in Seattle. It now was many miles over due. The attendant filled the gas tank. We could return in the morning for the oil change. With the long twilight I hadn't realized that the time was 8:30 p.m. I had driven for another 12 hours.

We backtracked to the Tok RV Village, a large, almost-empty park that advertised hot showers and a laundry. We needed both. While doing laundry, I picked up a local paper. Meteorologists had been surprised by a rapid-moving, late Arctic front. Yesterday, a 50-degree Southern front had been hit by the Arctic front dropping the temperature by 20 degrees. Thirty-degree temperature and 35 miles-per-hour winds had toppled trees and dumped snow. Today, the ground still was warm so that the snowflakes had melted as they landed. Traffic cleared tracks on the highway, but now the highway was beginning to re-freeze.

The sun finally set. The snow flurries began to stick and accumulate.

Hot showers, clean clothes warm from the dryer, a hot meal, and we were ready to snuggle down for another cold night.

May 2. How could my dogs know the time was 6 a.m.? I scarcely breathed. Sam poked my exposed ear with his cold nose. He prodded me with his front paws.

Okay. Okay. I struggled out of my zipped-up sleeping bag. Chris ignored the dogs' pitiful yipping. Sweats, coat, *mukluks*, gloves, and toboggan caps. We were ready to face the day. Fresh snow topped yesterday's snowfall and obliterated our tracks from the laundry room. I let the dogs lead me away from our small neighborhood of RV's, so their excited yipping and shuffling in the snow wouldn't waken anyone.

At the back of the RV park, the dogs discovered rabbit tracks in the snow. I let them follow the tracks into some frosted bushes. Wanting to share with Chris their find, we went back to coax him out.

While Chris dressed, I checked the thermometer. The temperature was 30 degrees inside and 20 degrees outside. We explored the winter wonderland of the unoccupied sites and the bordering forest. Besides recognizing the rabbit tracks, we recognized the split-hoof tracks of deer. One unusual pair of tracks appeared to be a wolf, or very large dog, trailing a rabbit.

I took videos of Chris "ice-skating" on glazed-over puddles. He lost his balance several times and landed hard. He was too well-padded with extra clothing to be hurt. Thin ice cracked and shattered out from under him. It sent him sprawling into a snowbank.

Cold and wet, we retreated to the RV for dry clothes, trekked to the bathhouse to change, and then back to the RV for hot oatmeal and cocoa. At 8 a.m. we unhooked the electricity to drive to the service station.

With an hour to wait while the oil was being changed, we left the dogs inside so we could explore this major crossroad town. Most of the businesses were closed for winter. We walked along the highway and crossed the Tok Cutoff, a major highway that had only a stop sign. We sloshed through slush and continued north skirting snowdrifts and icy patches. Broken, low clouds permitted steaks of sunlight. The air was crisp and very still. Our crunching footsteps broke the silence, as did the diesel engines of infrequent transport trucks.

A small, log building with a sod roof beckoned with a sign announcing Burt Paw Lodge. Chris found a curtain of long icicles hanging from the roof edge. He broke off the longest. It was half his height. Swishing it like a sword, he followed the sound of barking dogs.

Under a shed were several fenced kennels housing sled dogs. Some had young puppies. Signs painted on scraps of lumber invited tourists to visit the small, outdoor exhibit of dogsleds, harnesses, and rusted trapping equipment. Chris pulled me to a sign that read "sled dog pups 4 sale." I tugged him into reality. No way could we get a puppy!

A gift shop opened onto the covered porch of the quaint log building. We tried the door and found it open. A very talkative saleswoman in her mid-40s invited us in to warm up and look around. I explained about "just waiting" for the oil change and "just looking" for postcards. The woman showed me her collection of cards and unique gifts of Alaska; animal furs, carvings, birch-bark baskets, mounted animal heads and horns, and *ulus* (Eskimo skinning knives). She talked about the unique items as if she were the curator of a museum.

As I was paying for our picture postcards, another potential customer emerged in out of the cold. With his back to us he glanced around at the mounts on the wall. He was middle-aged and well-dressed in an Arctic parka, insulated pants, and clean, leather boots. His graying, bristly sideburns were ineffectively hidden beneath a fashionably long, auburn wig or hairpiece. The back length did not quite hide his dusty-gray, unshaved, nape hair.

The salesperson and I exchanged knowing glances as the man exited without speaking or buying. We both giggled.

"We get all kinds," she chuckled.

"I was wondering if he was looking for a replacement!" I hooted.

Gus was waiting. The dogs were ready to go. I turned left on the Tok Cutoff and headed south toward Palmer. The tracks on the roadbed had been cleared by previous traffic. I relaxed to contemplate Tok. The name of this tiny but major village seems to be in question. One story is that during the building of the AlCan it was a supply depot on the southern extension from Fairbanks and called Little Tokyo. Another story is that the settlement took its name from a famous sled dog named Little Tokyo. In either case popular opinion shortened it to Tok, which is pronounced with a long "o."

The Tok Cutoff was completed in 1942 simultaneously with the Alaskan Highway. It was a military shortcut to Anchorage. The AlCan continued north to Delta Junction to meet the existing southern road from Fairbanks.

The highway began to climb the floor of a very gradually rising valley between two mountain ranges. Fresh snow had accumulated on old packed snow. This softened the rocky landscape. Spruce, interspersed with birch, cottonwood, and aspen filled the lower slopes.

Higher yet icy waterfalls cascaded from the mountain passes. Near Mentasa Pass falling snow covered the tracks left by previous trucks. I crept along ever so cautiously.

Above the white mountain ridges, dark clouds caused a reverse silhouette. The strange sky made me think of the higher white clouds as islands of whipped cream on a chocolate sky.

An occasional mailbox was the only speck of evidence of human habitation in these spruce forests. Glancing down the accompanying snowbound gravel tracks, I could see tiny cabins, with wood smoke trickling into the sky. An occasional junkyard was thinly camouflaged in white.

At the tiny village of Cristochino a plowed gravel and dead grass airstrip followed the left side of the road between snowbanks.

Running north/south, the single landing strip was lined with tiny two- and four-passenger private planes dusted with snow, with their tires and pontoons half-buried in the snow. A puffed-out air sock indicated a strong wind from the north.

Cresting a long, gentle descent out of the mountains, I saw a mountain peak covered with snow in a range to the southeast. It must be Mt. Wrangell, 14,000 feet, in the Wrangell-St. Elias Range. I recalled reading that this mountain is a semi-active volcano. Glaciers glistened in high mountain valleys.

Below to my left was the very wide, shallow Cristochino River that filled a broad valley. Now I understood what was meant by the term *braided river*. Many icy, shallow steams channeled, converged, and separated in the wide riverbed. Rapidly flowing, frigid water tumbled ice chunks and silt over the soft tundra, which was underlaid by permafrost.

At the village of GlennAllen I took a quick, right turn to the west. The Tok Cutoff became the Glenn Highway. An amazing number of ice fields were in the snow-flecked, rugged, brown mountains. Streams of frozen, vertical flows and horizontal ice flats which were small or distant glaciers appeared. Lower slopes were a deep green with spruce beneath a frosting of snow.

A distant ice field attracted my attention long before I saw a sign for the Matanuska Glacier. It was huge and very close to the highway. The glacier looked as though it were a tremendous, thick, frozen lake that hovered above a rubble shoreline. The road to the terminal of the glacier was closed, so I pulled onto the shoulder for photos. The glacier appeared to be receding. Moraine rubble, dropped far in front of the glacier's tongue, spread over a wide, long area almost to the base of the cliff where I was parked. We wanted to go see it close-up—to touch it and experience a glacier. Perhaps on our way home.

I expected the town of Palmer to be more than just crossroads with service stations and small shops. Could this be all of Palmer, the town that hosted the famous Alaska State Fair with gigantic vegetables? More of the town that I couldn't see must be there. I turned right on the Palmer-Wasilla Cutoff, also called Alaska 3. On the outskirts of Palmer we passed experimental farms, dairy herds, and fields plowed for spring crops. More was here than I realized. Palmer was the headquarters for a government-subsidized farming community established in 1935. Colonists arrived in this fertile valley to establish homes and farms. Today gigantic vegetables (100-pound cabbages) and bumper crops make the Matanuska Valley famous. That name again—*Matanuska*. Oh, yes; that had been the name of our ferry.

Chapter 13

Wasilla

To welcome us to Wasilla, wisps of brilliant white, angel-hair clouds appeared in the bright, blue sky. Here in the valley trees wore a web of fine branches eager to bud out. Wasilla was a real town with a small mall, a large grocery/department store, and a few traffic lights. I pulled into a parking lot to call Anna for directions to the camp.

I continued west out of town on the Parks Highway (a continuation of Alaska 3). For several miles Chris and I watched for the B & J Rainbow station with a large rainbow painted on the end wall. At the traffic light I turned right onto Pitman Road. We were to proceed one-and-one-half miles and to turn right at a pink sign. My odometer read about three miles without seeing a pink sign. We turned around in a driveway and slowly made our way back. Chris's sharp eyes notice the small, pinkish sign almost hidden by a network of branches.

We turned onto a paved road that soon became gravel. *Where is it? Are we there yet?* We slowed and peered down each narrow track that led through thickets of alders, birch, and cottonwood— bare branches glazed with dripping ice. *Were homes hidden in the forest? Moose? Bears? Wolves?*

We turned into a postcard-like drive, bordered by spruce and birch-log fencing. A rustic sign based by a snowbank announced "LaVerne Griffin Youth Camp." We had arrived! In my journal I noted: Thursday, May 2, 2002, 5:30 p.m.

I parked Gus near the log fence. Chris and I walked to the manager's house and knocked. Dogs inside barked. No one arrived at the door. Puzzled, I turned to Chris. Less than an hour had passed since I had talked to Anna on the phone, so where was she? We walked between bulldozed snowdrifts toward a large building labeled "Dining Hall."

Calling out "Hello", we stomped the snow off our boots and entered the warm building. A man emerged from the kitchen to introduce himself as Mickey. Through my emails with Anna, his wife, I felt as if we already knew one another. Anna had driven into town and would be back soon. He showed us the wooded RV sites and apologized that the water and sewer lines still were frozen. Leaving Chris with Mickey to clear the site of fallen branches, I retrieved Gus and inched my way through the narrow, snow-lined drive. Following Mickey's hand signals I successfully backed into a campsite between the birch trees.

The dogs seemed to know that the time had arrived to get out and visit. Mickey ruffled Sam's ears and petted Lady. He shared with me that his Sheltie at age 16 recently had died. The dogs began to bark. Walking toward us were Anna and their daughter, Alysha. We hugged. At our first meeting we felt as though we were old friends.

The kids quietly eyed each other. Anna, Mickey, and Alysha showed us around the camp. They pointed out winterized cabins and summer cabins that had no heat, the group cabins, and two small trailers that had been expanded by wooden additions.

We entered the dining hall. Anna showed me the kitchen, dish room, and storage areas. A door labeled "Ptarmigan" stopped me in my tracks. *What's is this?*

Alysha laughed, "A Ptarmigan is the Alaska State bird. It's pronounced tarmigan. The P is silent."

A short hall connected the dining hall to a recently completed chapel addition. Large, double-paned windows admitted the late-evening light on both sides of this lovely room. At the far end of the chapel, flanking the speaker's platform, large windows and double doors led onto a deck cantilevered over the sloping hillside. Beyond the lacy, bare branches of birch and cottonwood I could see the icy surface of a frozen lake.

Anna invited us to eat dinner with them. We entered their home through an arctic entrance—an enclosed porch—where we left coats, boots, and the winter's cold. Another door led into their warm home. While Mickey started dinner, Anna showed me around. She explained how the house expanded from two connected mobile homes. The house was expanded by room additions for Larry and Sharon's growing family.

Alysha introduced Chris to Princess, a golden retriever, and Little T, a black lab. Both dogs were large, playful puppies that wanted attention. Chris caught a sight of Callie, a shy, calico cat, and Angel, a fluffy, gray tabby. Angel rubbed on his legs to be picked up. Alysha also had two cockatiels in a cage. Clint, her brother, was visiting his cousin in Anchorage but would be home in a few days. Clint's pets included tree frogs and geckos.

While Anna showed me around their home, Mickey prepared dinner. Anna explained that her husband had been in food service in the military. Her experience was in bookkeeping, so he was in charge of the kitchen and dining hall, while she took care of the camp's paperwork. This proved to be an excellent arrangement for them.

Mickey made us feel right at home with a delicious dinner of tacos. We shared travel adventures. Reared in Alaska, they had lived for a brief time in Kentucky. Alaska was in their blood, so they returned to Anchorage without jobs. Through their home church in Anchorage Mickey and Anna were familiar with the camp . Hearing that their friends were leaving as camp directors, they applied for the job. Here was an opportunity to rear their children in beautiful, spiritual surroundings while Mickey and Anna used their individual talents. Hearing how the Lord brought this family to the camp intensified how grateful I felt that He directed us here, as well.

An overcast sky and nightfall prompted us to borrow a flash-light and to walk quickly back to Gus. This frozen land, so different from East Texas, welcomed us. We were happy to be here, excited to be able to explore this part of God's creation, and content to experience each day doing whatever we could to be of service to Him.

Friday, May 3rd. This morning again was bitterly cold. Inside temperature was 30 degrees. How I wanted to burrow under my sleeping bag topped with blankets and ignore the dogs as Chris did. They were insistent. I was curious to see the camp in the morning light. Like a sourdough I pulled on my *mukluks,* heavy jacket, hat, and gloves. I grinned at applying the term *sourdough* (meaning old-timer, or resident) to myself. We really were *cheechako*s—new comers.

Light snow fluttered and drifted. I walked the dogs to the lakeshore, where they walked out onto the ice to lick it. Sam climbed snowdrifts breaking through the crust. Lady preferred the solid but frozen ground.

As the morning warmed up a little, Chris and I worked with Anna learning the routine of cleaning and sanitizing the few cabins that previous weekend campers had used. She showed us the bath-house and explained that the showers didn't need to be sanitized until after the next camp.

Anna invited us to go grocery shopping with her and Alysha. She drove back down the gravel road on to the paved road and retraced our route from yesterday. We laughed at the neglected sign at the intersection with Pitman road and added sign repair to her "to -do" list. Anna was an excellent tour guide. The town of Wasilla had spread along the Parks Highway and left the original townsite look-ing as though it were a storybook village. She pointed out the Wasilla Post Office, the library, and a small museum, then proceed-ed to a well-stocked grocery store.

On the way she explained that if they were hosting full-service camp, volunteers ate with the campers and staff. *Full-service camp* meant that we helped cook for the group. If the group at the camp was *self-service*, meaning campers provided for their own meals, then volunteers' meals were on their own. She added that most of the time plenty of leftovers were in the freezer at the end of a ses-sion, so that volunteers and staff could have meals together between sessions.

Grocery-shopping with Anna truly was an experience. The store was quite large and modern, with a larger selection of fruits, vegeta-bles, meats, and specialty items than in the small grocery where I shop at home. I was unprepared for the unusually high prices and

Anna's willingness to pay them. Anna said the prices were typical for early spring when so much had to be shipped in. Fruits and vegetables grown in the Matanuska valley during the summer would bring the prices down. I consulted my shopping list carefully before I picked up groceries for Chris and me. A large portion of the store offered clothing, housewares, and even furniture. I thought I was in a very large department store that happened to carry groceries—something I didn't expect to find here.

That afternoon we quite literally followed Anna and Alysha out onto the lake. We walked on water—ice, that is! They showed us tire tracks on which trucks and a snowdozer had cleared the ice for skating. We walked toward a dark spot on the ice to find the frozen remains of a bonfire that had not melted through the ice. Ice fishermen had made holes through the ice with saws and measured the ice to be 35-inches thick. Now I felt a lot more confident walking over the crevasses and hearing the ice creak and groan.

We continued exploring while we walked on the ice far out from the shoreline. Alysha led us to inspect a boat dock. We could jump off the dock to land on the ice without causing it to crack. Farther along the shore we were shown the swimming beach with a "swim at your own risk" sign. You wouldn't catch me swimming anytime soon, if at all.

A self-service group arrived around 4 p.m. Chris and I retreated to Gus. Mickey loaned me a small electric heater. After a supper of hot soup and cocoa we played board games for a while. Trekking on the ice had tired us both, so we readily went to bed although twilight lingered.

Saturday, May 4. Another very cold morning that was made more bearable with the heater. While I walked the dogs, I found Mickey at the firepit building a campfire. He gave me our assignment for the day—to pick up branches downed by the recent storm. When the weather warmed up and the snow melted, leaves to rake would be there. Soon volunteers would be arriving to make repairs and prepare the camp for summer. We would be cooking and doing KP duty. Mickey encouraged me to relax and enjoy not having much to do. He said I'd later make up for being a slacker.

Chris and I lazed around for a while and then spent the morning dragging fallen branches to the fire pit to be burned. We again took time to walk on the ice and to explore more of the camp. A large, flat meadow still covered by snow would emerge as a ball field. We discovered additional cabins that I hadn't noticed before. These still were closed up for the winter. Near the bathhouse we located the Smurf house—so named by the kids because of its bright-blue color. Beneath the kitchen was a storage area aptly called the Down Under. Another storage building behind the chapel had been named the Outback.

From the dining hall porch Anna yelled for Mickey. We ran to see if she needed us, too. In the kitchen a scratching noise emerged from one of the sinks. Anna admonished Mickey to "get it out." A tiny, mouse-like shrew had fallen into the sink drain and was trapped. Mickey was there to the rescue. He poked a pair of long-handled tongs into the opening, gently pinched the tiny mammal, and then released it outdoors.

I walked the road past the manager's home and took a right to check out the storage sheds and maintenance buildings. Walking on to the main road, I took pictures of the entrance signs and then returned to camp.

Sunday, May 5. Was the weather warmer, or was I acclimating? Checking the thermometer this sunny morning, the temperature was 40 degrees. Was spring on the way? The dogs and I walked down to the edge of the lake. Patches of snow reflecting the bright sun were soft and soggy. Ice along the shoreline appeared to becoming slushy. The dogs stepped off the boat dock onto the ice. Cracks like mini-canyons spider-webbed in all directions. The ice creaked. *Would it be a dangerous place on which to walk?* I wasn't about to try.

Today was our first Sunday at camp. For more than a year the congregation of Pioneer Baptist Church had been holding services on the camp. It usually met in the chapel. This morning a camp group was using the chapel, so church met in the Snack Shack. We met Pastor Larry and his wife, Ann, while we waited for Anna and Mickey. Jack arrived on a four-wheeler. Two other couples joined us in the tiny room that was warmed by a space heater and by the warmly dressed congregation of 13. Anna led our singing and treated us to a solo.

Pastor Larry's sermon included mention that he and Ann were sad to be leaving soon. As church planters they had enjoyed their assignment in Wasilla and would miss everyone. They were looking forward returning to the Lower Forty-Eight and to their grown children and families. The new pastor, John, and his wife, Carolyn, soon would be arriving soon from Missouri.

After lunch, we joined Anna and Alysha for the 45-mile trip to Anchorage. Alaska 1 south from Wasilla passed over frozen marsh between the base of the Chugach Mountains to the East and Knik Arm of the Cook Inlet. Anna instructed us to be on the lookout for moose. As we neared Alaska's largest city, I noticed that both sides of the highway were lined with high, chain-link fencing. Anna said that the fence was to keep moose off the highway. She pointed out sections of the fence where smart moose were supposed to go back off the roadway into the forest. She said the moose usually just stopped traffic as they licked salt off the roadway. If a car hit a moose, the police called a special patrol that hoisted the carcass onto a truck, took it to a slaughterhouse, then distributed the meat to the poor. We didn't see any moose.

On the right we passed Fort Richardson Army base. An overpass leading to Elmendorf Air force Base, also to my right, was the first sign that we were entering Alaska's largest city. To my left we passed Merrill Field, an airport housing hundreds of small private airplanes in hangars or tied down on the taxi strips. Most of these four- to eight-passenger planes were equipped with pontoons or skis, or both.

We stopped downtown at the Log Cabin Information Center, a long name for a small log cabin. The cabin was topped by a sod roof, which looked as though it were an unmowed meadow of tall, brown hay. Although advertised to be open year-round, the cabin was closed. I hoped to return another day.

Downtown, I was surprised at how much snow was piled by snowplows onto vacant lots and along the roadway. Snow was piled under trees and in bare yards. Snowdrifts banked the edges of sidewalks. *Where would it all go as it melted?*

Anna followed Highway 1 as it turned South, then turned West to Earthquake Park. We learned about the devastating 1964 earthquake that hit the coast of Anchorage. The north side of Fourth Street collapsed. It dropped homes and businesses a dozen feet or more into the Knik Arm of the Cook Inlet. Third Street had been reinforced and rebuilt, but First and Second Streets were considered an earthquake risk, so rebuilding was sparse.

Following the coast to the west and northwest were a net work of hike-and-bike trails that led into downtown. During the brief summer months Anna and her kids had ridden bikes on the trails. She encouraged me to bring Chris back when the weather was warmer.

After picking up Clint at his cousins' house, we made a stop at Mickey's parents' home in a pretty suburb of winding streets and hills. Mickey's dad, an avid salmon fisherman, showed us his fish smokers. He pulled out trays of salmon steaks to give us a sample. The fish strips were boneless and delicious. The Alaskan chef showed us how he packed the smoked salmon into jars to be vacuum-sealed.

Returning to camp, Chris disappeared with Clint while I walked the dogs. At dusk through the slushy snow I returned to the RV to put the dogs up. I heard a hissing noise. Not able to locate the source of the sound, I took the dogs back outside. No snakes are in Alaska, so what would cause a hiss? I was afraid it might be a sign of a propane leak, although the tank valve still was sealed from the ferry.

Not wanting to sleep with a potential danger, I tied the dogs to a distant tree and walked back to the campfire as I looked for Chris. He was as baffled as I was about the sound. We went with Clint to look for his dad to ask his opinion.

Mickey shook his head when I mentioned a snake hissing. His grin verified that no snakes, not even snow snakes, are in Alaska. I thought, *I like it here even more!*

Mickey pulled on his parka, picked up a flashlight, and led us into the night. Our shoes crunched on the re-freezing snow crust. I asked Chris to stop the dogs' yapping so we could listen for the whispering noise. Mickey listened intently and then went inside the RV. My house on wheels was so small that he didn't take long to check it out for noises.

Joining me outside in the cold he said, "Valve stem."

"What?" I asked.

"Valve stem's leaking. Inside dual, passenger side." He replied as he kicked the outside tire. "I'll fix it tomorrow."

Thanking him profusely, we said "good night" as he walked into the night.

Monday, May 6, the weather definitely was warmer. The temperature hovered round 42 degrees all day, with drizzle in the air. While Chris and Clint got to know each other, I spent the morning with Ann, the pastor's wife. She had taught a children's class on Wednesday nights, oversaw Vacation Bible School, and taught a children's class on Sunday. In the large pantry closet were boxes of children's materials that had been donated throughout the years. Another storage area was crammed with sporting goods, odds and ends, and more children's materials. Ann and I sorted and separated supplies. She wanted to make sure that the new pastor and his wife could find materials.

We decided to clean the storeroom first and then organize all of the children's materials and sporting equipment in that room,. This would give Mickey more room in the pantry. I was talked into teaching the missions class for the kids on Wednesday nights. Previous volunteers had brought a large variety of craft materials for Vacation Bible School. The materials had been left for the camp. I had plenty of materials from which to choose.

After lunch Chris and I got to know the bathhouse quite well. We were initiated as potty patrol—sanitary supervisors. Alysha and Anna showed us where to find cleaning supplies, huge rolls of paper towels, and toilet tissue. I was entrusted with my own keys to the storage and laundry area. We were given the combination to padlocks on the supply cabinets. We were officially "on staff."

Clint delighted in showing us how to sanitize the showers. First he and Chris hung the heavy rubber floor mats on wall hooks in the shower area. Then he sprayed the mats and shower stalls with a sanitizing solution. While the sanitizer did its work, Anna and Alysha shared their method for making sure the sinks and toilets were sanitized.

Clint pulled off his shoes and told Chris to do the same. Clint pulled a long garden hose through the bathhouse to the showers. He grabbed the pistol-shaped nozzle and aimed a strong stream of water at the rubber mats. Pretending to be shooting bad guys he took aim at the mats, until Chris talked him into letting him take a turn. We women were happy to let the "men" spray the "ladies" room, while we swept the water down the drains.

Chris and I felt a little strange about having access to both the "ladies" and "men" rooms. Our routine would be to check the bathrooms twice a day during weekend camps to make sure they had sufficient paper towels and toilet paper. After each camp session, we would work with Alysha and Clint to sanitize. During weeklong camps, we would do it more often.

Tuesday morning the temperature again rose above freezing. The melting snow was running groundwater that was not muddy. The layer of dead leaves on the rocky ground made it spongy. I noticed shaggy bark on some tall gray trees that were splotched with black. The bark was peeling off in wide bands around the diameter of the trunk. This must be birch bark—from which Native Americans made canoe. I didn't peel the bark from the trees but kept looking until I found some that had fallen to the ground. On the outside it was a dove gray color. On the inner side it was colored reddish-tan.

Mickey arrived with an air compressor to loosen the lugs on my no-longer-hissing tire. With the outside dual off, we could see that the inner tire definitely was flat. *Thank You, Lord, that this didn't happen in the middle of the Yukon.* Mickey loaded the tire into his truck. I went with him to town to have the stem replaced. In just two days the area looked more like spring, although no leaves were on the trees. The snow almost was gone; the sky definitely was brighter.

Wednesday was our day off. I didn't think we deserved a day off yet, since we hadn't been doing much work except for hauling branches, but I didn't argue. Mickey needed to go into Anchorage to the association office, so we followed him. On my map he pointed out several places of interest and left us on our own.

The lure of a chocolate waterfall drew me to visit the Alaska Wild Berry Products store first. What a fun place! On the wooden front porch we were met by two large, carved, wooden bears. Inside the front door, a huge, stuffed grizzly bear raised above our heads. There, across from the entrance, a chocolate waterfall! Beginning near the ceiling several large copper pots mounted on the wall poured silky liquid chocolate from pot to pot. Twenty feet of creamy, brown confection cascaded down into a tremendous copper cauldron and wishing-well mounted on rocks. A sign near the base of the fountain warned us to resist sticking fingers into the 3,400 pounds of liquid chocolate.

At the rear of the store a row of windows allowed us to watch the candy factory at work. In one area jellies were being cooked and bottled. In another area the candymakers were making a variety of goodies. *Oh, my!* We were encouraged to try samples! Besides offering candies, jellies, and preserves, the store carried a huge variety of souvenir items. We had a tough time limiting our purchases to postcards and a few souvenirs to take home.

Downtown I found the Anchorage Museum of History and Art but couldn't find a parking lot large enough for Gus. A double parking space with two meters was just barely long enough. Chris stuffed the meters with quarters; I picked up my city map. Off we went.

Walking through town we were attracted by the windows of Wolfsong of Alaska, a museum and gift shop. The purpose here was to educate the public about Alaska's most misunderstood and controversial animal—the wolf. Displays of mounts and impressive artwork captured my interest. Chris was drawn to running videos.

Continuing down the sidewalk we approached a massive mural of whales adorning the side of a many-storied building. The cluttered show window of a trading post caught my attention. Inside were fascinating artifacts: hand-crafted bone carvings, birch-bark baskets, totems, masks, knives, antique guns, and so much more that my mind was boggled. Intricate beadwork decorated soft skins made into bags, scabbards, and wide belts labeled "baby straps." On the wall behind the register was the head mount of the largest walrus ever harpooned before doing so except by natives for subsistence became illegal. Its tusks were more than four-feet long.

Walking along the streets I became absorbed in people-watching. Tourists wouldn't be here this early in the season. These people were Alaskans by choice. Most of them previously had been *cheechakos*. They dressed in camouflage as if to blend in with nature. Blue jeans, browns, beiges, and greens prevailed. Men wore beards. Men and women wore their long hair in ponytails. Most sported hiking boots, while others wore rubber waders or *mukluks*.

Young people seemed to be experimenting with who they wanted to be. Here was no class system, no lineage that mattered. Neither property, education, speech, nor religion mattered. Gumption did. They fantasized with portraying a colorful self-image within a social weightlessness. They tried on a new identity. Alaska is a frontier where a former life can be left behind.

The Anchorage Museum of History and Art was housed in a large, cream-colored, contemporary building. One of the outside walls supported a very large, tile mosaic of a snow owl. Near the entrance a circular, bronze sculpture depicts native animals: polar bears, walrus, moose, and salmon. As we entered the museum we saw a three- to-four-storied carved totem, topped by an eagle, gracing a prominent wall. The ground floor contained galleries that featured many examples of contemporary Alaskan art, from stone carvings to masks to paintings. I was drawn to the sleek, minimalistic lines and sparing use of colors but confused by symbolism to which I had no reference.

In the children's area the wall was painted with images of fantastic sharks, other fish, and a snorkeling diver. The mural complimented a traveling exhibit of Ketchikan artist Ray Troll, in conjunction with his children's book *Sharkabet; a Sea of Sharks from A to Z.*

Completing our tour of the downstairs, we went to the upstairs Alaska Gallery that featured the history and anthropology of Alaska.

Here were mounted muskox and other animal hides, kayaks, harpoons, displays of parkas and fur clothing, dogsleds, relics of Native Alaskans, Russian fur traders, American explorers, and much more to challenge the imagination. So many of the artifacts were strange to me. Having only read about the Far North, my concept of how life had been in the Arctic severely was challenged.

As I returned to camp, I commented to Chris that the snow was gone. The trees were looking less dead, but we still saw no signs of budding leaves. The roadsides were beginning to show a hint of green. Ditches and small ponds now were free of ice. *When would our lake begin to thaw?*

While we were away, a group of volunteers from South Florida had arrived to help prepare camp for the summer season. We were introduced to several middle-aged couples; a young couple with a precious toddler; and a young man, Jeff, whose wife had been unable to travel here.

Thursday morning we worked in the kitchen with the Florida women preparing breakfast. The Southerners commented about the cold. Jeff entered the dining hall and was muffled so tightly that he caused all of us to laugh. He pulled off heavy mittens, unwrapped a long muffler, removed his knit ski cap, took off his jacket, and began to unlayer several sweaters. I wore only a sweatsuit and light jacket. The temperature outside now was above 40 degrees. We teased about the shock of going from Florida's 90s in the Lower Forty-Eight to Alaska's spring. Jeff took the teasing goodnaturedly. He was energetic and eager to work

The work team broke up into small groups, gathered up rakes and old tarps, and began to clear up the piles of dead leaves. The leaves were quite soggy, stuck to the gravel, and were heavy to rake into piles. Several of us spread out an old tarp so that we could rake the leaves onto it. One of the men brought a rusted truck to the area where we worked. Teaming up we picked up the tarp. Chris and one of the men climbed into the truck bed. We hoisted the tarp in, turned it inside out to dump the leaves, and pulled it back out. Off went the truck to dump. Off we went to attack another layer of leaves.

I asked Mickey whether we could burn the piles of leaves rather than having to haul them off. He said that during the previous summer a forest fire had raged out of control near the camp. As it got closer, the church members and others started a prayer chain to save the camp.

Miraculously the firewall spilt as it approached the camp. I learned that fires would begin to burn roots underground. Often the fire would appear to be put out but could continue to burn and smolder beneath the forest floor. Later, sometimes days later, fire would erupt in a distant location. Fires only were safe in fire pits such as the one we had near the dining hall.

Early afternoon, with chores completed for the day, we loaded the 15-passenger van with Floridians and two Texans to visit the musk ox farm north of Palmer. We were so crowded that I sat on a small, plastic step stool between the front bucket seats.

I had read about the musk-ox farm but had not seen a sign for the farm on the Glen Highway when we arrived from Tok. Since my college days I've been curious about Musk Oxen. While I worked on a master's degree in art education, I had learned to spin wool and to weave on a variety of looms. I had read about this odd, Arctic animal and its famous wool. The musk-ox's wool undercoat, call *qiviut*, is reported to be to softest, finest, and warmest wool known. Softer and more elegant than cashmere, *qiviut* is said to be "light as smoke." I wanted to see and to feel it.

Our Florida driver was on his second volunteer trip to the camp, so he was familiar with the Matsu Valley. But we couldn't find the farm. Even though he was a man, he agreed to stop for directions. The farm was still closed for the winter, but it would open on Sunday, Mother's Day. We vowed to return after church and dinner.

The group decided to explore Anchorage with me as tour guide. Me? I'd made only two trips to Anchorage. The driver wasn't sure he remembered how to get around town. We knew we couldn't get lost, since he was willing to use a map.

Circling from Fifth Street, which was one-way going west, to Fourth Street, a one-way street heading east, we passed the Log Cabin Visitors Center. Its brown, hay-like roof had a tinge of green. Everyone had different ideas about where he or she wanted to go.

The driver pulled over to the curb in a no-parking zone, so we could unload to wander around town. We agreed to meet across the street at a café near a bronze sled-dog statue. The statue marked the beginning of the yearly Iditarod Races.

Chris, in the front passenger seat, and I exited first and stood by waiting for the others. A group of young, longhaired Alaskan Natives walked past and made fun of us "tourists" piling out of the van like circus clowns exiting a tiny Volkswagen. The three guys and two girls in jeans, athletic shoes, and sweatshirts were distinctive with long, shiny, black hair and almond-shaped eyes. Their accent was distinctive, but the loud laughing and obvious rudeness was classic of some teens everywhere.

Yes, we were tourists. Many others like us who arrive in the summer season provide the economy for their jeans and sneakers. I would have liked to talk to them but was not brave enough. As they wandered on down the street, we split into groups to explore in different directions.

We wandered in and out of several trading posts and shops, then returned to join the others for a meal at a restaurant that commemorated the sled-dog races. Dogsleds, harnesses, and animal pelts decorated the walls. Photographs of famous dogs, winning dog teams, and their owners were displayed prominently. The waiters returned with our orders and eagerly answered our questions.

Two dog-sled races are run from this location. The World Champion Sled-Dog Race, run in February, is a three-day sprint event. The better known Iditarod is run in March. This race commemorates the running of sled dogs in 1925 to take life-saving diphtheria serum to Nome to stop an epidemic.

The Iditarod race starts in Anchorage for spectators and the tourists who brave the March weather. The race is run for several miles north. The racers stop. The dogs then are loaded onto trucks and taken to Wasilla, where the race is restarted. This is the official start of the 1,000-mile run to Nome on the Bering Sea.

Chapter 14

The Kenai

Our Florida friends had prearranged a cruise tour out of Seward on the East Coast of the Kenai Peninsula. Tickets for the Kenai Fjords Tour were at a group rate—$30 off the regular price for the eight-hour tour. The young couple with the little girl believed the trip would be too cold for their daughter and wanted to sell their tickets to me. Without consulting my budget I grasped the opportunity to be a tourist. First, I had to clear being absent from the camp with my boss, Mickey.

Mickey laughed. He reminded me that I was a volunteer and didn't have to work if I didn't want to do so. The cooks and other volunteers would be gone, so not much would be going on around camp. Most volunteer groups from the Lower Forty-Eight planned a day or two for sightseeing. Who could travel all the way to Alaska without experiencing some of the Alaskan wonders?

Anna promised to check on the dogs while we were gone for the day. Chris and I packed backpacks with hats, gloves, and extra sweats. I added my video camera, the 35-mm camera, extra film, videotape, and batteries. Our tour included a stop for a salmon bake, so we packed only a few snacks for the drive.

The alarm woke us at 4 a.m. for a quick, warm breakfast. By 6 the South Floridians and the South Texans, bundled against uncustomary May chill, loaded into the van for the four-hour drive to Seward. Following Alaska 1 through Anchorage, we continued south to follow the coast of the Turnagain Arm of the Cook Inlet. The highway crossed a broad, wet marsh. A boardwalk enticed us to return and watch the birds feeding in the marsh.

The highway was carved from the base of the Chugach Mountains rising to our left. The terrain and scenery with icy waterfalls was awesome. We watched eagles fishing for salmon and kept watch for moose and bear.

Suddenly the driver pulled onto a wide shoulder at the base of the cliffs. He pointed out tiny, white dots speckled high on the craggy walls. We grabbed jackets and tumbled out of the van in search of Dall sheep. Sharing binoculars and the telephoto lens of my video camera, we could make out a small, scattered herd of these elusive animals. Several of the sheep were lying on narrow ledges, with just their wooly, white backs and their curled horns evident. Two spring lambs leaped, cavorted, and tiptoed precariously close to the sheer drop-off of the steep slopes.

The tide was out of Turnagain Arm. This left miles of quicksand-like mudflats, dotted with birds fishing in the shallows. The tidal flats filled the bay with a sea of mud. Narrow channels of flowing water meandered and crisscrossed the flats.

One of our group members, who had been reading up on Alaska, told us about bore tides in the Arm. He said that because high tide water entering Cook Inlet has to squeeze into a relatively small area, as much as a 40-foot difference could exist between high and low tides. A bore tide is a foaming wall of water that surges into the Arm at high tide. It can be six or more feet in height above the regular high tide and travel at speeds of 10 knots. Some bore tides, forced by the strong winds, have covered the highway and caused extensive damage. As the tides recede, whales and other sea mammals have been stranded by these unusual occurrences.

Angling around the southern end of the Arm, the highway crosses a salt marsh. Rounding the tip of the thin finger of the arm, past the remains of the village of Portage that was destroyed by the 1964 earthquake, we began to climb the Kenai Mountains onto the Kenai Peninsula. The Kenai Range runs the length of the central and eastern side of the peninsula which separates the Prince Williams Sound of the Gulf of Alaska to the East and the Cook Inlet, a large bay, to the West. This southern part of the state of Alaska has a surprising number of glaciers and huge ice fields. It is considered to be Anchorage's backyard playground for winter sports, hunting, and fishing.

The highway that crossed through a glacial valley and then followed a pass through the Kenai Mountains is supremely scenic. The marshy tidal flats quickly became alpine terrain. We traveled through the Chugach National Forest. We passed several mountain lakes that followed icy streams and into thick forests.

Ninety miles south of Anchorage, the highway forks with the Seward Highway continuing south to the eastside of the peninsula to the town of Seward. The right fork continues to the West Coast and follows that coast to Homer.

At last we reached Seward. The tiny village is squeezed between Resurrection Bay to the east and mountains to the west. Seward once was Alaska's leading port city but later was eclipsed by Anchorage. The 1964 earthquake devastated the town. Today it is a major tourist center, since it is the most northern terminal for cruise ships and is on the Alaskan ferry system. Fishermen flock to Seward for surf- and deep-sea fishing.

Hikers and other outdoor enthusiasts use Seward as a gateway to the Kenai Fjords National Park. Many others, like us, were interested in wildlife and glacier excursions. The large harbor has docks for the largest cruise ships and the ferry. A city harbor for fishing charters, as well as sightseeing charters, and an assortment of private fishing boats crowded along the banks. While we waited to board our charter, we watched kayakers and canoers brave the biting winds and icy swells. I walked across the main road from the Kenai Fjords Tours office to a general store to look for postcards. Bracing the video camera against the strong winds, I took photos of the quaint village, docks, and sea birds.

Time to board our pristine mini-cruiser. Buffeted by the sharp wind, our group joined others to file down the wooden pier. The ship was small compared to the ferry. It was built with three enclosed decks plus outdoor observation decks on each level. Inside was a snack bar, comfortable upholstered seats, and groupings of tables and chairs.

Although the sun was climbing, the biting wind drove us off the outdoor deck. Chris and I found a forward, second-floor observation deck where we could stand by the frosted bow windows or sit comfortably and see the sea. Doors led to outside passages along the sides of the boat. Another set of doors opened back into another lounge.

On the drive from Anchorage Chris had developed a headache. The swaying of the boat while still at anchor worsened the headache and soured his stomach as well as his disposition. I gave him some medicine for his headache and a soda to help his stomach. He didn't appreciate my sympathy. He just wanted to lie down and be left alone.

As the boat left the dock, our captain and guide, Jorge, began his running commentary. He pointed out where the tourist cruise ships soon would be docking to initiate the summer season. He slowed to an idle. Between the boat and the shore he pointed out adorable sea otters bobbing on the surface. I ran outside with the camera. Floating on their backs, their cute kitten faces and soft, gentle eyes implored us to cuddle them. Jorge gave us interesting otter information. Their luxuriant, thick undercoat traps air that insulates their bodies and makes them buoyant. The boat drifted closer to the whiskery, inquisitive little animals. They actually were about four-feet long and weigh up to 80 pounds, but from the deck they looked to be about the size of large, very wet cats.

Jorge told us to watch closely for surfacing sea otters. He said that they could dive up to 60 feet to pluck sea urchins or clams from the bottom. We hung over the rails with our cameras snapping.

We watched as a surfacing sea otter flipped onto its back. Using its chest as a tray and a flat rock as an anvil, the otter banged a clam on the rock until it cracked open. Finishing its meal the otter began grooming its fur with its forepaws. It swished itself clean by doing a barrel roll and then dove for another dinner course.

Passing the sea otters, I hurried back into the sheltered deck. I had just pulled off my cap and gloves and unwound my muffler when Jorge announced whales on the horizon. On went the cap, gloves, and muffler. I joined the crowd that was returning to the outdoor deck. Far off the bow were several dark specks. Through the video-camera telephoto lens, I could make out black humps and an occasional spout.

Jorge assured us that we would get closer. He mentioned that all the ships in the area were in constant radio contact. Each captain or pilot notified the others when wildlife was spotted. I hadn't given much thought to the extreme mobility of whales and that their habitat extended from the Arctic Ocean to Hawaii. As we approached, Jorge identified the black bumps as humpbacks. One of 14 species of whale, the humpback does not have teeth. It has long strips of baleen—strips of tough keratin—that hang from the upper gum line. The whale takes enormous quantities of water into its mouth. It then forces the water out. The baleen screen traps krill and small fish, which the whale swallows.

Slowly and quietly approaching the whales, we witnessed whale gymnastics. A huge, 40-foot long, 30-ton whale hurled its body out of the water in a spectacular leap. Another whale repeated the display. Several blew towering waterspouts into the air. Whales dove with tremendous splashes of their tails.

Returning indoors, I asked Chris whether he had seen the whales. His reply was that he'd seen plenty of whales on the ferry trip. How quickly kids become complacent!

Chris was feeling a little better by the time we docked at Fox Island for a salmon-bake lunch. The shore of this wooded island was littered with flat, black stones. The slate-looking pieces had been tumbled by the changing tides until they were smooth and rounded. A landscape gardener would have had to pay a small fortune for decorative stones such as these. Here was an unending supply. Jorge encouraged his departing tourists to try skipping the stones. The tide would return them to shore.

A boardwalk led from the dock to a sheltered, outdoor pavilion. To one side a huge, wood-burning grill was covered with salmon steaks. A young woman attended the fish and turned the fillets with tongs. Her smile was as intriguing as the aroma of salmon and wood smoke. She loved her summer job, the secluded island, and Alaska in general.

Chris and I joined a rapidly moving line to pick up a plate of freshly baked salmon, potato wedges, salad, rolls, and desert. We found seats in the sun at a picnic table on the pavilion. Chris wasn't hungry. He began throwing bits of bread to a bird perched in bushes beyond the pavilion railing. The bird ruffled its deep, iridescent blue feathers. It raised a crest. From having read about them, I recognized a Stellar Jay.

The jay hopped back and forth along the railing. It gobbled bits of bread thrown by other diners. It seemed to know that its prospects for a snack increased if it fluttered back and forth. Chris crept closer to place bread on the railing. The bird hopped a few feet away, cocked its head, and watched as Chris sat back down. The jay eyed Chris, hopped closer, and retrieved its snack.

A pair of black and white magpies joined the bird's lunch counter. They squawked and fussed and tried to drive the jay away. Fellow tourists debated which species was the smartest. I interjected that I'd heard that ravens were the most intelligent.

Tossing the last of our crumbs to the birds, we cleaned up and then joined the group to re-board the cruise boat. The clear, turquoise sky and warmer winds enticed me to stay on the open deck. Chris went inside.

The captain announced for us to look closely at the rocky islands near shore. We rounded an outcropping splashed by the waves. On small islands were thousands of Stellar sea lions. Light brown, 1,500-pound males that were up to nine feet in length covered the rocky rookeries and waited for females to arrive in June. The males arrived early to stake out their territory and to defend it against other males. They don't eat for two months.

We witnessed huge males fencing with their necks and driving each other into the surf. Many peacefully were sleeping like huge, surf-tumbled rocks. The islands were so covered with sea lions, I wondered whether space would be available for the females.

Leaving the sea lions behind, Jorge explained that harbor seals were smaller and much lighter in weight than were the sea lions. They spend most of their time in coastal waters and rivers. Fur seals spend most of their time in the open ocean. I had thought seals were seals.

We approached another rocky cliff pounded by waves. Jorge told us to watch for a different kind of rookery. Thousands of white birds swarmed around the rocky wall and screamed with a piercing call. These medium-sized birds were Arctic Terns. They soared on long, pointed wings. A forked tail made them look as though they were white swallows. The terns' heads were topped with a bright, black cap. The birds' bright-red bill and red feet appeared artificial on these hyperactive birds.

The terns were nesting in crevasses and on ledges. They obliterated the rocky walls. Parent birds vigorously defend their nests. Jorge directed our attention to a cave-like crevasse that we slowly were approaching. Birds were flying, landing, and diving into the sea. Suddenly from the crevasse thousands of additional birds streamed into the sky. They threatened us with their ear-splitting call.

We saw one of Alaska's most unusual birds, the Horned Puffin. These black birds with white faces and huge bright-orange, yellow, and red beaks are most bizarre. They seem comically out of place as they roosted and nested on the rocky coast. They would appear more natural as yard ornaments—like pink plastic flamingos.

Jorge announced a side trip to a shallow beach where a black bear had been sighted. As we slowly approached an inlet, I noticed several other tour boats quietly idling in the bay. Sure enough, a black bear wandered across the beach. It stopped to sniff the air and to dig into the rocky soil.

Jorge explained that black bears can be tan or cinnamon as well as black. The black bear is smaller than is a grizzly bear. Black bears have straight noses and are less bulky. The grizzly usually is tan and has a prominent hump on its shoulder, is more massive, and has a dished forehead.

As we turned to leave, I overheard someone comment that the tour people probably fed the bear to make sure we got to see one.

What a glorious day this had been! Around 6 p.m. the cruise boat returned to port. The afternoon sun still was high in the sky. A tired group of *cheechakos* (outsiders, non-Native Alaskans) fell into the van for the ride back to camp.

Before we descended the Kenai Pass to Turnagain Arm, Jeff talked the driver into stopping in a pulloff surrounded by snowbanks. He insisted that we had to play in the snow. He climbed a snowy embankment to a high meadow covered with old snow. As Jeff stepped onto the snow crust, it crushed. He sank to his knees whooping, "Come on!"

Although none of us wore boots, we joined Jeff in his first-ever snowball fight. At Jeff's insistence, Chris retrieved the stool from the van. As he turned it upside down, Jeff tried to use the stool as a sled. It got stuck in the soft snow. Chris and Jeff trudged off through the deep snow in search of something to use for a sled.

One of the older women called out, "Watch this!" as she flopped backward onto a snowbank. She swished her arms and her legs to make a snow angel. None of the rest of us wanted to chance getting snow into our clothes. She was a lone snow angel.

Getting cold and hungry the men yelled for Jeff and Chris to work their way back through the soft drifts. We piled back into the van to warm up and wait for the adventurers to return. In a dumpster at the side of the parking lot, they found a cardboard box. The makeshift sled stuck in the soft snow and soon was abandoned.

As we passed through Anchorage, our stomachs began a chorus of growls. After much discussion, we decided to stop at a family-style restaurant for a late dinner. Chris ordered fried halibut, while I had a halibut burger. The fish was delicious. Halibut is a huge, flat, flounder-like fish with mild, white flesh. Our server said that the largest halibuts are more than 400 pounds. The men in our group began to plan a fishing trip.

Back at camp, at 11 p.m. a fantastic sunset over the lake greeted us. Tired, full, and overflowing with tales of our adventures, we tourists made our way to cabins and RV's.

Mickey set out coffee, cereal, milk, juice, and muffins for a casual breakfast. This permitted us to sleep late. We thanked him by raking leaves with gusto. The day was warmer. The last remnants of snow had disappeared from sheltering trees. Wet birch, beech, and cottonwood leaves lay matted in thick piles. At least we didn't have to rake the entire 60 acres!

To make the job easier, each group of rakers spread an old tarp on the ground. Piles of leaves were carried or raked on to the tarp.

Cooperatively, at least four of us grabbed corners of the tarp and lifted it into the truck bed. More leaves were piled on top. With the truck bed overflowing, one of us drove the truck to a spot near the maintenance buildings with the others seated on top of the leaves. The driver backed up to the growing pile. Four of us grabbed the four corners and pulled the tarp off the truck to dump the leaves. We felt as though we were a little like the four friends lowering their sick friend through the roof to Jesus.

For dinner we had a potluck supper and hot-dog roast outdoors at the fire pit. I dragged my Dutch oven out from Gus's basement storage, cleaned it up, and in the hot coals made apple cobbler. All of us volunteers looked forward to bed, even though the sun still was shining.

Sunday, May 12. Mother's Day. No campers were at the site this weekend, so we had church services in the chapel. A group from North Carolina had arrived to help rake leaves and prepare cabins for the summer session. Volunteers doubled to 26 the attendance at Pioneer Baptist Church.

Fun-loving Jeff arranged for the use of the camp van to visit the Musk Ox farm on its opening day. Again Chris and I were invited.

With our Florida friends we piled into the van to return to Palmer and find the Musk Ox farm. A freshly painted sign on the highway directed us to a large, red barn backed by fenced pastures. Large, gray knolls dotted the pastures' grasses.

The barn housed a gift shop, small museum, and a special art exhibit. I felt scarves and caps knitted from *qiviut*. The fiber was unbelievably light and soft, as though I were holding goosedown. A woman explained that the wool is brushed from the oxen as they shed in the spring. Traditionally Native Alaskans plucked the fibers from shrubs on the tundra that the Musk ox had rubbed against.

The fiber is sent to co-ops in Native villages where women knit caps, scarves, shawls, and tubular turtlenecks from traditional designs. The co-op, called Oomingmak Musk Ox Producers Co-op, from the Inupiat Eskimo name for the musk ox (or bearded one), sends the finished items to the farm and associated gift shops for sale. The proceeds are returned to the villages.

As I passed through a small museum, I learned that the musk ox once lived with mammoths and wooly rhinoceros on the steppes. They were unafraid of humans. By 1865 non-Native men had hunted them to extinction. In 1930 the United States bought 34 animals from Greenland to reintroduce them to some of their original range. Here in Palmer is the world's only domesticated herd.

According to the workers, the animals are not as gentle and slow-moving as they appear to be in the pastures. The males do courtship battle by bashing heads. Their heavy, drooping horns grow from a four-inch thick horn covering a three-inch thick skull on the top of their heads. Aggressive charging and bashing between two grown bulls is like a car hitting a concrete wall at 17 mph. The ground trembles.

As we exited the back of the barn, we approached double-fenced pastures. A public-address system repeated warnings to stay behind the fences and not to try to pet or feed the animals. Parents of young children were cautioned that the wooly mothers of those adorable, fluffy calves especially were protective of their babies.

Perhaps because the herd and scattered individuals were mostly at a distance, they weren't as large as I expected. The females were about four-feet tall and weighed around 350 pounds. The early calves, the size of an Old English sheepdog, hid behind their mothers. Males were kept in separate pastures. They were about five feet in height and much heavier—about 600 pounds. Their horns were impressive. The ones in the distant pastures looked as though they were dark brown haystacks with horns.

As I left the barn, I joined some of our group members across the road. They had found saddled horses tied to a fence. A chestnut mare which was not saddled had by her side a two-week-old paint colt. The baby was wearing a halter with a short lead but was not tied. The inquisitive little fellow wound between his mother's legs and under her belly. I offered my hand and coaxed him to emerge from behind mom. He sniffed my fingers. She nickered. He pranced back to safety.

A couple from our group joined others and mounted up for a short ride down the road. The five-minute ride cost $5. At the stables an hour's ride would be $35. I opted to wait to see if our finances would permit a longer ride. Five minutes only would be a teaser for me. I never had outgrown my preteen love for horses.

The afternoon warmed up to 50 degrees. The sun was high; the sky was clear. On such a beautiful day no one was ready to return to camp. We decided to explore Hatcher Pass.

Fishhook Road wound and climbed into the heart of the Talkeetna Mountains. The sheltered, shadowy, north side of the slopes held patches of snow. The higher we climbed, the more snow remained. A wide pulloff at the head of a long, deep valley gave us the opportunity to try to see all the way to Palmer at its mouth.

The view was a photographer's or painter's dream. The sun created brilliant patches of dazzling snow and dark-contrasting shadows. Here was a true example of atmospheric perspective. The receding, overlapping walls of the side canyons would challenge an artist's palette as the colors grayed and muted in the distance.

We returned to the van to continue climbing steeply. Rounding more outcroppings of rock, we crossed a snowbound, icy roadbed. The road abruptly ended and was blocked by drifts. Beyond the drifts and a "road closed for the season" sign were the abandoned buildings and old mining equipment of the Independence Gold Mine. Once spring returned to the pass, this would be opened as a state historic park.

Jeff and Chris unloaded some flattened cardboard boxes they had brought "just in case" they found snow for sledding. They trekked onto the pristine snow and promptly sank through the crust. Now thigh-deep in soft, wet snow, with their shoes filling and toes freezing, they trudged toward a distant slope to try out their makeshift sleds.

I lost my footing in the deep, soft snow, fell backward, and had to accept a helping hand. Staying on the snowpacked roadway seemed to be the prudent way to admire the scenery. I was beginning to experience why the Eskimo dialects have 200 different words to describe the different snow conditions.

The clarity of the light in the high pass is that for which landscape artists strive. Distant mountains snagged glaring rays of the setting sun. The sky was an indigo blue that near the horizon lightened into turquoise. I almost could see to heaven. The purple shadows lengthened across the brilliant snowfields as the sun slowly descended. The temperature dropped. Our group drifted into the sunny areas where it was at least 20-degrees warmer than in the shade.

In answer to blasts from the van's horn Jeff and Chris, our explorers, returned. As we left the high peaks of the pass, Chris noticed a large cabin nestled in the hills and surrounded by snow-drifts. A sign almost buried by snow announced the Hatcher Pass Lodge. A narrow, plowed track led toward the cabin, so we took a detour.

The track widened into a parking lot with snow machines, trucks, and a snow dozer that recently had been used. We got out to investigate. We didn't expect anyone to be about. A footpath of trampled snow led to the rustic A-frame cabin's second level.

Single-file we tramped up slippery wooden steps to the south-facing arctic entrance. A large, metal grate in the floor encouraged us to stomp and scrape the snow off our boots. An "Open" sign was on the outer door, so Jeff pushed the door open.

The lodge's manager and his wife attended a small lunch counter, where we ordered coffee, hot chocolate, and slices of freshly baked pie. While I waited for our order, I glanced at the menu and the posted lodging rates. The expense was way over my budget, even though accommodations included a sauna.

As I carried my steaming cup of cocoa, I walked out onto an encircling balcony to watch the violet shadows encroach on the remaining sunlight patches of snow. Near the crest of a long slope two tiny skiers were making zigzag tracks in the powder. I wondered if they were based at this lodge. How did they get to the top? I didn't see snow-go machine tracks or a lift. I lost sight of them as we said goodbye.

Monday morning was clear and warmer. The weather seemed almost springlike, especially after the snow of yesterday. We all felt a little guilty and worked to make up for our pleasure trip. Mickey assured us that this wasn't necessary. God gave us Sunday as a day of rest. Except for kitchen duty, he didn't expect us to work on Sundays. Again I raked leaves until I thought I'd drop.

For a change of pace I helped the women from North Carolina take down all the curtains in the cabins. They planned to launder the curtains. As soon as a dryer-load finished, we hung them back up. We were too smart, or lazy, to let the curtains get wrinkled and then have to be ironed. I'm sure that raking, walking, and climbing on chairs was healthy exercise, but by lunchtime my shoulders ached.

That afternoon I was raking leaves when I heard an elderly woman call out as she fell. I rushed over to her. She said she tripped on some rocks. Her left wrist hurt. I gently helped her to sit up. I removed her watch and rings. Others from her group rushed over. I gave her watch and rings to a woman that she knew.

I sent Chris to get some sticks from the woodpile. He hesitated because he didn't know that I was thinking of a splint for her wrist. Someone was holding a sweatshirt. That would do nicely. I borrowed it, cradled her arm in the shirt across her chest, and tied the sleeves together over her shoulder to form a sling. All that Scout training was paying off. Some one brought the van. She was hurried off to the hospital.

Tuesday was another leaf-raking day. This was getting old and tiring. At least no snakes are in Alaska. Chris and I had raked leaves at a camp in East Texas to get rid of the copperheads. I'd rather rake here.

By afternoon the Florida men were making headway as they tore down the old porches from the cabins. Piles of discarded lumber needed to be moved to a dumpsite. Chris and I took over driving the old Ford pickup truck and alternately hauling lumber and leaves.

Time for a break. I walked to the lake. The "No Swimming" sign had emerged from a snowbank. The ice was beginning to thaw and pull back from the bank. The surface was crumbly. I kicked it with the heel of my boot and shattered it into large chunks. Lifting some of the ice, I was surprised to see 10- to 12-inch-long icicles penetrated into the lake. The ice crystals glittered as though they were glass prisms hanging from a chandelier.

Cleaning canoes and checking for leaks was on our "to-do" list. The cleaning we could do on the shore, but how on a frozen lake do we check for leaks in a canoe? I noticed some short, thawed channels and poked at the ice with a canoe paddle. I could lift 12- to 24-inch-thick blocks enough to see the dagger-long ice crystals hanging below the surface. No longer could we "walk on water." Although still thick, the ice was too unstable and rotten.

Anna joined me on the dock to poke at the ice. I asked her how long before the lake thawed. She said that for several more days the broken ice near the shore would refreeze during the night. She showed me where distant ice had begun to change color. It got darker as thick, submerged blocks fractured and the surfaces thawed.

Ice breakup is a time for celebration, she said. When the rivers and sea ice begins to groan, creak, and snap apart, Natives anticipate spring. Especially in the town of Nenana, near Fairbanks, this is an important event. Here old-timers place wagers in the Nenana Ice Classic, a betting pool to guess the time when the ice will "go out" or begin to break up. A large, wooden tripod is set up on the frozen Tanana River. A trip wire connects the tripod to a clock on shore. The wire will break when the ice and tripod begin to move downstream and will stop the clock. The person with the closest-guessed time wins the pot.

Here on the lake, the ice "rots" and sinks. I could understand the ice melting and appearing rotten or mushy. My limited experience with ice is that it floats, not sinks.

A group of men from home—the west side of Houston—arrived to insulate and complete the camp's shop building. A second group from North Carolina moved into the cabins for a week of work. These volunteers were there to clear property for the construction of the new Pioneer Baptist Church. This tiny congregation soon would have a building to call a church home.

With dinner and dishes done by 7 p.m. and our bodies aching from raking and hauling leaves, we volunteers looked forward to hot showers. A bonfire blazed in the fire pit near the dining hall. Its warmth and cherry flames beckoned me to join other volunteers who sat on logs and swapped tales. Even though my body said "bed", the long evening was deceptive. How strange to consider bedtime when outdoors was so bright!

I hadn't seen Chris (or Alysha or Clint) since dinner, so I walked home to take my things and to look for him. I passed the lake and noticed that the sun finally was beginning to descend beyond the birch-edged ice. The sky was filled with vibrant yellows and oranges. Time for some obligatory sunset photos.

Swapping my towel and toiletry bag for a camera, I hiked back to the lake. The kids zoomed past on their bikes and were oblivious to the time. In the weak heat of the vanishing sun I found a spot to sit. At 10:30 p.m. I took my first photo. For the next hour I took pictures at 10- to 15-minute intervals as the wispy clouds refracted the sunlight from brilliant golds to deep reds, indigo, and magentas with purple streaks against a glowing burnished sky.

By 11:30 I was out of film and the sun still had not officially set. I called Chris to return to the RV. Breakfast duty would be on us too soon.

Wednesday's weather made me think of Houston's changeable conditions. Although the sky was fairly bright, drizzle fell all day. That didn't stop any of us from working. Raking and hauling leaves still had to be done, as did the porch construction, shop-building, landclearing, and of course cooking, feeding, and cleanup for all the volunteers.

Thursday, May 16, marked two weeks at camp. I felt as though I were a resident and not a visitor. Other volunteer groups have arrived and gone or would be leaving this weekend, but we would stay. I enjoyed the feeling of being useful and needed.

The sky cleared. The weather became warm enough to pull off sweatshirts while we raked. Again Chris and I took over hauling the old lumber from the porches under reconstruction to a pile by the storage sheds. The old pickup with a crazy quilt of blue and silver paint had a standard transmission that slipped and was tough to get into gear. The brakes, too, had seen better days. Chris begged to steer the truck. I let him hold the wheel while I struggled with the clutch, gears, and brakes. He begged me to let him drive. This was as close to driving as I'd allow.

On one of our trips to unload leaves, I backed up to the refuse pile and didn't set the brake well. Chris and I were on opposite sides of the tailgate and were pulling on an old tarp topped with a huge pile of leaves when the truck began rolling backward. Chris jumped onto the tailgate. I jumped to the side as the tailgate rammed into the huge leaf pile and stopped the truck.

Hey, I didn't know I was so strong! Thank God neither of us got pinned behind the tailgate. Chris jumped from the truck onto the leaf pile and laughed. He wanted to do it again! One of the volunteers—a mechanic—took the truck to the shop for repairs.

After dinner Anna and Clint launched a canoe into some of the melted water by the dock. Chris and I lowered another canoe into a clear puddle. We struggled to let out the straps on life jackets, so that we could get them over our jackets. Climbing aboard we shoved off the dock. Each crew struggled in vain to canoe over and around submerged ice chunks. Paddling around the perimeter of the dock took more effort than I expected. Crushed ice blocks floated up under the canoes. It impeded progress both forward and backward.

Chris smashed his paddle down on the ice slabs and splintered them into shards. Not a good idea, Anna cautioned. We can't chance splintering a paddle, too. Reaching the far end of the dock we gave up, circled the end of the dock, and fought our way back down the other side. Anna and Clint called it quits, too. We hauled the canoes out onto the dock to wait for "breakup."

Friday, May the 17th, warmed from a chilly nighttime low of 40 degrees to a pleasant high of 70. The birch and cottonwood trees, bare and dead-looking only a few days ago, were shimmering with chartreuse leaf buds. Several of the work teams left camp to return to the Lower Forty-Eight. The campground host, Ira, and his wife Kathy, arrived from their winter home in Arizona. Kathy retrieved two huge fucshia plants from a greenhouse in which they had wintered. She hung the hanging baskets from the dining-hall eaves. Their coral-pink-and-white blossoms shouted "spring."

I straightened my back and rolled my shoulders to loosen the tightness. Waving my toilet-bowl brush, I laughed aloud. What a sense of humor God has! He led me to earn a doctorate in education to clean toilets is Alaska!

Laughing, I made sure that I properly had sanitized the shower stalls and cleaned the sinks. Humming to myself, I finished mopping. This was fun. Next to washing dishes cleaning bathrooms at home was my least-favorite job. Today I would help cook and "do" dishes for more than 100 people for all three meals.

Before lunch started, I had time for a walk to the partially frozen lake. Birch and cottonwoods were bursting with new, lime-green leaves. I sat on a wooden bench in the brilliant, but weak, spring sun at the far end of the swimming pier. Only the mallards and loons braved getting their feet wet.

At age 9 I had accepted Christ as my Savior. Three years later, while I attended a youth conference, I felt compelled to let go of the back of the pew in front of me and respond again. I knew that my Lord was calling me for special service—not as a missionary or as a pastor's wife, but to work with children. I made plans to go to college and become a teacher. Those plans were put on hold when I married and was blessed with two delightful daughters.

Then divorce. The marriage had been a mistake. I had chosen to be married to a non-Christian; therefore, our marriage was not blessed. I was devastated, but the divorce was inevitable. I knew that even though I was forgiven, I felt out of God's will. How could He use me now? How could I serve Him? As I kept trying to seek His plan for my life, the stigma of my big mistake weighed on me.

My daughters survived being parented by a single mom who took college courses and worked to support them. Their mom was a teacher at a time when their friends had two parents and stay-at-home moms. Teaching supported us, but I felt unfilled. Had God forgotten what I thought of as my calling? Didn't He have some way I could serve Him? Had divorce negated His plans for me?

I thought my daughters needed a father; I wanted a companion. I hated being the odd one—not part of a couple. I convinced myself that the new man in my life was a Christian and that the Lord's will was for us to marry. How we blind ourselves and see only what we want to see! I drifted away from church and followed my husband.

Our marriage lasted only seven years. Two divorces couldn't be any worse than one. After all, sin is sin. Again I prayed for forgiveness.

My girls were in high school when they met a very young couple who had a newborn son. The parents could not cope with the struggles of parenting a preemie and asked me to babysit on weekends to give them a break. I willingly accepted this opportunity to serve. I thanked the Lord for putting me in the life of this frail infant. Babysitting became a private adoption. I knew God had been listening to my prayers. My mistakes had been forgiven. He had not forgotten his plans for me to work with His children.

Across the icy waters, gray-flecked white trunks of birch trees bowed from the bank. Their lacy branches tipped with emerald hints of spring delicately reflected in the glassy lake. I realized that only through reflection could I now see how God had been preparing me for His Plan in spite of my bad decisions. He knew my heart as well as my weaknesses.

Several throwaway teens from my classes became weekend foster kids. I obtained state licensing as a foster home. Additional foster kids became a part of our ever-changing family.

Yes, God could use me in spite of my big mistakes. I had acknowledged His love for me and had prayed that I would recognize His will while I dealt with these kids. Oh, the trials of being a single parent to a house full of teens! Today I can laugh and tell others, "Never ask God for patience; He will give you kids!" I learned extreme patience and to have an unceasing prayer life to deal with pregnancy, drugs, and runaways. I perfected prayerdriving on many trips to therapy, counseling, meeting at schools, and rehabs. I often thought a husband would be helpful, but the Lord knew that I needed only to rely on Him.

A newspaper article featured the need for "forever families" for tough-to-place, adoptable children. Little Nick was 5 years old; my oldest daughters were grown. I called immediately. Being a single parent was not a deterrent. Six months later I received a phone call and learned that 3-year-old Darrell legally was free for adoption. Prayer always had sustained me. Now I prayed earnestly that the best home would be found for Darrell even if it was not with me.

Blind and retarded because of abuse, his developmental delays would be a lifelong challenge. I wasn't sure that I would be the best parent for him. The Lord planned otherwise; Darrell joined our family.

Today I still struggle to understand God's purpose for Darrell's life. I wasn't able to "fix" him, heal his blindness, or educate him for a normal life. Now at age 23, he remains blind, profoundly retarded, and unable to care for himself. With many regrets and much remorse, when his care became too great, I had to place him in a residential-care facility. His story is not "happily-ever-after."

What was God's purpose for Darrell's life? Why was he placed in mine? While writing his story in my book *Adopting Darrell*, I reconsidered Jeremiah 1:5, "Before I formed you in the womb, I knew you. Before you were born, I sanctified you." My God knew me, too, and knew I'd choose to mess up. He loved me so much that He forgave me.

Many years ago the Lord had given me a vision of earning a doctorate degree in education. Then he taught me perseverance. Completing a bachelor in fine arts degree required nine years. A masters in art education was completed in just four years. He made possible my studying, teaching, and parenting the two boys and three older girls who, through adoption, joined my family. A year later I adopted a sibling group of four. I now was a single parent of eight kids ages 8 to 14. In May 1989 I met my final educational goal. I completed the doctorate in education. At graduation all but one of my kids helped me celebrate.

The following year my oldest adopted daughter gave birth to a son but was unable to parent. The infant joined my family to make a dozen. With the oldest three kids grown, I had only nine at home when we set out on a family adventure.

My distant cousin, a paleontologist, extended a vague invitation for my family to visit on his summer dinosaur dig in Montana. Much to his surprise, I accepted. I always have had a love for travel. My kids were fascinated with dinosaurs. What a challenge! I spent three weeks, covered 3,000 miles with nine kids in a van and pop-up camper. With the 2-month old baby in a backpack and

Darrell in a wheelchair, we visited Yellowstone National Park, the Royal Tyrell Museum of Paleontology, Dinosaur National Monument, and all of the dinosaur museums in between. My kids and I got down on our knees in the hot, dry badlands of Montana and gently picked fossils loose from the surrounding rock.

I was disturbed that we repeatedly were told that dinosaurs lived millions of years ago. Genesis 1:24 says that "Then God said, 'Let the earth bring forth the living creature according to its kind: cattle and creeping things and beast of the earth, each according to its kind'; and it was so" (New King James Version).

On the dig we helped excavate a jumble of bones from different species that had been found in a small canyon. The scientists told us that the bones indicated that the bodies had been washed together in a flood, then quickly covered with mud. Later, visiting Dinosaur Monument, we saw a mountain of mixed fossils. Again the remains were jumbled together "as if by a massive flood." Why would no one admit that only one worldwide flood had occurred? Noah's Flood. Noah was instructed to take into the ark a male and female of every living creature. Could he have taken baby dinosaurs?

Returning home I began to study Creationist's views of dinosaurs and Noah's Flood. I learned that Job 40:15-24 describes an animal familiar to the man, Job. Called the behemoth, it was a huge, strong, mammal that ate grass. It had strong hips and a thick truck like a cedar tree. Could this be a description of a T-rex? Scientist today doubt that T-rex was a meat eater.

Job 41:1-34 describes a large sea creature that shoots fire from its mouth. Could the Leviathan have been a Brontosaurus? Could Chinese legends of fire-breathing dragons be oral history of extinct dinosaurs?

I prayed that my children would understand Romans 1:20: "From the time the world was created, people have seen the earth and sky and all that God made. They can clearly see His invisible qualities—His eternal power and divine nature. So they have no excuse whatsoever for not knowing God" (*Ryrie Study Bible*).

A breeze shifted the splintering ice crystal on the lake's surface. Reflections rippled and shattered.

I felt secure in the knowledge that I once again was in the Lord's will. My struggle to parent teen-agers with multiple emotional issues often was overwhelming. Besides forgiveness what I needed was to depend solely on the Lord. With His guidance and constant prayer my kids and I survived their teen years. They all accepted the Lord as Savior, but not all of them have followed in the Christian lifestyle.

One by one they became adult enough to be responsible for their own lives. I despair over many of their choices but trust these young people to the Lord. Except for my responsibility for the youngest, my parent days are over. In spite of my mistakes I believe I am fulfilling God's plan for my life. I had been able to serve the Lord by loving and caring for His children. I had retired from teaching and soon would retire from parenting. I knew that I wouldn't retire from serving.

Low over the spruce on the far Eastern shore, a majestic eagle began soaring directly toward me. I held my breath. It was a juvenile bird—dark brown with just a hint of white on its tail and on what would become its misnamed "bald" head. Silhouetted against the cloudless azure sky it glided overhead. I turned to follow the flight of this king of the sky.

A tiny, white bird flew determinedly toward the eagle. It dropped down and bombarded the eagle's back. Some nerve! The eagle continued on its flight path and ignored the tern's repeated harassment. The tern flew aside as the eagle settled onto a bare birch among the spruce across the lake. The gutsy little bird must be protecting a nesting site, I thought, as it braved its foe and flew down repeatedly to attack the resting eagle.

After I retired, much to my surprise, the Lord wouldn't let me rest, either. I was living a long-time dream to drive to Alaska to celebrate my 60th birthday. After wearing out the pop-up camper, I had bought a 20-year-old motor home. What a learning experience! By the time I retired in 1998, all of my children but the youngest, Chris, were grown. We had worn out two other RV's. Chris and I upgraded to a four-year-old motor home. In my first book, *Grandma's on the Go!,* I chronicled our adventures.

As I walked toward the dining hall, the stoic eagle and the persistent tern reminded me that God still is not through with me. He has been as patient with me as the eagle is with the aggravating tern. The tern's perseverance, as it attacks the much larger and stronger bird, encouraged me to keep on trying to understand His will. Here I am volunteering in Wasilla, AK—cooking, doing dishes, and cleaning toilets!

The sun warmed my back. I raised my eyes towards the expanse of heaven and knew that He allowed me these experiences so that I might speak and write to encourage others to discover and follow His plans.

On Saturday I joined Mickey to cook breakfast for six men from North Carolina—our only remaining work team. They hurried off to the site of Pioneer Baptist Church to complete clearing the large lot. After lunch two of the men stayed at the shop to cut letters for a sign on a band saw. They showed me how to use the saw. Later that afternoon I taught Chris how to cut out letters. He and I made a sign for the RV park area.

After dinner Chris and I and Anna and Clint tried the canoes again. The surface ice now was far enough from the shore that we thought we could take a little tour of the lake. Large quantities of ice still were near the center of the 150-acre lake. Chris and I followed Anna and Clint out along the Eastern shore. They soon found themselves surrounded by ice slabs. Chris and I tried to pass them, but slightly submerged ice blocks surfaced and surrounded us. Both canoe crews strained to plow forward.

Chris, in the bow of our boat, tried to smash the ice with his paddle while I struggled to propel us. We flipped long shards of glittering crystals onto the surface ice. Suggestions were shouted between the two crews. We agreed to turn our boat around and head back to the pier, as we struggled against the wind. Gusts blew us further into the icy lake. Anna and Clint turned their canoe around to face the shore and then became icelocked. I backpaddled and hoped to open an ice-free channel so we could turn around. Blocks of ice drifted up under the canoe hull. We were firmly trapped. Icebound.

Chris and Clint called crazy comments back and forth across the ice that separated us. I was cold. My shoulder muscles ached. My ungloved hands were freezing. Ice blocks closed in and surrounded us in all directions. We tried poling over the ice by using our paddles like ski poles to shove our canoe/sled forward. We made little progress.

The wind blew us toward the center of the lake and away from the ice-free shore. Determined to break free we tried to follow a trail of crushed ice left by Anna and Clint. As we alternately poled over the sheets and paddled through icy mush, we struggled forward.

The budding trees, greening underbrush, and clear-blue sky of spring seem to laugh at winter's final joke. Exhausted, we reached the dock. We, too, could laugh. How silly we'd been to challenge God's timing for breakup!

Later that afternoon I stood on the chapel balcony overlooking the lake. To my amazement all of the ice was gone! Melted, or rotten, or sunken, or windblown. It was gone. Only near the far Western shore was any hint of the entrapping ice.

Sunday. The clear, warmer weather was a temptation to skip church and play. With such long daylight hours, that would have been foolish. A large group of youth campers passed us on their way to the lakefront. To my astonishment an excited young woman and her brave youth pastor waded into the 38-degree lake. To applause from her friends he baptized her quickly. Blankets were thrown over their shivering bodies as they all trooped back uphill to the fire. They were on fire for the Lord.

Only kids would be brave enough to do that, I thought. But, no! Later that afternoon, two volunteers—men from North Carolina— jumped off the pier. Immediately they climbed back out. They were grateful for the towels and blankets their amused friends with cameras provided.

Except for when we prepared, served, and cleaned up meals, Sunday was our day of rest—or day of play. Anna, Clint, Alysha, and Chris went out to paddleboat. I took a canoe solo. In only one day spring had arrived. Swimming near a thicket of birch on the shore, a river otter or muskrat glided just below the surface. Its cat-like face and bright eyes caught sight of us. It glided toward a submerged tree and dove out of sight.

Anna directed us toward a secluded cove—a loon-nesting site. We cautiously drifted toward a brush-pile nest near the shore. The nest slightly was above the water surface. The loons are a protected species and could not be disturbed. Through my binoculars I saw a bird low in the nest. Keeping its head lowered it slipped over the edge and dove. We watched in silence. An eternity seemed to pass before the loon popped to the surface many yards away. Still further out a second loon surfaced and called with its haunting voice. The first one answered but glided toward the center of the lake. Together they were leading us in two different directions away from their nest.

We pretended that we hadn't seen them and silently paddled away. A pair of swans flew overhead. They surprised me with their grace. Again we froze with delight and drifted while we watched them land on the lake.

Returning to shore Anna told us that she had been a volunteer at a bird rescue and rehabilitation center. She is trained to work with raptors. She had the honor of releasing a juvenile eagle on the lake.

Monday we had no campers. Anna invited us to go into Anchorage with her and Alysha. While she ran errands, we could visit the Alaska Native Heritage Center.

A large bronze sculpture of "Raven the Creator" greeted visitors near the entrance. Legends from before the Russians introduced Christianity in the late 1700s reflect Alaskan Natives' animistic beliefs. The highly intelligent ravens, which live year-round in all parts of Alaska, were thought to have mystical powers. The birds have shown an unusual ability to learn and to solve problems. Perhaps this is why Alaskans have so many legends of the raven's ability to provide for the needs of Native Alaskans

Passing through the entrance, we followed the sounds of drumming. On a stage to one side of a recessed, circular gathering place several Natives in costume presented a dance. Both men and women wore a *kuspuk*, a calico pullover shirt with a hood. It was designed like a parka and trimmed with ribbons and braid. They wore pants and *mukluk* boots. The five men sat crosslegged on the floor and tapped rhythm on shallow, tambourine-like drums. Four women gracefully danced in place. Their feet did not move.

In each hand the dancers held a feather fan. Their hand movements, reminiscent of the hula, told the story of a hunter and a hunted seal. Some of the men acted as if they were paddling a kayak; then they pulled imaginary arrows from a quiver on their backs to shoot the seal. When the seal dove underwater, the men held their breath, blew out their cheeks, and shook their heads as if diving and surfacing.

Storytelling preserves Native Alaskan oral traditions, imparts important social traditions, and explain nature and its creatures. Stories were told, not written, and heard, not read. Meaning and nuances are lost when stories are translated into writing because of the special relationship between the storyteller and audience.

At the end of the performance another woman wearing a *kuspuk* answered questions from the audience. She was asked whether mothers carried their babies in their parka's hood. She replied that a soft, leather baby strap was worn across the mother's chest and over her shoulders. The strap supported the baby's bottom, while the baby leaned against her back. The baby was "worn" under the parka or *kuspuk*. "Like this," she said, as she turned around and pulled aside the wide neck of her garment. Nestled against her neck was a black-haired, sleeping baby.

She introduced him as her nephew. She was babysitting.

We followed Alysha to the Hall of Cultures, where several artists had small studios to demonstrate and exhibit their work. Beautiful beaded jewelry, drums, and masks captivated me. I wanted to stop to talk to each one of the artists, but the kids hurried me along to see the exhibits.

Artifacts representing the cultures of the five major culture groups taught me that Alaska's people are not all Eskimos. I learned that Alaska has 11 distinct cultures that speak 20 different languages. What we *cheechakos* (foreigners) call Eskimo are the Inupiaq and Yupik cultures. Igloos only are temporary winter hunting shelters. In the exhibits outdoors we would see actual habitats.

The kids quickly tired of looking at museum stuff and insisted that we go outside to see the villages. Representative structures had been reconstructed around the perimeter of a small lake.

Our first stop was the Talking Circle, a circular area partially flanked by low bleachers. An older man and a teen-aged girl encouraged us to touch a large assortment of furs: wolf, fox, seal, bear, moose, and others.

The girl pointed to a vertical pole with an extended horizontal bar about eight feet off the ground. Suspended from the end of the bar was a leather cord. Tied to the free end was a tennis-ball-sized leather sphere. She asked Chris and Alysha if they wanted to learn some Eskimo-Native American games. Both kids shyly declined.

The small, wiry man who appeared to be in his 50s walked over and lightly touched the leather ball which hung about three feet from the ground. He then squatted and jumped flat-footed. Extending his legs straight out in front of him, he kicked the ball.

Not believing his agility, I gasped. He gave us a slight smile and touched the ball to stop its swinging. Again he jumped. This time he kicked both legs to the side and hit the ball squarely. After a couple more incredible displays of strength and balance the girl took her turn.

The girl squatted on the ground and leaned on her left hand. Balanced on her hand she kicked upward and hit the ball with her right foot while she held her left. Again the kids were asked to participate. After much coaxing Chris agreed. The ball was lowered to a few inches off the ground. His kicking was unsuccessful, but at least he tried.

We learned that games such as these, requiring excellent coordination and strength, are part of the Eskimo-Native American Olympics. Natives place great value and have respect for physical fitness. Training for competition keeps individuals in physical form during the winter darkness.

Leaving the Olympians to demonstrate for other visitors, we followed the trail to an unusually large, wooden, modern-looking structure. This clan house represented the Eyak, Tlinget, Hiada, and

Tsimshian cultures of the Southeast Panhandle. These peoples lived along the coast of the Inside Passage. On our short walks off the ferry, I had not seen evidence of their culture.

The impressive cedar-plank dwelling was nearly square with a gabbled roof. We entered through an oval opening through a tremendous totem sentinel. Four huge, interior logs topped with massive beams supported a plank roof. The lodge, about 20-by-30 feet, typically would house four to six families. Each family had as living quarters a low platform along the wall. The central area was excavated and served as a large hearth. Woven, cedar-bark mats provided screening and floor coverings.

Artifacts consisted of intricately woven sea-grass baskets, skin cloaks and the remarkable Chilkat robe. Woven of mountain goat wool and cedar-bark strips, these fringed blankets only were worn for ceremonies. Black and yellow dyed fibers contrasted with the natural light-gray wool. The design consisted of flat, stylized eyes, animal heads, and geometric shapes. In no other culture have I seen this artistic style.

In college I raised Samoyed dogs. These dogs, known for their thick, fine undercoat, originated along the Alaskan coast. The Salish tribes raised the small, wooly dog. Its hair was pulled or brushed out and combined with goat wool for weaving.

The afternoon sun glared through the low entrance. Shafts of light enticed us to leave the gloom of the windowless lodge and continue our tour. The dirt path edged the lake and then turned abruptly toward a large, earthen mound covered with short grasses.

On one end of the mound the kids discovered an open doorway and entered the dwelling by walking down a sloping, dirt ramp. We found ourselves in a dim, open space below ground. A young man explained that these dwellings actually would be pits four-to-six-feet below ground. The roof was wood covered by sod. The dwellings often were built with whale-bone frames covered with sod. Sleeping platforms for several families were placed around the outer walls. They had no fire pit or hearth. Cooking was done outside.

Our guide showed us a small hoop that hung vertically from a strip of leather from the ceiling. The kids were encouraged to try to throw a small harpoon through the opening of the hoop. He explained that the Aleut culture lived on the rocky necklace of islands that extend southwest from the Alaskan Peninsula to Asia. With harpoons thrown from their kayaks they hunted Stellar sea lion, seals, and whales. Boys played games such as this to develop their coordination.

The kids said "yuck" when he showed us a waterproof rainsuit sewn from strips of sea-lion intestines. Pretty ingenious, I thought. The hunters wore a decorated wooden visor or elongated hat to keep the rain and ocean's glare out of their eyes. The hat was similar to the crownless visors we use today but much more highly decorated.

Continuing down the trail, we arrived at an open-front, sod building. The Inupiat, also known as Northern Eskimos, built sub-terranean multi-family sod dwellings similar to the Aleut. The open front strictly was for visitors. Inhabitants used an underground tunnel that extended up into a large living area. The passageway trapped cold air so that it did not enter the house. My adventurous kids were encouraged to crawl through the tunnel. I declined.

Inside this community house was a display of harpoons, lances, and hunting and fishing equipment. We learned that this dwelling represented winter homes. All Native cultures used temporary camps with tents or lean-to's during the short summers while they traveled to hunt or fish.

The next dwelling represented the Yupik or southern Yuit Eskimos. This partially dug-out building had a doorway but most often had an underground entry tunnel. A central hearth and raised sleeping platforms completed it. This was a men's house where men and boys lived and worked. Usually the women and younger children occupied another dwelling. In the men's house planks for dancing and ceremonies could cover the hearth.

The last house on our tour was a pioneer-style log cabin. These homes of Athabascans Native Americans were scattered in the vast interior of Alaska and the Yukon. Their language ties them to the Navajo and Apache of the Southwest.

Three women wearing calico *kuspuks* pointed out a small, log cabin built on stilts. It was called a *cache* and was used to keep food and supplies out of the reach of bears. A log ladder leaned against the base of the cache.

The Athabascans built varied house styles: log and sod dugouts with entrance tunnels, plank or log cabins, and portable caribou or moose-skin domed tents. People living along major salmon rivers were not as nomadic as were those who lived inland. Inlanders spent summers fishing and drying fish and in the fall hunted caribou and moose. The clans traded with their neighbors and adapted practices from them. They used dogsleds to travel their trade routes in winter. In summer the dogs carried packs on their backs.

We learned about a ceremonial event call a potlatch. To mark a special event one clan would host another. Before the gathering the host clan manufactured and collected gift items and food. The invited clan members were given fine gifts during formal presentations which were followed by a feast and dancing. The hosts usually gave until they were destitute.

Leaders competed with each other to give more wealth and food in order to obtain status. Later the hosts would be invited to a return potlatch that would be given by their guests. This lack of selfishness enabled the clans to assist each other during tough times.

Returning to the main building, I examined gift-shop items and tried to absorb expressions of Northern Native culture. I bought postcards resisting beautiful books. Alysha showed Chris a pair of Eskimo yo-yos. Two stuffed cones of sealskin were attached to either end of a leather thong. She tried to demonstrate how to work them, but the gift shop was too crowded. I bought a pair so they could take them outside.

In front of the building a teen-aged girl dressed in a lovely blue *kuspuk* was twirling a set of yo-yos. Seeing Chris's yo-yo she offered to give him a lesson. She advised him to hold one fur cone in one hand while he twirled the other in a circle in front of him. Then he was to twirl the second cone in the opposite direction. With practice they would fly past one another.

Tuesday, May 21. Although tired from yesterday's adventures, I quickly accepted Anna's offer to go gold-prospecting. Early in the day we loaded into my motor home kids, dogs, and food. Our first stop was in Anchorage to search Anna's mom's garage for tools and gold pans.

Marie, Anna's mom, was a delightful, energetic woman. A widow, she lived in a split-level older home in a hilly subdivision of well-kept, hill-climbing homes. Her love for flowers was evident in her carefully tended yard and houseplants. Anna clearly got from her mom her enthusiasm for life. Marie declined our invitation to go gold-prospecting with us. She had to go to work. In the garage she showed us where to hunt and to take whatever tools we needed. Anna unearthed camping equipment—remnants of family camping. She selected two shovels and gold pans.

Marie owned and used an ancient, 21-foot Class C motor home that was reminiscent of my 1976 Jamboree. She was stylishly dressed for work and was fresh from the beauty parlor. I had a tough time imaging her roughing it in a vintage RV or gold panning.

Marie shared how their family had bought mining rights in a forested valley with a river flowing through it. Long ago some gold had been found there. No one had been on the property in several years. She wished us luck. Wow, now were going to experience the "real" Alaska!

As we loaded our prospectors' tools, Marie excitedly told Anna to mark June 31 on her calendar. On this date her church would be taking a group on a 26-glacier tour out of Wittier. She had arranged for tickets for Anna and her kids.

Grabbing my hand she said, "I'm trying to get two more tickets, so you and Chris can go, too."

I thanked her profusely for thinking of us. Anna would let us know whether she got the tickets.

Driving south on the Seward Highway, Anna directed me to turn in at the Big Game Alaska Wildlife Center. For a small fee we were able to walk up-close to many native animals in large pens. Anna explained that rescued, injured, or orphaned animals were housed here. The ones that could be rehabilitated would be returned to the wild. Others would find homes in zoos or remain here as a part of a wildlife-awareness education programs. Herds of buffalo, moose, caribou, and antelope grazed in separated pastures. Some of the animals had signs of injuries. A large grizzly had his own cabin in a double fenced area. To the delight of visitors three tiny, black bear cubs cavorted in an enclosure. Their mother had been killed in a forest fire. Fortunately a ranger had rescued them. They were so cute and playful—just like kittens. I wished we could stay to watch them be bottle-fed.

We drove south past the Turnagain Arm to the Portage cutoff. The riverside glacier center was closed, but we watched huge chunks of ice flow toward us from the calving glacier that was out of sight. Anna directed us to a parking area with a hiking trail that led to another glacier.

Since the day was relatively warm, we wore T-shirts and jeans. As we climbed into the mountains, the air became colder. Snow appeared in the shadowy crevasses. Soon we were hiking in soft snow that soaked into our shoes. We tried to avoid icy patches on the trail. My Southern body had difficulty adjusting to the changes from warm sunshine to cold shadows. Our jackets had been left behind.

The glacier became visible. It hung as though it were a huge, bluish ice pop between mountain peaks. We approached a steep climb and decided to backtrack. We'd travel there another day and be better prepared for the climb.

Further south, as we drove around the base of a mountain and crossed a river, Anna excitedly called out for me to slow down. I crept along the shoulder as she searched the forest for a secluded road. There it was, she hoped. I turned right onto the weedy gravel lane. Hidden from the highway, a metal gate stopped our adventure.

Anna shrugged and got out to investigate the lock. To our relief the padlock wasn't snapped closed. She pushed back the gate. I drove through. She closed it behind us. The road led deep into the forest. Snow that first appeared in the hollows soon blocked the road. Tracks of four-wheelers continued through the slush and mud, but I wasn't chancing getting stuck. We pulled over onto a wide shoulder.

Chris and I pulled on knee-high rubber boots. Anna and Alysha had fishing waders. Somehow we shouldered shovels, an ax, gold pans, and cameras. The temperature was too warm for jackets, so they were left behind. Sam and Lady on their leashes led off down the two-track lane.

Anna searched the forest and deadfall that encroached on the road as she looked for landmarks. She waded through soft snow on several short forays into the woods. After much searching she found a post several yards into the brush and woods. Attached to the top of the post, a small board sheltered a Mason jar. She shouted to Alysha that she'd found the claim. What was so important about a glass jar?

Anna unscrewed the jar from its lid that was nailed to the post. From inside she extracted a yellowed, folded paper. On it were surveyor's marks for the claim. We almost were there, I thought. We hoisted our prospectors' tools, pushed through thick, snow-laden brush, and began a descent through the spruce. The tangled undergrowth reminded me of the thickets in East Texas, except that I couldn't identify the plants beneath the dead-looking birch, cottonwoods, and tall spruce. Snow in low, sheltered spots looked deceivingly firm, but each footstep broke through the crust. In spite of knee-high boots, cold wet snow filtered in to soak my socks. My boots were too tight to wear over shoes and so loose with just socks that the snow pulled loose with each step. More than once I lost my balance and landed ungracefully.

The poor dogs were too short-legged to plow through the snow, so they tried leaping, with their bellies dragging. Where the snow had melted, we slogged through mud and tangled undergrowth. Our descent toward the river became gloomy from shadows cast by the surrounding mountains. I wondered if we'd run into a bear or a moose. The dogs' barking should warn the critters away, I hoped.

The sound of rushing water encouraged our prospecting team on. The fast-flowing river carried chunks of crushed ice. Anna and the kids stepped off the bank into the swirling, frigid, white water. I stayed on the bank with the dogs to watch out for bears. Anna showed Chris how to shovel into a gold pan the watery gravel from the river bottom. She then filled the pan with water and swished the gravel around. Into the river she sloshed the lighter stuff. She stuck her fingers into the icy water and poked at the gravel. Satisfied that no hint of gold was there, she dumped the pan and repeated the process.

The miners seemed oblivious to the cold water, snow, and the damp, chilly air. I was freezing. Who would have thought that in late May we would need jackets? The shadows deepened. I no longer could see the sun beyond the mountain peaks. My watch showed 8 p.m. No one agreed with me that time had arrived to get back to civilization. How would we ever find our way back after dark? My adventurous sprit was failing. Anna hadn't seemed to be following a trail—just her instincts. If left to me, I'd just climb up—up toward where I hoped the road might be. This Boy Scout was so unprepared. No compass. No map. And no food.

The others finally admitted being cold and hungry. Emerging from the gloom of the thick forest, I sighed in relief. The sun was still casting a golden glow on the magnificent landscape opposite us and along the roadway toward civilization. Like 99 percent of all gold miners, we returned emptyhanded.

To show Anna and Mickey how greatly I appreciated experiencing Alaska, I worked exceptionally diligently at all the chores necessary to keep camp running. On Thursday a group arrived for the night. Friday we hurriedly cleaned cabins and sanitized the bathhouse. Two new groups were there for the weekend. Some confusion arose as to our responsibilities for cooking and serving. Which group would use what facilities at what time? What was I supposed to do?

During my free time on Saturday, I sat on the swim beach and watched Alaskans brave the warming lake for a swim. Chris joined Alysha and Clint. They pulled off their shoes to jump fully clothed off the dock. They surfaced sputtering, shivering, and laughing. Chris tried to throw water on me to get me to join them. No way! I love to swim but only in much warmer water. I threatened to leave and not return with a towel and dry clothes for Chris. With teeth chattering he agreed to leave me alone.

During Sunday-morning church service the director of missions from Anchorage conducted a commissioning service for Anna and

Mickey. This made official their positions as directors of the LaVerne Griffin Youth Camp. Many years ago, LaVerne Griffin had a vision of a camp for youth. She and her husband bought 60 acres of property bordering the lake. They hiked in with backpacks from the Parks highway. Later a road approached the area. An extension reached the camp. Given to the Baptist association, the property was slowly developed through the efforts of hundreds, maybe thousands of volunteers. Mr. and Mrs. Griffin have passed away and left a legacy to young people of all ages and denominations.

The new pastor of Pioneer Baptist Church—John and his wife, Carolyn—were introduced and welcomed to Alaska. They originally were from Hannibal, MO, and were very excited about living and working in Alaska.

We now had three summer missionaries: Caesar from Brazil, who was a college student in Texas; Jessica from Australia; and Kevin from Georgia. Ira and Kathy, retired volunteers who wintered in Arizona, were our camp hosts. They claimed Alaska residency but left before the weather turned too cold. These folks, added to the volunteers from North Carolina, Florida, and Texas, made this trip so much more meaningful than if I had been on vacation.

Lorna, a young mother originally from England, brought her four children to visit Anna and her kids. Chris joined them for a swim. Lorna's openness and energetic spirit made her an instant friend. Although Chris was older and much larger than her boys, he, along with Clint, was invited to spend the night. What fun for him to be making friends so far from home!

On Thursday I learned that Marie had gotten tickets for us at a reasonable price for the 26-glacier tour. Anna and her kids took their RV to Anchorage to run errands. On Friday we would join them at Marie's church.

On Friday, ready for another adventure, we met our friends and many strangers to board large, yellow school buses. How nice to leave the driving to someone else and to sightsee along the Turnagain Arm! At the entrance to the Whittier tunnel we waited for our turn to drive through the three-mile long tunnel through the Chugach Mountains. My new friends and fellow travelers clued me in on the story of the tunnel, the only land approach to the town of Whittier.

One set of train tracks ran through the tunnel. Eastbound trains alternated track time with westbound trains. Years ago cars and trucks were loaded on the train's flat cars for the trip. Today we would wait for the westbound vehicle traffic to emerge from the mouth of the mountains; then we would take our turn. Tunnel traffic—train and motor vehicle—was tightly scheduled and controlled. If a driver missed his time, he must be prepared for a long wait.

Traffic lights changed from red to yellow. A long, single line of passenger cars, commercial transport trucks, RV's, and pickup trucks loaded with fishing equipment played follow-the-leader past our buses.

The lights turned green. Our turn had arrived. Our bus was directed to merge into the line of eastbound travelers. The tunnel was dark. Very dark. The bus's headlights illuminated the two silvery ribbons of train track that disappeared into the shadows under the old van preceding us. Occasional signal lights blinked from the sidewalls. It was as spooky as a coalmine or a narrow wild cave.

The tunnel was long. Very long. Three miles at 30 mph equaled an unusually long time in the dark heart of the mountains. At last, light at the end of the tunnel. We let out our collective breaths and blinked in the brightness.

The Klondike Express, our tour boat, was tied up at the end of a long, wooden dock. A gangplank led onto the stern. Two hulls, like a catamaran, stuck out from the stern with a lifeboat suspended in between. Above the twin hulls rose a squarish but sleek, enclosed observation cabin with open decks on both bow and stern. The kids and those of us young-at-heart passengers raced up the outside stairs to the open upper deck.

As soon as the tour boat left the dock, a brisk, damp wind forced me to layer sweaters and a jacket over my T-shirt and hide in the protection of the wheelhouse.

Over the PA system the captain directed our attention to glaciers that hung in the clefts of mountains soaring on either side of the bay. How could he remember all those names? Whittier, Billings,

Northland, Lawrence, and many more. How did someone determine that these were glaciers and not just leftover, winter snows? I lost count and went inside where it was warmer.

Glaciers form when snow repeatedly falls on unmelted snow. The weight and pressure of the new snowfalls cause the old snow to re-crystallize into grains of ice. Glaciers can become thousands of feet thick and miles long. Gravity causes the ice mass to move downhill. Many types of glaciers are in Alaska: the alpine glacier that forms on mountain slopes; Piedmont glaciers, which are two or more glaciers combined; valley glaciers are alpine glaciers that settle into a high valley; and tidewater glaciers that end in a tremendous cliff face of ice along the shore of a bay. Moving glaciers grind and erode the mountains. They sculpt and refashion them into U-shaped valleys called *fjords*.

In the distance crunching sounds were followed by a muffled "boom." The captain explained that he slowly would approach a calving tidewater glacier. He then would cut the engines so that vibrations would not cause avalanches. Calving icebergs could be dangerous to the boat. As the tour boat crept nearer, the aqua-colored projecting wall of the glacier loomed beautifully forbidding. Sedan-sized chunks of ice and smaller icebergs floated past with only a small portion of their bulk visible above the icy surface.

One of the ship's crew used a dip net to scoop smaller glacial chunks up for the brave tourists to taste. Chris said the ice tasted carbonated, like a soda. Another louder "boom" drew our attention to the glacier's many-storied face. A cave extending above and below the bay's surface was calving or shedding huge chunks of ice from the interior. With close observation and patience I was able to photograph a boxcar-sized chunk breaking off from the cave's ceiling. It made a tremendous rumbling, roaring crash that sent ice and water splashing. Ice chunks shot up unexpectedly from beneath the bay's surface to float in the turbulence towards us.

Surging glaciers can move as much as 200 feet in a day and violently calve unexpectedly. Since early exploration in the late 1700's Alaska's glaciers have been retreating. This exposes once-covered land. This bay once was solid ice.

As we left the base of the calving glacier, we passed several smaller, less impressive ones. A gull rookery scaled the high wall of a cliff. Squawking birds swarmed as though they were bees over the crevasses where other birds were nesting. Many flew over the boat. I wondered if they would dive for bread crusts like the sea gulls in Galveston do. I had heard that some species were migratory. Maybe some of these birds followed us from Texas.

During the return trip to port, we got out our picnic lunches to join the others with hot chocolate or coffee. I don't remember the ride back through the tunnel. I slept. The late sunset was deceiving. The time almost was midnight as we followed Anna in her RV to the parking lot of her church, where we boondocked for the night.

Saturday, June 1. The warmer weather brought out Alaska's infamous mosquitoes. Southeast Texas has swarms of trophy-sized bloodsuckers, so I was prepared with repellent. Alaska's 30-plus species hatch out in succession during the spring and early summer. They are huge and fierce. The mosquito is celebrated as Alaska's state bird. Deet is recognized as perfume. By reapplying repellent, wearing long sleeves and long pants, and by staying near the campfire we survived early-morning and late-evening attacks.

The weather, despite the mosquitoes, was too fine to stay indoors. We volunteers sat at the picnic tables close to the fire as we shared stories and swatted. The kids lined up dead bodies to count their revenge. In the craft room I found a sheet of construction paper and transparent tape. As rapidly as they killed them, the kids taped dead mosquitoes to the paper. Within 30 minutes they had immortalized 86 critters.

Monday, June 2. Morning devotionals for volunteers and staff met in the dining hall after breakfast cleanup. This morning my attention drifted to the parking lot beyond the south windows. Without thinking about interrupting our meeting I jumped up and yelled, "Moose! Moose"!

Trotting down the drive toward the dining hall was a real, live moose. The meeting abruptly adjourned as we all rushed to the windows. The knobby-kneed, long-legged yearling with huge, batlike ears and a bulbous nose was so ugly it was cute.

The moose looked around, pranced back and forth, then took off around the chapel. We followed him from window to window. Anna said that the mother moose probably had run the teen-ager off as she prepared to calf.

Anna showed me a photo of three adult moose kneeling on their front legs to eat early grass. They seemed to be praying for an early spring.

The Anchorage newspaper began to report moose mama and moose calf sightings, including one born on the grassy mound of an overpass in town. A report emerged of twin calves near downtown. The paper reported urban bears eating out of bird-feeders, eating dog food, and getting into trash cans—all inside of the city limits. And I think I have problems at home with raccoons!

Later in the week Chris and I ran errands in Wasilla. I had seen a sign for the Iditarod Trail Race Headquarters and was confused because of the bronze dog and sign in Anchorage. We drove to a tiny town, Knik, near Wasilla. Here we saw a fascinating video on the history of dogsledding as a sport and as an economical means of transportation in the wilderness.

Dogsled racing began in the early 1900s. In the winter of 1925 a diphtheria epidemic in Nome threatened the entire community. Twenty dog sled teams mushed in relay around the clock from Knik, the railroad head, through blizzards to take the serum to the dying town. A small, brindle-gray mutt led his team for 340 miles on the last leg of the trip. Today Togo, the mutt, is preserved in a display case.

In 1973 the Iditarod races again began to commemorate the 1925 race. Races are run on the first Saturday in March starting in Anchorage at the bronze dog. The race then restarts in Knik, near Wasilla. Competitors travel more than 1,100 miles to Nome. In 1995 Doug Swingly won the race with a record time of nine days and two hours. Susan Butcher has won four times.

Many photos of famous dogs showed dogs that looked like Togo, a non-descript mongrel. I thought all the dogs would be silver and black Siberian Huskies or snow-white Samoyeds. Only a few dogs were pretty. Most teams consisted of 12 to18 dogs harnessed in pairs to a central line. Mushers, breeders and trainers look for double-coated dogs with stamina and heart, regardless of their looks.

Chris took a dogsled ride on a wheeled sled pulled by six rangy, medium-sized dogs. Most were shedding in clumps. Lying on the track, harnessed and attached to a central line, they were so "chilled out" that I doubted they could be convinced to walk, much less pull. Chris took his seat. The musher yelled something like "mush." The dogs exploded down the trail and jerked the front wheels of the sled off the ground. They raced through the woods. Returning to their starting point an assistant intercepted the lead dog before he could race on.

The musher and his helper tied the dogs to stakes. On the parking lot Chris and I examined a pickup-style truck with a two-tiered dog box on the rear. Each side of the box had four small, wire-mesh doors on each level. The musher led a dog to the truck. He held tightly to its collar while the energetic dog ran along on its hind legs, with its forelegs beating the air. An upper door was swung open. The man lifted the dog by its collar, his arm under its hindquarters. The dog bounced. The man lifted. In he went.

In a little more than a week we would be leaving to work during a Vacation Bible School in a small, rural church in Fairbanks. I set to work. I had been experimenting with creating birch-bark baskets and birdhouses. I wanted to leave a special "thank-you" gift for Anna and Mickey. On a large thin sheet of inner bark I drew in ink a soaring eagle with the following verse:

"But they that wait upon the Lord shall renew their strength; they shall mount up with wings as eagles; they shall run, and not be weary; and they shall walk, and not grow faint" (Isa. 40:3 KJV).

I lashed four small, leafless branches into a rectangular frame. Using raffia, I stretched the bark and bound it onto the frame. I also made an extra-special gift. One of Alaska's national treasures is a moose nugget, scientifically known as moose scat or poop. The pecan-sized droppings dry out into odorless pellets that look and feel as though they are hardened sawdust. Souvenir shops sell millions of moose-nugget specialties. Some are painted gold. They sell nugget earrings, necklaces, swizzle-sticks, key-chain fobs, and much more. Tourists love them.

I replicated an idea that used pecans to make a basket. I glued dry nuggets together in the bottom of a Styrofoam bowl. Additional nuggets were glued around the inside in alternating rows like bricks on the inside of a cistern. When the glue dried, I peeled off the Styrofoam to reveal a nugget bowl. Ash and spruce cones were glued on as finishing touches.

Chapter 15

Denali

June 13. During morning devotionals we had a tearful farewell. Chris and I were presented with certificates of appreciation and a magnet with a loon painted on it. Anna and Mickey were intrigued with the eagle wall-hanging and the birch-bark birdhouse. They got a great laugh out of the moose-nugget basket.

Time to say "goodbye." As much as we wanted to stay, we had a purpose to visit Fairbanks. On our way north following Alaska 3, the Parks Highway, we would visit Denali National Park.

The day was warm in the mid 70's. The sun was brilliant. The atmosphere was crystal clear. A perfect day to see Mt. McKinley. Off to our left ran the Alaska Range under a mantle of snow and ice glittering in the sunlight. I pulled over to photograph North America's highest peak, the south peak of Mt. McKinley at 20,320 feet. A showpoint of Alaska, Mt. McKinley also goes by the native name of "Denali."

A right turn led us to the quaint, bohemian, funky town of Talkeetna. A dilapidated, wooden wheelbarrow filled with potted spring flowers rested at the base of a rickety board sign that was handpainted "Welcome to Beautiful Downtown Talkeetna." Small, ancient, clapboards and log cabins lined the few, short blocks of the one main street. We parked at the dead-end near a small RV park and riding stables. A stroll back up the street led into a couple of gift shops, a few restaurants, and the offices of flight tours, walking tours, guided hikes, boat tours, and fishing outfitters. Talkeetna is the base for Denali climbers—tourists looking for the unusual, artists, and independent minded Sourdoughs.

On the Inside Passage Ferry we had met a middle-aged woman who wintered in Seattle and worked on the railroad that ran from

Anchorage through Talkeetna to Denali and Fairbanks. She recommended a visit to this hippie-artist-tourist Mecca. We weren't disappointed. The tiny village overflowed with friendly folks. From the server who took our lunch order at the Roadhouse, the couple who shared their outdoor picnic table, to the laid-back salesclerks in tiny crafts shops, people were warm and genuine. Tourists were welcomed as being no different, no more eccentric than Natives.

I wished I had planned to spend at least one night here. However my plan was to reach Denali National Park this afternoon so, hopefully, we could get a campsite. We might find vacant sites at the Teklanika Campground, 29 miles into the park from the visitors center.

The park road branched to the west from the Parks Highway. A large parking lot was concealed behind spruce and native plants. A rustic pole sign welcomed us to Denali National Park and Preserve. A short walk led to a beautifully designed, large, contemporary log chalet—the park headquarters and visitors center. Several young people clad in hiking boots, shorts, and windbreakers and shouldering tremendous backpacks walked toward us. Each carried a long, metal cylinder. On closer inspection, these were bear-proof, food-storage canisters. Some hikers wore whistles around their necks. To warn bears of their presence others had strings of bells around their ankles.

While Chris looked around the gift shop, I hurried to the reservations desk. We were able to reserve one of the few vacant RV sites at Teklanika; two nights for $40. The campground is the farthest distance that a private vehicle can travel into the park, but only if you are registered at the campground. I registered for an early-morning bus tour. The bus would pick us up at the campground and take us to the Eielson Visitors Center, 66 miles from the entrance.

No private vehicles were allowed past the campground. As we drove east on the only park road, misty rain began to fall. No traffic met us on the narrow, two-lane road that led deep into a valley north of the Alaska Range. Isolated, tired, and hungry I was disappointed by the lack of wildlife and a dreary overcast that blurred the landscape.

An eastbound tour bus crept past. As we approached the Sanctuary River bridge, a sign warned that only registered campers could travel beyond this point. At the head of the bridge a few cars were parked. This was evidence of tourists exploring on foot before they returned to the visitors center.

The road led past a tiny, isolated ranger station that appeared deserted. A bored-looking young woman in a ranger's uniform stepped outside to check our camping pass. I asked her what being out so far by herself was like. She replied that she didn't mind the isolation. She read a lot.

The road deteriorated to rough gravel with periodic frost heaves. Another tour bus approached. I pulled over to a wide spot on the limited shoulder and held my breath as it crept past. The road angled south in a wide valley over constantly changing terrain: mountain ridges; fast-flowing, chalky-white streams of murky glacial silt; meadows of low-growing alpine shrubs, but no animals.

A rustic, wooden sign directed us into the campground. I found no ranger station or host, so I drove through looking for an empty site. As we wound our way through low spruce and arctic bushes that separated the campsites, the sky cleared. A magnificent rainbow appeared over the mountain range. I stopped. Tears filled my eyes.

"A sign," I thought. "A promise that we someday will return to Alaska."

I backed into a site bordered by young spruce. We slathered ourselves with mosquito repellent and walked the dogs. A Dutch-oven dinner over a smoky charcoal fire helped to ward off the attackers. As the sun slowly descended the mosquitoes, immune to repellent, ascended to drive us inside. Thus far Denali was a disappointment.

We got up extra early to pack our backpacks with lunch, snacks, drinks, repellent, cameras, and film. Ponchos topped our warm clothes. Buzzing mosquitoes covered the screen door and were intent on attacking their victims. Through the screen Chris sprayed them with repellent so we could slip outside. Their relatives buzzed and swarmed around our faces and followed us in a cloud.

We hiked down the gravel track away from the vegetation toward the park road and left most of our tormentors behind. Other adventurers joined us to wait at the bus shelter. The shuttle had left the main visitors center at 6 a.m. and soon would arrive to pick us up.

A green Bluebird bus ground to a halt. We kept cameras handy and stashed backpacks in anticipation of seeing animals early in the day. The driver apologized that it didn't look like a "mountain day." The fine mist and haze, as well as high clouds, probably would hide Mount McKinley. This was an informal tour. The driver welcomed questions. He would be in radio contact with other tour-bus drivers so they could alert each other with animal sightings.

The driver told us to keep our eyes open, to scan the mountain ridges and valleys for antlers, the cliffs for specks of white and for anything that moved. "If you think you see an animal, holler out and give the clock direction. We're headed high noon."

We all intently peered out the windows. A rider sighted movements in the brush at 2 o'clock, to our right. The driver crept to a stop as three caribou raised their tree-branch, paddle-and-spiked antlers above the bushes. He said that they were a part of a herd of 1,500 to 2,000 caribou that roamed the park. Camera's clicked. Videos whirred. Excited naturalist "wannabes" shared viewpoints with strangers.

At Sable Pass, 13,900 feet, tundra had replaced trees. Tundra is a mixture of low- to medium-plants above the tree line. Cool temperatures and strong winds eliminate tree growth. The low vegetation is thick and spongy. It is an ideal hiding place for small mammals and their predators, as well as large and small plant eaters.

Sable Pass followed a roiling, boiling, shallow river. The braided ribbon channels crisscrossed the valley floor. Fast-moving water in just a few days could cut new channels. Glacial flour and silt gave the flow a chalky-gray tone. The driver stopped and blocked the road. He announced, "Look closely at 11 o'clock. I think there's a bear in that thicket."

The entire busload silently scrambled to the front of the bus. The Bluebird crept along until we were alongside a gray-brown mound several yards from the road.

The mound moved. We didn't move. We held our breath.

"Grizzly", whispered the driver as the bear lumbered onto its feet. "Blacks have a dished face," he continued to whisper. "Grizzlys are sorta Roman-nosed." He paused. We could hear the bear scratching at the tundra.

"Black bears can be cinnamon brown to blond. Brown bears can be blond to almost black. The difference is blacks are 50-percent smaller than brownies. Blacks around 200 pounds vs. 1,000 pounds for a grown grizzly. Grizzlies are brown bears that live inland and eat more vegetation than meat. Grizzlies and coastal browns like fish," he concluded.

The bear shuffled off out of sight into a ravine. With photos taken, we let out our held breaths.

Dall sheep appeared as tiny, white specks high on the shear mountainside. Through the telephoto lens of the video camera we could see kids scampering along the rocky ledges.

At Polychrome Pass the bus pulled over for a rest break at a line of porta potties. Many of us climbed to an overlook to get a closer look at the brightly colored volcanic rock. Although the sky was hazy, we had a spectacular view of the vast tundra to the south. The distant Alaskan range rose skyward. The mountain peaks were frosted with perpetual snows. Lower slopes and shadowed crevasses held thawing snow.

With powerful binoculars some of our group located a small pack of gray wolves that hunted on the flats. I was surprised to learn that even though the wolves lived in packs, only the Alpha male and Alpha female bred. The other pack members helped feed the litter of the fittest pair.

"Wildlife photographer at 12 o'clock."

I was sitting near the front of the bus and caught his joke. Ahead of us a van was parked in the road. On a platform on top of the van, a man in a camouflage jacket focused a huge camera mounted on a tripod. An assistant, hands crammed into warm pockets, walked around the van and intently watched the tundra. She handed lens and film up to the photographer and quickly returned her hands to her pockets.

Our group waited patiently until the camera, tripod, and photographers safely were back inside their van. I wondered about their credentials. He must be famous to get a permit to drive this far and to take photographs.

Other tour buses were at the Eielson Visitor Center. One group would travel an additional two hours to go 20 miles to Wonder Lake the end of the road for tourists. Near the gift shop Chris and I joined a group of kids enthralled by a ranger's stories. They saw mounts, plaster casts of prints, and scat (animal poop). The kids were spellbound by the small jars of animal waste that she passed around for their inspection, identification, and comments.

Noon and time for a picnic lunch. Ground squirrels insisted that we share. They were brave. They climbed on the tables and begged for handouts. Lunchbags on the ground were fair game. The squirrels were sneaky. The ravens were quick and adept thieves.

Suddenly someone rushed to the picnic area calling, "It's out! It's out! McKinley!" We experienced mad rush to the observation deck. We only had been able to see the base of McKinley and the Alaska Range, but clouds and haze had obscured the famous peak. Now it was visible only 33 miles away. It looked so close and loomed much higher than I expected. All too soon clouds returned to obscure its majesty and mystery.

All too soon the Bluebird was returning east. The urge to nap was kept at bay by random appearances of Dall sheep, caribou, moose, two more bears, and many birds I could not name.

At the rest stop two bicycle riders carrying bulging backpacks waited for a bus to give them a lift back to civilization. The young man dressed in a heavy jacket, gloves, and helmet rearranged gear in his bike panniers. A young woman pushed her mountain bike a distance from him and let it drop to the ground. Her glazed eyes stared vacantly. I was about to pass her on my way to the outhouse.

"You look tired. Are you OK?" I asked.

"No," she replied and she looked past me towards the mountains. I hesitated. Should I walk on? Offer to help in some way?

She glanced at me, "A bear. On the trail." As she recalled her terrifying experience, the girl was shaken visibly. I stopped.

"We were riding down a trail, a couple of miles from the road where the bus let us off. A bear raised up on its back legs and roared. It lunged at us."

"What did you do?" Neither rider had signs of injuries.

They slowly had walked backward down the rough trail and kept their bikes between themselves and the bear. The bear had followed. The rocky, twisting trails, tough enough to negotiate traveling forward, must have been a nightmare to negotiate going backward. The bear trailed them almost to the park road, then it lumbered off into the tundra.

"It took us a couple of hours to get to the road. When the bear disappeared, we rode here to catch a shuttle." She paused, "I'm going home."

In the park, bears have the right-of-way. They demand it. Park visitors repeatedly are warned to make noise, never leave food or food wrappers, to use bear-proof food containers, and never to approach a bear. Be aware; learn how to avoid encounters and protect yourself. Black bears will climb a tree after you. Grizzlies will shake you out of the tree. Mother bears are particularly protective of cubs and very dangerous, as are mother moose that have calves.

I wanted to give the young woman a hug, but she turned away.

On the return trip my concentration, looking for animals, was less intense. I lost count of the number of bear and moose we saw. Too many caribou, sheep, and eagles were seen to count. We saw a rare, Arctic fox pouncing on voles on a mountain slope. Denali was everything I expected and more.

That evening we battled mosquitoes while we hiked with the dogs to the Teklanika River. It was bordered by clumps of scrub and willows budding with fuzzy catkins. The intermittent, shallow river must have been a wide torrent during the spring thaw. Evidence of water-borne rock and shallow streams crisscrossed the river valley. Now the river meandered like strands of wet hair through the center of the flood plain.

Chris joined a couple of young boys who were trying to skip rocks. I searched for unusual rocks and tumbled stones. I found many that were composed of bands of different colored sediments. Pulverized rock called rock flour colored the fast-moving, milky white stream.

Early Saturday morning we returned to the Visitor Center and then took a shuttle to the park's sled-dog kennels. Dogs were everywhere. A line of large, chain-link kennels housed mama dogs and large litters of adorable puppies. Older pups and grown dogs were chained to a series of widely separated doghouses. Walking the alleys between the rows of doghouses was like strolling through a small neighborhood in which the residents barked a welcome. Some dogs perched on the tops of their houses. Some sat and whined a welcome. Others barked and pranced at the end of their chains.

Most of these dogs didn't look like the Siberian Husky or malamute types I had associated with sled dogs. Now I was beginning to look past appearance and could see their spirit and energy. The park rangers used the dog teams to patrol the park in winter, because dogs have less environmental impact than snow machines.

Trainers invited us to visit a shed to see sleds, harness, and dog boots. We then were asked to move to a set of bleachers alongside a dirt track where a wheeled sled waited. During the summer the rangers hold four dogsled demonstrations a day.

A young ranger introduced himself. His accent gave him away even before he told us he was from Australia. As a student tourist he had visited Denali. He was so impressed that he returned there to work.

As trainers brought hyperactive dogs to the sled, they held each dog's collar with its forepaws batting the air and its back paws prancing and jumping in anticipation of a run. The dog could pull the trainer down and drag him if two of his four legs were not off the ground. Harnessed to the towline, they settled down waiting for the rest of the eight-dog team.

This musher did not ask for volunteers to ride on the sled. At the musher's signal, the dogs sprang forward at such a breakneck pace that the sled tipped over. Running along beside the sled, the musher made a grab for the handle and flipped it upright as the team raced out of sight behind some trees. Soon the team reappeared and tore down the track. Trainers helped stop the team in front of the bleachers. They were ready to go again but were returned to their doghouses.

Leaving Denali and continuing north to Fairbanks, I contemplated the dogs. The American Kennel Club recognizes more than 300 species, from the tiny Chihuahua to the monstrous St. Bernard. Sled dogs are not recognized as a breed. They are bred for specific characteristics of stamina, heart or desire to pull, and a rangy body type with a double coat.

Are the great differences in dog characteristics evidence of evolution? I don't think so. All domestic dogs originated from a single species, probably similar to a wolf, that sought the warmth of human's fires and an easy meal of garbage. Humans learned that they could breed dogs for specific purposes. Mating two dogs that could herd, or hunt, or fight produced pups with the same characteristics. Eventually the dog became the most variable animal in terms of color, size, and shape.

Centuries of breeding for selected traits and interbreeding for certain characteristics have actually caused deformities. As dominant genes have produced distinctive breeds, those breeds have become weaker in other traits. "Pure breeds" are much weaker than mutts. Could a Chihuahua live with Eskimos? How would a Saint Bernard survive in Mexico? Most pampered pets could not survive without the care of their owners.

My Shelties are descendants of small herding dogs bred on the Shetland Islands off the coast of Scotland. Here the cold, damp, harsh winds and rugged terrain called for a miniaturized Collie-type dog that could survive the harsh conditions. The dogs are intelligent, co-operative, and are easily trained. The Shetland Islands also are home to the miniaturized Shetland pony, sheep, and cattle.

All dogs, regardless of breed, are still of the dog "kind." If a mixture of purebred dogs were allowed to interbreed, after a few generations their descendants would look like a typical nondescript mutt. Add a few wolves and coyotes to the mix, and their descendants would resemble the pair of dogs on Noah's ark.

Dogs and wolves interbreed so readily, if permitted to, that dog/wolf mix breeds are not allowed to race in Alaska. The wildness of wolves easily can dominate the domesticated dogs' gentleness.

Chapter 16

Fairbanks

Arriving in Fairbanks I parked and called the pastor of Gold Rush Church, to let him know we had arrived. He was a bi-vocational pastor and had an auto-repair shop to support his family. The pastor was working on a car engine and said he soon would meet us.

A maroon van speckled with gray rust inhibitor pulled in alongside us. A bear of a man unwedged himself from the driver's seat. He was more than six-feet tall and at least 250 pounds. A full beard covered most of his grease-stained T-shirt. His shoulders and chest were broad and his arms muscular, as if he singlehandedly tore out auto engines. The burly pastor wiped his hands on his faded jeans. I accepted his handshake. He was the picture of a typical Sourdough, from his shaggy ponytail to his worn, dirt-crusted hiking boots.

"Can't get your rig to my house." He drawled with a pause long enough for me to wonder what we were doing here. "Follow me to the church."

Relieved by the mention of a church, I quieted the yapping dogs and backed out to follow the faded van.

"Where are we going?" asked Chris.

"I don't have any idea," I laughed. "Another adventure."

I followed for several miles north past the University of Alaska campus and away from civilization. To the left a steep, gravel road led uphill into the trees. Perched on the crest of the hill a long, low, turquoise-blue building faced the road. A porch with redwood railing ran the length of the building front. Only later did I locate a sign on the edge of the highway that announced "Gold Rush Church."

"Over there," the pastor, a man of few words, directed me to park. Past the end of the building the graded gravel extended to a forest of cottonwoods, alder, and a few black spruce. We climbed out and stretched. Where would I hook up? Would we be boondocking?

Three middle-aged women in jeans and T-shirts walked down the porch steps to greet us. The shortest, heaviest woman was introduced as the pastor's wife, Charlotte. The others were members of a quilting circle that met weekly. She explained that a volunteer group from North Carolina had planned to lead the Vacation Bible School but couldn't be there.

Introductions around, without much conversation, we were invited to go inside. The church building was constructed from three, side-by-side military trailers. From the center of the porch a door opened into a very small sanctuary.

The podium, back wall, and part of the ceiling were draped with paper vines and artificial flowers. Strange, I thought, until I remembered that the Vacation Bible School theme was the Amazon jungle. I was given a short tour of the kitchen and bathrooms. One had a shower and was offered for our use. The rest of the building housed a couple of classrooms and the pastor's office. Here we met their youngest son, Josh, who was playing games on a computer.

I left Chris and the boy to warily eye each other and went out to hook up the electricity to an extension cord. I walked the dogs while I waited for the pastor and his wife to complete their Saturday tasks. The cloudless sky reflected the turquoise of the church. I was unusually warm. I checked the thermometer. Low 90s. We were further north, but the temperature was higher here in the interior in the summer where the sun never sets. Well, almost never. I had heard that on June 21, the summer solstice, the sun would not set at all.

This is different, I thought. Not quite primitive but definitely quaint. I was set back by the lack of conversation and tried to convince myself that I could be a listener and not the talker that I usually am. Questions were trying to pop out of my mouth. Be patient. Wait and see.

"Have dinner with us," the pastor commanded.

"OK, we'd love to." I wondered if I should contribute anything. They often hosted volunteers, so this probably was customary. After the women left, I tried to help Charlotte straighten up for Sunday school. She didn't talk. I stifled my questions. I didn't want to appear nosy.

Chris, Josh, and I crowded into the back of the van already loaded with boxes of groceries, tools, and Bible School crafts. The road seemed to circle north of Fairbanks. We turned up a narrow paved road, then a gravel road, then climbed and bumped up a single-lane track. Other tracks branched off into the forest and went up hills leading to small, partially hidden, weathered cabins. Most of these plywood constructions sprouted additions without the aid of an architect. I thought I could be in the hills of Appalachia.

The van turned on to twin ruts and began to climb a steep hill. We passed through a chasm of car bodies. Derelict vehicles in various stages of junkyard decay bordered both sides of the track. Weeds and large bushes threatened to help the autos decompose. A roofless Volkswagen bus was host to a tree that had sprouted from its floorboards. The rusted and bashed-in vehicles in stages of disassembly crammed the sides of the drive with later models parked adjacent to the base of a cabin.

At the crest of the long hill, tireless wrecks shouldered a plywood-faced cabin. To the right of a raised deck a one-story room was painted white up to where a shed roof once had sloped off to the right. Above that an unpainted addition under a left-slanted roof indicated that the new direction was the result of adding on. Attached to the back was a two-story, unpainted, plywood addition with a strongly slanting shed roof to the right. Directly opposite the porch steps and leaning against the rest of the cabin, another one-story addition, painted church blue, had a roof that slanted the opposite way.

A low railing enclosed the deck on the two remaining sides. Narrow boards on stones served as steps. Off to the side of the porch a chicken-wire fence tried to corral chickens, a few ducks, and a couple of turkeys. They shared the dry, scratched-bare dirt with a large, whiskered, white goat.

Four nondescript dogs were chained to sheds scattered about a clearing near the chicken pen.

An older boy burst out of the cabin. He bolted down the steps to help his mom and the rest of us carry bags and boxes from the van. Jimmy was his name, but he didn't wait to be introduced. He vaulted to the top of the porch railing, where he walked as if on a tight rope.

I stepped on the deck and surveyed the parsonage. Flowers planted in buckets brightened the porch. Jimmy jumped off the railing, raced to the open door, and charged inside. Chris followed Josh to meet the dogs. I waited for an invitation to enter or for a "make yourself at home." Walking around on the porch, I wondered what I was waiting for.

Jimmy burst out of the door, jumped on the railing, then jumped back down. He took a running start and vaulted over the railing. This caused chickens, ducks, and turkeys to scatter as they squawked. He untied the goat, retied it further from the porch, threw a couple of handfuls of grain in the air to scatter for the fowl, and leaped back over the railing. I chuckled at his antics.

"Boy!" boomed the preacher from the doorway.

"Fed 'em!" replied Jimmy as he threw back the barbecue-grill lid. "Doin' it." He swiped at the rack with a brush, then lit the propane. I confided to myself that the flame would sanitize the rack. Soon his dad emerged outside with a platter of pork chops to put on the grill.

"Go inside," he invited.

To the right of the door, a cramped kitchen was tented with plastic sheeting tacked to the ceiling. Mounds of dishes, pots and pans, and assorted appliances, utensils, and kitchen paraphernalia hid the counter tops. Boxes of canned goods and staples crowded the floor.

To my left, past a large, wooden table, Charlotte stood in the center of a small living area. She motioned for me to join her. I slid past the table and a buffet cluttered with paperback books, newspapers, kitchen utensils, and unrecognizable stuff. Above the cabinet, shelves held memorabilia from the kids' childhood: dolls, toy planes and cars, and trophies and ribbons from school projects and sports events.

She moved some newspapers and magazines from an over-stuffed sofa for me while she took a seat on a recliner. With few words, she admonished Jimmy to put away the groceries. She apologized for sitting and explained that she was asthmatic. She was recovering from bronchitis and often was very tired. This explained her hoarseness and bouts of coughing.

My offer to help was politely refused. We sat looking at each other. I wanted to start a conversation. Obviously she just wanted to sit and rest. I picked up an outdated women's magazine and thumbed through it.

The wall across from me was wallpapered with photographs of their children. From baby pictures and snapshots to progressive school photos, the growth and development of each child had been documented. Family group photos were scattered among the others. I saw several photos of the pastor and a single-engine airplane. He, like many other Alaskans, was a pilot. The collage made quite a statement as it covered the entire wall and the door that led into the blue addition. A bedroom?

Charlotte explained the plastic ceiling in the kitchen. Earlier in the spring a fire had burned the ceiling, some of the interior walls, and cabinets. Pink insulation peeked out from seams in the plastic. I tried not to be too obvious as I surveyed the two adjoining rooms.

I commented that I liked her photo wall. She pointed out the two boys that I had met and their two older kids. John, the eldest and an Eagle Scout, was on staff at a Boy Scout camp. Daughter Christi worked at a different camp and would be home the next afternoon for a break.

Chris followed Josh inside to flop in front of a small TV. Charlotte excused herself to go into the miniscule kitchen to make a salad and mashed potatoes for dinner. She ordered Josh to set the table. He jumped up to set it with mismatched plates and silverware. Josh dragged folding chairs out of a back room to place around the table. I wished that Chris would do his chores as quickly, without backtalk or comments, as these boys did.

Pork chops ready, we were given our choice of canned sodas. Our plates were piled with meat, potatoes, salad, and bread. It was an excellent meal to have been prepared under much less than ideal conditions.

After dinner I tried to help by scraping the plates. Jimmy vaulted over the porch railing to feed scraps to the animals. Josh put two large dishpans on the table. Into one went the dishes, utensils, and dish soap. Pastor poured water from a five-gallon jug into pots to be heated on the stove. He poured the hot water into the two pans. Josh's job was to wash the dishes. I asked for a towel and offered to dry. I assumed that their lack of water somehow was related to the fire—not much different than camping.

The family was so nonverbal, I felt like an intruder. I tried to ask about Fairbanks and about things to see and do. I carefully formed my questions in generality so I wouldn't seem nosy or condescending, but I was so curious as to their lifestyle that I was afraid I would offend. Was this family typical of the pioneer, free-spirited Alaskans?

I asked to use the restroom and was led down a jumbled hall off the back of the kitchen. A door opened into what appeared to be a large, walk-in closet or storeroom. Clothes hung on hangers and on hooks along two walls. Piled boxes of stuff cluttered the remaining space. At the back, a small porta-potty sat between boxes. OK. I can deal with this. I'll pretend I'm boondocking. I saw no sink or shower. I was thankful that I kept a small bottle of hand sanitizer in my belt bag. I made a mental note not to request use of the facilities again, unless I had a true emergency.

The sun was still high at 10 p.m. when the pastor drove us back to the church. He gave me a key to the building so we could use the shower, bathroom, and kitchen. His family took turns using the shower before they returned home.

Sunday. I didn't know when the sun set or rose. By 6 a.m. when the dogs were yapping to go out, the sky was bright. We went for a walk. Sunday school would not be until 10 a.m. I opened the building, straightened a few chairs, and waited. I had nothing to do. No Sunday newspaper to read. Just sit and wait.

Three couples, a single woman in her 40s, and four school-agers joined the pastor's family, Chris, and me for Sunday school and church services. We were warmly welcomed. The congregation was disappointed to learn that the expected volunteers would not arrive this year. Volunteers normally arrived early enough to canvas the area and invite children to Vacation Bible School. I wondered why the members had not done this preparation themselves. Perhaps they had gotten information too late.

After the service one of the men loaded a couple of bags of trash into his truck to take to the trash dump. His wife bragged to Charlotte that she had gotten a nice chair there. Seeing the puzzled look on my face, she explained that the city of Fairbanks had a public recycling center where people could drop off discards and help themselves to what ever was there. The need for landfills is reduced; less risk of trash fires exists. Always a bargain hunter, I added this information to my list of tourist sites.

Again we were invited for a meal at the pastor's home. I didn't want to be a burden and tried to decline. Charlotte insisted that we eat moose roast with them and then ride with the family to pick up their daughter, Christi, at the camp at which she worked. Another opportunity to explore more of Alaska. I agreed.

The moose roast was tender but a bit gamey. The ride south was long and boring. Only a few small places of interest broke the endless, flat tundra and patches of low forest. A huge Santa welcomed travelers to the town of North Pole. Strange, wooden creatures along the roadway announced the Knobby Shoppe. We didn't stop. The return trip was tiring. We were crowded. Christi was no more talkative than was the rest of her family. She listened to a CD player.

The kids were dropped of at the cabin. We returned to the church. Charlotte mentioned that the volunteers had planned to paint the walls in the two bathrooms. She asked if I'd like to do it. I readily agreed. Vacation Bible School was scheduled to start at 6 p.m. Charlotte would ask the pastor about paint. I could do something meaningful during the day to repay them for the meals. We'd still have time to sightsee.

Monday morning I disconnected the electricity and got out a map of Fairbanks. Off we went to see the town. By circling north on College Road I found Illinois Street that led into downtown. A large, empty parking lot just north of the Chena River had space for us. Facing the parking lot was a gleaming white clapboard church with a belltower and steeple. Flowers and flowering trees had been planted as soon as winter was over and were lovely against the bright blue sky.

We walked south on an auto bridge festooned with brightly colored flags and hanging baskets of blue Forget-Me-Nots, Alaska's state flower. A log visitors center surrounded by a garden adjoined the base of the bridge. The large, peeled-log structure was crowned with a green, shaggy, sod roof. Log planters supported a profusion of blossoms. After a long dull, frigid winter Alaskans enjoy the brief summer with a rainbow of colorful flowers.

Inside, a massive stone fireplace complimented the varnished logs. A friendly volunteer encouraged us to pick up brochures and to look around.

On a nearby plaza we saw a monument to E.T. Barnett, a steamship captain who set up a temporary trading post here on the Chena River in 1901. The following year prospectors found gold in the hills. Soon miners stampeded the area. Today Fairbanks still is a frontier town in spirit.

A rectangular, white obelisk marked Milepost 1,523 of the Alaska Highway. Since World War II, this has been considered the end of the road, even though now a highway to the North Slope exists. To local residents this is where the road ends and the wilderness begins. The monument lists mileage to major cities. Houston is 4,682 long, lonely, fantastically scenic miles away.

Situated in the Golden Heart Park is a bronze sculpture, The Unknown First Family, that commemorates the first pioneers to the area. The monument depicts a larger-than-life family clad in fur-trimmed parkas, trousers, and *mukluks*. Their all-important dogs are included. Mounted on a high, rough, stone base, the sculpture footing is washed by the spray of a fountain. Water cascades down the stones into a surrounding moat which was reminiscent of waterfalls.

We walked south through town and back up another street. Downtown was like a deserted frontier town. Not many specialty shops were open. The bank and courthouse had few customers, nor did the early opening bars.

Retrieving the RV, I drove through town with little traffic to turn west on Airport Way. We passed Pioneer Park, where I had been told I could find a free dump station. I circled around to take advantage of it.

A halo of cottony fluff drifted in the breeze from a small grove of black cottonwood trees. I walked over to investigate the catkins releasing seeds to the whims of the wind. Drifts of down enveloped the branches and coated the grass like snow. Broad, triangular leaves that were glossy, dark green on top and silvery gray underneath flashed gray-green in the breeze.

Continuing west we located Alaskaland. The parking lot, pitted from winter's ice, was sparsely occupied. June is not yet tourist season, but the gates were open. A classic paddle wheeler, the Nenana, is permanently on display. Its colorful history of transporting goldminers to the interior is memorialized with displays. A reconstructed Gold Rush Town with log cabins and clapboard cottages facing boardwalks lined a curving, hardpacked dirt lane. Many of the buildings housed crafts shops. Fortunately for my wallet most of the shops were not open.

One open shop drew me like a magnet. A young woman, seated at a spinning wheel, spun natural wool. From light fluffy roving, she created a fine, soft yarn. The woman was in college and just learning to spin. She and I shared experiences. While in college I had a sheep, sheared her, and spun her wool. The sheep's name was Sheba because she "baa-ed" a lot. I had learned how tedious carding and cleaning the wool is. I could spin on a drop spindle, a flax wheel, and the large walking wheel that was used in the South for spinning cotton.

Another student wove a houndstooth pattern on a four-harness, counter-balanced, floor loom. The memories this brought back! When I worked on a master's degree in art education, I had designed and built a loom very similar to this one.

The students and I discussed the interest in pioneer crafts that surfaced in the '70s around the time of the United States

Bicentennial. During the '90s many historical locations added craftspersons to demonstrate pioneer crafts of the era. The young women enlightened me by saying that Alaskan's interest in crafts had never dwindled in favor of "modern" ways.

I reluctantly said goodbye to follow Chris past the Harding railroad car and a tower of moose and caribou antlers to the Alaska Native Village. Here contemporary craftspersons worked on their specialties which were for sale. No one was working today. I was disappointed but enjoyed the small museum.

From here we wandered to the Mining Valley, past dredge buckets, sluice boxes, and other mining equipment. Mining Town had an assortment of boom-town structures. These originals had been rescued and relocated here.

Chris peeked into a building and discovered airplanes. Two men in their 20s were building a balsa-wood plane from a kit. Other models hung from the ceiling. Chris convinced me to buy one for him to build. The men showed us the large collection of antique airplanes: bi-planes, planes with pontoons, planes with skis, planes used by explorers, scientists, and the military. Bush pilots, a special breed of flier, land on ice, water, riverside gravel bars, or rough airstrips near isolated villages. They transported cargo and passengers. Many heroic rescue attempts would not have been successful without daring pilots.

Leaving Alaskaland we passed up the Alaska Salmon Bake and the campus of University of Alaska and found our way back to the church. At 5 p.m., the pastor and his family arrived upset because materials had not yet been delivered from another church. Nervously Charlotte showed me some information she had downloaded from the Internet. We looked over the crafts projects and materials. While in the children's classroom, Charlotte hinted that I might be willing to help her put up wallpaper borders as well as to paint.

At 5:45 p.m. another pastor arrived to drop off materials. His church the previous night finished its VBS. Six additional kids and their parents joined us for the opening led by the pastor. He continued with a Bible story and a missions video. After a snack prepared by the moms and free time outside, time arrived for crafts. I did what I could to help supervise outdoors and with the crafts projects, but with so few kids I didn't believe that I was earning our keep.

I declined Charlotte's dinner invitation. I offered to do the painting she had mentioned, as soon as the pastor purchased the paint. I would try to put up the wallpaper border, too, when she found what she wanted. The sun still shone brightly when I went to bed about 11 p.m. Chris stayed awake playing video games on our small TV.

Tuesday. By 5 a.m. the dogs were ready to go out. The sun already was bright. Did the sun ever set? We had seen people out and about at all hours. Alaskans didn't seem to sleep. They must make up for summer's lack of sleep by sleeping during the long winter when for about 60 days the sun does not rise above the horizon. With temperature reaching minus-40 degrees in winter, hibernating seemed like a good idea.

By mid-morning we were restless to explore more of Fairbanks. The main campus of the University of Alaska was founded in 1917. Satellite campuses are in Anchorage and Juneau. The University Museum is advertised as a "must-stop" for visitors. The contemporary, multi-storied buildings are a nice contrast to a signpost totem and several painted, carved totems in a flowering, forested setting.

Large museum displays divided Alaska into regions, with each display area including cultural artifacts and mining and scientific equipment. The state's largest exhibit of gold nuggets, flakes of gold, and objects made from gold is situated here.

A mummified steppe bison carcass in 1979 had been found preserved in permafrost near Fairbanks. While placer-mining, the prospector found legs with hooves and hide protruding from the frozen silt and muck. This carcass was not a fossil but a frozen mummy—a bison with blue crystals on its exposed hide. Named Blue Babe, the frozen carcass was rushed to the campus and refrozen to prevent its red flesh from decay. Blue Babe is exhibited with flesh and skin intact.

Wooly mammoths joined other wildlife exhibits. A mounted grizzly standing on its hind legs towered over us. Dinosaur bones dug from along Alaska's North Slope seemed out of place unless we remembered that before Noah's Flood the Arctic had been tropical. Fossilized ferns and other tropical plants have been unearthed with the dinosaurs.

Studying the Native cultural displays reinforced my understanding of the complexity of designs and use of materials of the diverse cultures. The contrast with Southwest Native Americans is apparent. However, a strange, strong resemblance exists between the basketry, beading, and quill work of Native Alaskans and Natives of the Lower Forty-Eight.

During the ride back to the church Chris began counting joggers and bicycle riders on the paved hike-and-bike trail that followed the road. He let out a yell and pointed. Cruising along the trail was a young man clad in a tank top, shorts, helmet, and skis! He used ski poles to push himself along as if he was on snow. I pulled over for a closer look. Small wheels had been mounted on the underside of the skis. Summer wheels are on dogsleds, so why not wheels on summer skis?

A gallon of white paint and brushes waited on the church porch. I fixed a quick lunch before I changed into grubbies to tackle the painting job. Both restrooms were small enough to use a chair to stand on and old newspapers to protect the fixtures and floor. By 4 p.m., I had given one restroom a first coat of fresh paint. It would be dry in time for VBS.

Charlotte seemed pleased with my progress. She became more talkative. Her enthusiasm for sprucing up the building was loosening her tongue for girltalk.

Wednesday morning misty rain and cooler temperatures kept us inside. I gave the restroom a second coat of paint and the second restroom a first coat. I needed a few groceries, so I decided to visit the local farmers' market that was held only on Wednesdays.

Housed in a small metal and plywood building, the market had an assortment of tables, counters, and shelves that held fresh vegetables, potted plants, cut flowers, and crafts. Handmade soaps and lotions, candles, decorative crafts, and jewelry crowded hand-knit sweaters, woven shawls, and mittens. Fudge, homemade cookies, and honey were alongside rhubarb pies and pumpkin bread. I splurged on a fat loaf of banana bread chocked full of nuts.

By early afternoon the sun dried away the clouds. I finished the second coat of paint on the second restroom. Charlotte arrived with her husband and the boys. They inspected my work and thanked me by giving me two tickets for a riverboat tour that very evening. The Fairbanks Baptist Association had arranged for area pastors and their wives to take this retreat as part of the Summer Son Celebration. Pastor couldn't justify leaving VBS. He and his wife previously had taken the Riverboat Discovery Cruise. They wanted us to go in their place. At five we would leave for the four-hour tour.

Charlotte again mentioned the wallpaper border. We measured the restroom walls and the walls of the children's room. She asked whether I would drive their van because she didn't have a license. I'm always ready to travel. We left the boys with Pastor to have a hurried ladies afternoon out. We visited a couple of paint and wallpaper stores. Charlotte found just what she had in mind with the bonus that the rolls of border were on sale.

We stopped to have a soda to celebrate our good fortune. Charlotte felt comfortable enough to share her story briefly. Her husband, originally from Montana, in the early '70s had traveled to the North Slope to work on the construction of the oil pipeline.

"I was a mail-order bride," confided Charlotte.

I grinned in disbelief. "Really?"

"Oh, yes," she replied. "Twenty years ago."

She didn't reveal how they first began corresponding—she in Seattle, he in Fairbanks. They exchanged photographs. He sent her a plane ticket. She flew north to meet her groom. They were married by a justice of the peace. At first they lived in a tiny apartment near downtown Fairbanks. The couple claimed a two-acre homestead in the hills 10 miles from town and five miles from the nearest road. For several years they backpacked the trail to clear their land and build a tiny cabin.

Today their original cabin is their kitchen. As their family grew so did the cabin. Charlotte confided that they never had drilled a water well because the rock was too dense and drilling would be too expensive.

Rainwater is collected in a cistern for washing. Drinking water is from free springs. A wood stove and propane were used for heat. They have had electricity for a long time and a phone too, except when winter storms tear the lines down. The Internet is a very popular pastime for the kids and more dependable than the mail service.

At their previous church Pastor was "promoted" from deacon to assistant pastor. He studied via the Internet. He then became an interim pastor at Gold Rush for a while. When the new pastor of Gold Rush felt led to return to the Lower Forty-Eight, he accepted the pastorate. The small congregation could not support him and his family, so he continued in his trade as auto mechanic. In his small plane he often flew to distant villages to make repairs.

That evening, following Charlotte's directions, I drove the RV southwest of town to the riverboat landing on the Chena River. A frontier, false-front-style building with a covered boardwalk faced the parking lot. The building housed offices, a boutique, an upscale gift shop, and ticket sales for the Riverboat Discovery III. Beyond it, the red-trimmed, glistening white, four-storied sternwheeler moored at a dock as it waited for us to board.

We joined a line of several hundred other passengers for the four-hour, 20-mile excursion down the Chena River to its convergence with the Tanana River. Chris and I walked the gangplank and climbed the outside stairway to the third-floor, glass-enclosed deck. We found seating by the windows.

The captain welcomed us aboard. His grandfather, Captain Charlie Binkley, had been drawn to the Yukon in 1898 with a dream of piloting paddle-wheelers in the Yukon and Alaska. He founded a family tradition. Ninety years later his descendants—grandsons and even some great-grandchildren—operate the Discovery tours. They carry passengers on the only authentic paddlewheelers remaining in Alaska.

As we cruised slowly down the river, we first stopped by a fenced clearing along the shore. As if on cue, which perhaps was the boats' signal blast, a herd of reindeer bolted from the trees to stare at passengers who stared back with cameras clicking. The herd knew that grain waited for it near the fence. Several calves cavorted and caused chuckles. As we drifted back into the main channel of the river, they drifted back into the trees.

Farther down the river we stopped by the Chena River Indian village. Three working fish wheels turned slowly in the current near the shore. Fish-drying racks near the summer shelters waited for the later salmon run. We were not able to watch them catch and dry salmon because Natives didn't occupy the summer village this early in the season.

The boat stopped at the waterfront home and kennels of Iditarod champion Susan Butcher. At the sound of the boat's signal sleeping dogs alerted the family of company. Susan, her husband, and their young daughter emerged from a large, log house. Dogs chained to kennels and dogs in pens greeted them with yips and insistent barking. Susan pulled out a cordless microphone so we could hear her over the din.

Susan and her dogs are four-time champions. She won the Iditarod in the 1980s and set speed records in each of these races. She and her husband breed and train dogs. Their young daughter already has begun to run her own dogs. Today she turned loose a litter of eight, two-month-old puppies. They cavorted and played with her. She rolled on the ground as she hugged one puppy after another.

The boat captain and Susan carried on a loud-speaker conversation while she explained the sport of dogsledding. He asked her how many dogs she had. She replied that she had counted 26 last night, but this morning she had nine new puppies. Her husband walked into a pen and, for all to see, held up a newborn pup. Its mother whined until he put the pup back with her.

We traveled down the Chena River until it converged with the broad-braided Tanana River. Sandbars and marshes obscured many of the channels. The captain explained that spring flooding shifted the sediment and made travel hazardous. He located the main channel and selected a wide, hopefully deep, channel in which to turn the boat.

On the return trip we ate a box lunch and enjoyed the scenery. I surveyed the other passengers. Some obviously were tourists, perhaps with a group tour. They were uniformly dressed in newly pressed and creased jeans and had long-sleeved, button-down shirts with the collar neatly peeking above a souvenir sweatshirt. Most of them wore maroon, navy, or hunter-green shirts advertising Denali and its wildlife. For the men wolves out numbered moose; women preferred Dall sheep with lambs or birds. They preferred white athletic shoes to boots. Everyone carried a jacket in case the temperature dropped before we returned. Tourists wore namebrand windbreakers or lightweight parkas.

Most Native-born Alaskans reveling in the "warm" weather had left jackets in the cabin. They were comfortable in faded jeans, plaid, flannel lumberjack shirts or hooded sweatshirts topped by a fleece or leather vest. Hiking boots were the footwear of choice. Ski caps or Western-style felt hats topped ponytails on men and women. Most of the men sported beards.

I thought about the Alaskans I had met. Many were ex-military who had been stationed either in Anchorage or near Fairbanks. Individuals who enjoyed an active, rugged, free-spirited lifestyle stayed on after discharge. Other Alaskans were runaway hermits—rugged individualists who left problems in the Lower Forty-Eight for a private, secluded life in the wilderness. Some, like the pastor, arrived to work on the pipeline. Men outnumbered women—more so in the wilderness and small villages.

In Anchorage I had noticed people with the Hawaiian, Tongan, and Samoan features. Many wore wildly patterned, colorful Hawaiian shirts. I learned that as many Polynesians travel to Alaska in the summer as Alaskans who travel to Hawaii for the winter. In Anchorage I had noticed more people with features of the original Alaskan Natives than I did in Fairbanks.

During the warm days many Alaskans in both cities wore shorts, tank tops, and sandals. If the evening turned cold they added sweatshirts. Ball caps, bush caps with earflaps, and Stetsons with conchos and feathers expressed individuality, as did Aussie canvas hats ornamented with fishing flies. I liked the fashion of individuality.

Thursday we slept late. After lunch the pastor dropped off Charlotte and the boys while he did errands. Charlotte and I tackled the wallpaper borders. We measured, cut, soaked the strips, and worked together to get it up in the right place. A folding chair in the bathroom on which to climb made the project go quickly. In the children's room we climbed on tables to reach the wall near the ceiling. The last strip had been hung with just enough time to clean up before VBS. What a difference the decoration made in brightening up the rooms! I was glad that I could be a part of it.

Since we had worked without stopping for dinner, I accepted Charlotte's invitation for a late meal. Their oldest son, John, had arrived home from the Boy Scout Camp. I listened attentively as he and his mother planned his upcoming Eagle Scout awards ceremony. Chris, an active Scout, had missed his troop's summer camp because of our trip. I hoped he also would achieve the rank of Eagle Scout. So few boys complete the necessary requirements that earning the rank of Eagle is a high honor.

I talked to John about the required service project that all Eagle candidates have to perform. Each Scout has to find a community need, present a solution, and arrange for donations of materials. To complete the project he must organize and lead the other Scouts in his troop.

Even in very cold, snowy weather the elementary school was required to hold surprise, winter fire drills. As they left the building, students grabbed their jackets, but many of the kids didn't have time to gather caps, scarves, and mittens. John's Eagle service project was to organize donations of caps, scarves, mittens, and large, bright, plastic pails for storage. One pail full of donated clothing went to each of the 10 classrooms of the youngest children and to the special-education class. As the class marched outside for the drill, the teacher or a designated student grabbed the bucket. Students could don the donated clothing. This past winter the project had been in use. It was greatly appreciated by the teachers, parents, and the kids who in a hurry couldn't find their own belongings.

Friday, June 21. The Summer Solstice is the longest day of the year. According to some sources, today would be 21 hours and 39 minutes of daylight. The remaining two-and-a-half-hours officially would be twilight and dawn, as the sun barely would slip below the horizon. Dusk would become dawn with no period of darkness. A festival would be held downtown. A baseball game started at midnight. I had acclimated to constant daylight now. How would not sleeping at all feel? I wondered if the pastor's family celebrated the solstice.

We spent the longest day of the year preparing for our return trip. Although church members said that the dogs didn't need health certificates to go through Canadian Customs, I stopped at a veterinarian's office. The vet's office manager said that we could be turned back at the Yukon border. I would have to drive back to Tok to get them. Rather than to take a chance I paid for the checkups and certificates.

Friends at the camp had given me a wooden bowl that was cracked from being out in the weather. They recommended that I visit the Great Alaskan Bowl Company while we were in Fairbanks. Off we went to find it.

A small mountain of logs, sawdust, and wood scraps near the factory's sign marked its location. In front of the building, hardwood logs, shaved flat on one long side, lined the entrance. A bowl-shaped depression had been somehow cut or carved into the upper side of the log. Many logs were planted with masses of showy, sunny flowers. The Alaskan favorite, the state flower, blue Forget-Me-Nots, spilled over the logs. Other log planters without flowers were tagged for sale.

Inside the warehouse/gift shop, aisles led between row after row of shelving displaying more than 100 different wood products. Small, hardwood salad bowls to huge serving bowls lined the shelves. Sized from seven inches to 22 inches, they were in many natural finishes. Some bowls were nested in sets. Other bowls were sold as salad sets or singly. Plaques, trays, and other wooden items as well as jellies, honey, and other souvenirs tempted tourists.

A long shelf was dedicated to the *ulu*. I already had purchased one of these knives for myself and several more as gifts. The *ulu* has a curved blade with a handle on top. The Eskimos developed it to cut the blubber from whales. Contemporary *ulus* are used by cooks and for decorative purposes. Some have scenes or wild animals carved into the wooden handles. Others have handles fashioned from antler or bone. Mine is rather plain but has a multi-colored, laminated, wooden chopping block with a bowl-shaped depression that exactly fits the shape of the knife.

At the back of the shop two large glass windows allowed us to watch the woodcarvers at work. An open bay in the back wall admitted a trailer-load of birch logs. With a radial arm saw a worker cut the logs into manageable lengths. A huge spike was driven into one side of the log. It was rotated on the spike so that the log hung horizontally. A curved saw blade cut a circular, concave hole. Out popped a small, shallow cone. The blade was readjusted to cut a larger groove, concentric to the hole. Out popped a perfectly formed bowl. The worker caught it. I marveled at the simple technology that carved bowl after bowl out of the same log. The remaining hollowed-out log was stacked with others to be used as a planter.

The bowls were stacked on a cart to be taken into the next room. Here they were hand sanded and then varnished. Some were engraved with what looked like a woodburner. Tired of watching, Chris wanted to explore the giant woodpile outside.

Along with broken bowls and splintered logs were some unfinished bowls that looked pretty good in spite of fine cracks. An employee drove up on a tractor and pulled a trailer of reject bowls and logs. He said we each could have a bowl and a planter from the pile. The scrap hardwood would be sold by the truckload for firewood.

On the way back to the church I saw a sign for the city's recycling and trash center—the ultimate scavenger's paradise. Large, metal trash bins lined three sides of a huge gravel parking lot. Signs indicated which set of containers was for garbage, trash, or vegetation. At the far end of the lot a covered, cement slab was a depository for furniture, books, clothing, and usable household items.

A woman dropping off several bags of workclothes commented that the center had limited pickin'. At the end of the college semesters, students who were moving dumped all sorts of good stuff that would be too much trouble to move with them. With our limited space, I passed on many goodies and limited my scavenging to a couple of books.

After VBS we again were invited to dinner. No one talked of celebrating the solstice. I didn't ask. On the way to the pastor's cabin we stopped at a public fresh-water spring so the boys could fill with cold water five- and 10-gallon containers.

On other trips to the cabin we had passed sections of the Alaskan Pipeline. Pastor stopped at a section of the pipeline that was raised high overhead. The huge pipes were bolted to a massive, metal spider web of supports and support posts. Sections of the 800-mile pipeline from Prudhoe Bay on the North Slope to Valdez are elevated on supports to allow passage of migrating animals and to keep the hot, flowing oil from melting the permafrost. The pipeline is laid out in a zigzag pattern to help it survive earthquakes. Some sections disappear underground to pass beneath Fairbanks' roads.

Pastor had worked building the pipeline. He related some of the challenges of constructing it over and under three mountain ranges, past active faults, and over many miles of boggy ground, called *muskeg*, that overlays the permafrost. After the oil started to flow, many of the workers were out of jobs, but instead of returning to the Lower Forty-Eight, they made their home in Alaska.

I learned that the oil bonanza benefited every community and turned Anchorage and Fairbanks into modern cities. Leaders of the state didn't want the economic boom to become a bust like the fur and gold booms were. They created the Alaska Permanent Fund to provide income for all Alaskans. Twenty-five percent of all mineral-lease proceeds is reserved for citizens. Annual dividends are paid to all residents who qualify. Funds are provided for the state legislature; monies are added to the principal so it continues to grow.

Many of the residents I had met talked about what they would do with their dividend, in the way we pre-spend our income-tax refund. Many people pay off bills or put money into savings. Children also receive the benefit, so large families reap a yearly windfall. Unfortunately large sums are also spent on alcohol, especially in the remote, bush villages.

The pastor and his family didn't suggest anything special to celebrate summer solstice, so I didn't mention it. That night Chris and I played board games by natural light until after midnight. I read without electricity until I fell asleep around 2 a.m.—at dusk. About 3:30 I woke to a bright dawn. If any "night" had happened, I missed it. The newspaper recorded 21 hours and 30 minutes of actual daylight before the sun slipped briefly below the horizon. The other two-and-a-half-hours were considered twilight.

Saturday morning, in spite of the bright sunlight, we slept late. In the early afternoon the pastor's family members drove up to invite us to go along with them to take John and Christi back to their respective camps. I had nothing planned, so we squeezed into the van with four kids and duffel bags of camp gear. Passing through town, we continued south on Highway 2, the Richardson Highway.

We first stopped at the North Pole. This is the real name of a tiny Alaskan town. At 101 Nicholas Drive a 15-foot, wooden Santa welcomed us to Santa Claus House. The white, multi-storied alpine-style building was decorated with murals of Santa in his sleigh with all eight reindeer, Santa with a group of children carolers, and Santa in his workshop with elves. Red ribbons tied in elaborate, painted bows adorned boughs of holly. Painted snow topped decorated Christmas trees.

Attached to the building a fenced area corralled a herd of real reindeer. The small, lively deer crowded the fence to be petted. Some of them rubbed onto the trees and peeled velvet off of their antlers. Young fawns hid behind their mothers.

Reindeer are not native to Alaska but were imported from Siberia in the 1890's. Scientists consider reindeer and caribou to be the same species, although caribou are larger and rangier than the small, more delicate reindeer. Perhaps Santa should use caribou to pull such a heavy sleigh, but Rudolph the Red-Nosed Caribou?

The kids, tired of petting the reindeer, raced each other to the entrance. Inside we rummaged through aisle after aisle of Christmas decorations, gifts, and toys. Santa sat on his throne surrounded by Mrs. Claus and assorted elves. Kids of all ages shyly sidled up to visit with him. One of his "elves" was ready with a digital camera. Photos could be purchased from a computer printer. Santa took a break to stretch. He walked over to me and offered his hand. His beard was real. Who could resist a photo with Santa?

My favorite area was a room devoted to the display of many wonderful nativity sets. Elaborate Renaissance figurines of all sizes; wooden, stone, glass, and metal figures; as well as contemporary designs were for sale. With so many beautifully crafted crèches I searched for something really special. I bought a tiny igloo with Mary, Joseph, and Baby Jesus dressed in parkas.

Driving further south I was pleased when we stopped again. Along the roadside an assortment of strange, wooden animals grazed. See More the Knotty Moose greeted us and presided over an array of crazy critters created from spruce and birch burls. Burls are large, wartlike growths or galls caused by fungi, bacteria, or insects on the trunks of trees. They cause faster wood growth. The tree trunks with the woody, roundish growths were combined and joined as the legs, body, and head of fanciful animals. My favorite was a giant mosquito that towered over my head.

A gift shop of peeled and polished logs was surrounded by a knobby, burl-log porch railing. Hanging baskets of flowers welcomed visitors. Inside the world's largest burl counter had been cut from a four-foot-wide burl. It was a beautifully grained and highly polished slab of wood. Here Alaska-sized ice cream cones with too many choices of flavors and too many calories tempted us.

Charlotte insisted in sharing a family tradition with us. Whenever the family traveled this route, it always stopped for a double dip. Who could resist? I couldn't.

Ice-cream cone and napkins in hand, I wandered through the store gazing at the realistically mounted wildlife displays and Alaskan-made gifts. My favorite, the hand-made birch baskets, were tagged with the now-familiar silver hand or tagged "Authentic Native Handicraft." I was tempted to buy one. Birdhouses made from "log" twigs sporting sod roofs with live plants were difficult to resist.

After we left the store, the family presented us with a scroll-saw clock cut in the shape of Alaska. It was their way of saying "Thank You" for helping out. I cherish it.

Chapter 17

Returning South

Sunday morning, June 23, my dogs and I were up very early. Rather than stay for church this morning, we had said our "good-byes" yesterday. I wanted to get an early start on our 4,682-mile (plus detours) trip back to Houston.

Again I blinked back tears. Our new friends had so little materially but so much quiet friendship to share. The northern end of the Richardson Highway looked familiar as we passed Santa at North Pole and Knotty Moose and friends at the Knotty Shop. The desolate highway followed the Tanana Valley alongside the braided river. Tundra alternating with forest was devoid of any evidence of human inhabitation. Remote, tightly guarded entrance gates identified Fort Wainwright and Fort Greely.

Several hours down the road we arrived in Delta Junction, where the Richardson Highway branched off from Highway 2. A Milepost marker commemorated the Northern End of the AlCan. At this point the builders of the Alaskan Highway had connected with a primitive road already existing between Delta and Fairbanks. To my disappointment the visitors center was closed. Without fanfare I would begin the final stage of my birthday dream: to drive the AlCan from one end to the other—1,500 miles from Delta Junction to Dawson Creek, British Columbia.

Hours passed as quickly as did the changing scenery. We stopped in Tok for gas and to revisit the Burnt Paw shop. The Main Street Visitors Center now was open for the tourist season. It had a small museum and gift shop. I asked about the naming of Tok. I heard a third version. Tok was named for a husky puppy—the mascot of the 97the U.S. Army Corps of Engineers. Was the pup Tok named for Tokyo?

A visit to the All Alaska Gifts and Crafts would be my last opportunity to study Native crafts, jade, ivory, and jewelry. A nice display of mounted animals would give an incoming tourist a good preview of things to come. Lady dog had chewed a hole in Chris's Eskimo yo-yo, so we bought new ones.

The route from Tok to the Yukon border and onto Beaver Creek now was unfamiliar. In six weeks all evidence of winter's snow and ice had been transformed. Summer flowers, brilliant green birch, willow, alders, cottonwoods flashing gray-green leaves, and the deep green of spruce replaced the silvery haze of late winter.

Chris asked to stop at Ida's to eat. I wanted to visit with the cook. Entering the small café, we found it deserted. I called out. No one emerged from the kitchen or from behind the counter. The tables were set with placemats and tableware wrapped in napkins; menus were stacked neatly by the register. The front door banged open and startled the silence. A man who was not the cook entered. He had walked from across the road to tell us that the restaurant temporarily was closed while the cook worked on a woman's car.

Continuing on, the two-lane highway showed winter stress. Faded pink flags marked patched pavement and frost heaves that were being scraped. Long, gravel sections had no shoulder. Repeated repairs had left a dropoff. Suddenly a muffled boom woke me from daydreaming. I stopped as far off the road as I dared. I saw no traffic in either direction. I made a quick check of the tires. The outside dual on the right rear had blown out. It was perched on the very edge of the dropoff. I sighed a quick prayer. If I had driven off the roadway, the RV could have turned over.

Chris retrieved a bright yellow towel that I could use as a warning flag as I tried to use my cell phone to reach roadside assistance. I couldn't get a signal. No vehicles passed in either direction. I saw no mile-post markers, no villages, no evidence of civilization. We were intruders in the wilderness connected to other humans only by a very long, thin ribbon of gravel.

Discouraged, I prayed. *How could I get help?* We couldn't stay here on the road and become a target for a drowsy driver. I strained to listen for an engine. Time passed slowly. From the opposite direction a tiny speck of dust grew larger as something approached. Two women in a sedan slowed down as I waved my towel. I asked the driver if she could give me an idea of where I was. The passenger held a Milepost on her lap. She replied that they had just crossed over the Danjek River Bridge. She recalled that they had passed through very few villages in the direction I was headed. No villages were between us and Beaver Creek, some 70 to 80 miles behind us. I thanked them and said I would try to get help from someone going south.

I tried the cell phone again. Nothing. I stood behind the RV with my yellow towel and waited for a vehicle I could wave down.

A minivan slowed to a stop. I approached the female passenger and explained my problem. The driver got out to check my tire. He said I had enough air in the inside dual so that I could drive on it if I took things easy. The inside tire looked good. I told him where I thought I was. He didn't know the area either. He offered to follow me until I could find a wide area in which to pull off the roadway.

With trepidation and relief that we were not totally alone in this isolated wilderness, I slowly drove south. The bridge over the Danjek River was reassuring. Once over the narrow, metal frame bridge, I saw a gravel track to the left that led to a gravel pit on the side of the shallow, silty river. I could wait here until road construction crews arrived in the morning.

The couple in the minivan followed me as I turned in.

They offered to stop at the next village to try to find a wrecker to send back to me.

I thanked them for getting us to a safe place off the road. We could stay here and dry camp, but what if construction crews did not arrive in the morning? I got out the Milepost to get a better idea of our location. The guidebook traces the Alaskan Highway through the Northwest Territories and Provinces of Canada to Fairbanks from south to north. I had to work from north to south by locating Tok and following the guide backward.

On a small map I finally saw the Danjek River and a bridge. Continuing to read the entries backwards, I located the Kluane Wilderness Village and an advertisement for 24-hour tire repair.

Now I had a goal. At best guess the village was less than 20 miles in the right direction. As a last resort in the morning we could ride our bikes to the village.

I'd try to send a message. On a sheet of notebook paper I wrote a description of the RV and our location. With my yellow towel I stood by the roadside and waited for another car to flag down. Soon another car going in the right direction stopped. The driver gladly agreed to deliver my note to the tire shop.

Chris got his bike down off the rack. He had a great time jumping the gravel piles and skidding his bike like a motorcross biker. Kids deal with stress so much better than adults do. For him this stop was a welcome diversion.

I sighed a prayer of hope and busied myself fixing supper to keep from worrying too much. My mind buzzed as I tried to analyze the situation and figure out if I had dealt with our predicament sensibly.

Chris reluctantly parked his bike to eat a quick meal. Then off he went while I did the dishes. Even in the outback of the Yukon, woman's work never is done.

I heard an engine—a low, deep, heavy engine. It didn't pass the gravel pit. The sound got closer. I opened the screen door and was met by a beautiful, dust-covered, dented wrecker. Little more than an hour had passed.

"Need help, lady?" A burly, bearded mechanic in stained, greasy coveralls and hiking boots stepped down from the truck cab.

"I am so glad to see you!" I greeted my rescuer. "Are you from the tire shop?"

"Yep," was his only answer.

Within less than another hour, the spare tire was on, the bike was on the rack, and we were on our way. I followed the wrecker driver through more gravel construction sites toward Kluane. I was grateful to be riding in the RV and not on a bike.

An approaching pickup truck threw gravel as it sped past in the opposite direction. A small rock cracked my windshield. At the tire shop I walked around to the front of the wrecker. The flying gravel had shattered the truck's windshield.

The small tire shop stocked only one tire that was the right size. I had it mounted and the spare tire returned to its spot as a spare. A hand-lettered sign read:

200 miles from Tok
100 miles from Beaver Creek
100 miles to Hines Junction
200 miles to Whitehorse
400 miles to Watson Lake

The work done, the shop foreman offered to let us dry camp on the parking lot for the night.

Monday, June 24, the road followed 50 miles along the south shore of the beautiful Kluane Lake. The highest mountains in Canada border the largest lake in Canada—the Kluane. The pristine Wilderness National Park could be accessed by three tiny villages. They once were relay stations or highway-maintenance camps. Each twist and curve in the highway presented astonishingly beautiful scenery. Patches of purple wildflowers and pink Fireweed beginning to bloom filled the open spaces.

Before we reached Haines Junction, we encountered 100 miles of construction. The bright, pink flags marking potholes now were faded white and tattered. Speed was reduced to 15 mph. Sometimes I saw a flagger, a lead car, and heavy equipment. Sometime I made it on my own.

Burwash Landing looked much as it might have during the building of the AlCan, a settlement of trailers, RV's for construction workers, heavy equipment, and very little else. Washboard roads continued. While I waited for the lead car, I talked to flaggers Several were young women who enjoyed the outdoors, scenery, and the excellent salary.

The sun slipped overhead and behind us. I turned north on the Klondike Highway and looked for the Lakhini Hot Springs. We had not had an opportunity to visit the Chena Hot Springs near Fairbanks and wanted to experience natural hot water in the Arctic. The road became gravel as it led through a mountain valley to dead-end in a dry parking lot. We grabbed our swimsuits and towels to join a line of swimmers waiting to purchase tickets at the bathhouse.

After changing, Chris and I met up to walk through an enclosed breezeway toward an outdoor swimming pool. Out of its shelter I caught my breath and wrapped my towel tighter around my shoulders. The breeze was cold! Steam rose from the clear, blue-green water in a large, two-part, rectangular, cement pool. Two sets of steps led down in to the extremely hot water. The heat didn't bother Chris. I took one slow step at a time. Very slowly. Had I read something about abrupt temperature changes causing heart attacks?

Chris crossed a wall into the larger pool. Water flowed over this wall as well. He encouraged me to follow him and said that the water was not as hot. He was right. The larger pool was more comfortable. Later we learned that the small end of the pool was where the natural hot spring entered the pool and was hotter than the other section was.

Our skin began to look sunburned, as though we were boiled lobsters. I was uncomfortable. Chris loved it. I climbed out to sit on the top step with my feet in the heat and the towels around my shivering shoulders. This would take a lot of getting used to. I could say I'd done it. One more thing to add to my list of accomplishments.

From the hot springs I had a relatively short drive to Whitehorse. On our way north we had stayed on the bypass and not visited the town. Today we turned down Two-Mile Hill road to see the Gold Rush town that had grown as stampeders who had run the Whitehorse rapids stopped to dry out and get supplies. Early miners thought the foaming rapids of the river reminded them of the flowing manes of white horses. Thus the river was named and the town named after the river.

We circled through the small town and remarked on the quaint shops. A grand sternwheeler was moored in the Yukon River. Visitors were welcome to watch restoration, but the interpretive center would not be open this late in the day. We followed the largest fish ladder in the world up the Yukon. This series of steps help returning salmon reach their spawning beds.

Tired from a long day and our swim, we welcomed a familiar Wal-Mart. I counted 54 RV's taking advantage of boondocking on an unpaved lot at the foot of the paved lot. We joined the stream of traveling customers heading into the store to stock up. Wal-Mart stores willingly permit dry camping. By the evidence of RV'ers returning to their rigs with aqua shopping bags, it's a successful relationship.

Tuesday, June 24, while leaving Whitehorse, Chris called and pointed to a wooly mammoth, then another, and a third smaller one. A sign, "Yukon Beringia Interpretive Centre", tempted us to stop.

The wooly mammoth family sculpture was a hint of displays inside. A cast of the largest wooly mammoth skeleton ever found towered over us. Displays traced the Ice Age inhabitants of the sub-continent: great woolies, lions, scimitar cats, giant short-faced bears, camels, and giant ground sloth.

The earliest evidence of humans in the New World is said to have been found in the Blue Fish Caves near here. This area of Canada was ice-free, unlike the rest of Canada, during the Ice Age. I don't agree with scientists that the earth is millions of years old. Biblical Creation indicates a young earth. So I just subtract a couple of zeros off the dates on the display signs.

A volunteer announced that everyone could go outside for a demonstration of the *atlatl*. He set up wooden targets of animals at varying distances, then showed the visitors how an *atlatl* was slung to throw a spear into a target. The *atlatl* is a wooden device that allows the hunter to gain distance and force with his thrown spear. The volunteer encouraged visitors to try their luck. Chris hit a wooden mammoth but missed the rest of the wooden wildlife.

Back on the road our next stop was the Tlingit Heritage Center north of Teslin. A line to totem poles guarded a boardwalk from the parking lot to the center. Tlingit totems here and many locations in Alaska were of great significance to the tribes that didn't have a written language. The poles recorded history and day-to-day events of importance. These five, single-figure poles were newly carved and vividly painted. Each seemed to represent an animal figure with humanlike arms and legs.

Masks and artifacts connected this culture from the Yukon to the Tlingits of southeast Alaska. Many fine-twined baskets made from spruce roots were decorated with colored patterns woven from maidenhair fern or thin strips of cherry bark. I discovered a basket design that I had seen before—the rattle-top basket. The removable lid of the basket had a separate compartment in which puffin beaks had been placed. The beaks rattled when the basket was shaken. I wondered at the extent of trading that must have transpired to get puffin beaks from the icy waters of the Kenai to the interior of the Yukon.

From my early college days the flat, geometric designs of Chilkat dance blankets had fascinated me. Here I saw beautifully woven, Tlingit blankets with similar designs and learned that the two tribes are related. The blankets are not actually woven but are made with a cedar-bark warp wrapped with fine goat wool that is then twined with two or three strands of goat wool. Using natural dyes on the goat wool creates the abstracted designs. I wondered whether the white Samoyed-type dog had been used for its wool. I once had a Samoyed dog and was able to spin his soft hair into acceptable yarn.

We found a provincial park that was open for the night.

Wednesday, June 26. What a sight! The Watson Lake Sign Post forest crowded the side of the highway. Sixty years ago an Army soldier working on the construction of the AlCan put up three signs on one post: his hometown, his location, and his destination. Signs have been added steadily ever since. Today more than 49,800 signs cover posts and trees on several acres. They feature street signs, city-limit signs, small advertising signs, and best of all personal, handpainted family "we-were-here" signs. We wandered around and through the signpost forest laughing and pointing at odd signs from strange places. How I wished for a board and some paint so we could add our own sign!

While I filled up the gas tank, I started a conversation with a man who was filling up a class A bus. He was heading north. I warned him about the construction and gravel that had broken my windshield. The man laughed and shook his head. He already had thrown gravel and broken out both of headlights on his own tow vehicle.

Within the next two hours continuing down the AlCan, we saw a huge, dark-brown bear and then a female, black bear and her cinnamon cub. A herd of horses, oblivious to traffic, grazed on both sides of the road. In the next 20 miles while we followed the Liard River, we crept through a herd of buffalo, or were they bison?

Two bicyclists—one pulling a trailer—crept up a hill. These were the first of several brave bike riders carrying panniers and backpacks, sleeping bags, tents, and gear. They were brave to negotiate the mountains and mammals.

Chris noticed the sign, "Liard River Hot Springs Provincial Park." Alysha had told Chris that this was a "must" stop. So we did. The entrance gate had a "campground full" sign. We drove on to check out the hot springs.

The parking lot near a sign and path to the hot springs almost was full. Let's go! We changed into swimsuits, grabbed towels, and donned a windbreaker against the cold breeze. At the trail head a large warning sign read: "Beware of Bears." I read aloud that bears frequented the area, so caution was advised. Walking the boardwalk trail a person should make noise and be wary. Past this point neither food nor pets were allowed. Occasionally sirens would sound to scare off bears. A different signal would warn swimmers of a bear sighted in the area.

With trepidation I followed Chris on the boardwalk through the woods and over wetlands. Strange water plants, marsh plants, and some larger shrubs on drier mounds were out of place in Arctic clearing. Chris flopped on his belly on the boardwalk as he looked for fish in the flowing, shallow water. I scanned the edge of the wetlands for signs of bears.

The boardwalk led into the forest. Shadows closed in. The wooden trail carved a dark-green tunnel through the forest. I imagined I saw bears behind every tree but didn't tell Chris. Massive ferns and tropical plants crowded the walk as we approached the hot springs. A few people passed us on their way back to the parking lot. They didn't seem concerned about bears.

Wooden stairs led up to a bathhouse and a long, wooden deck that bordered one side of a clear, steaming stream. On the opposite side of the stream a natural bank was draped in vegetation. Bathers sat on the steps that lead into the water. Braver souls sat in the hot water. Chris scrambled down into the water. I slowly eased in. Very slowly. Downstream a small dam held water in a chest-deep pond. The water here was too hot for me. I stepped over the dam and sat below its overflow. The steaming water flowing over the dam and over my shoulders relaxed the tension from driving and watching out for bears.

Two couples in their 20s settled into the water near me. I tried not to listen to their discussion of a bear attack. A couple of years ago a young woman had gone to the upper spring where the hottest water bubbled from the springs. A bear surprised her and attacked her. Her screams got the attention of a man who tried to fight off the bear. Another man ran for his rifle in his truck. He raced back to shoot the bear. Both the woman and first man were killed. The bear died of the gunshot. Most ironic: the shooter was charged with killing the endangered bear. The case still is in court.

Other patrons entered the stream. I worked my way into the shallower stream. The cold air on my shoulders and hot water up to my waist caused a dilemma. Do I sit with my whole body in the heat, or get out and freeze? I settled back under the waterfall while Chris splashed and played. He was oblivious to the heat and cold. Massive ferns grew on the riverbanks, with frond tips floating in the water. Rising steam encouraged unusual growth in the tropical foliage. What would this arctic jungle be like with a covering of snow?

My fingertips turned pruney. My stomach growled. Time had arrived to leave this weird wonderland. The gloomy shadows of the forest broke as we used the boardwalk to cross over the open wet-lands. A female Mallard duck and her ducklings paddled in the warm water. They dove to nibble water plants. Their little feathery tails waggled like flags.

Chris lay prone on the boardwalk to try to catch minnows swimming in the shallow water. He dipped his hand in and pulled it out quickly. The water was unexpectedly warm. How had the minnows adapted to the heat? Ducks and other wading birds also had adapted to the temperature. I wondered whether they migrated in the winter or just stayed near the hot springs. I scanned the edge of the woods for bears.

Since the campground was full, we cooked supper over the grill before we continued southeast. We passed several avalanche areas with signs warning against stopping. One area recently had been cleared. So much rubble was piled on both sides of the road that several buses could have been covered. A black bear grazed near the road. Another bear and her cub appeared oblivious to the sparse traffic. We passed a herd of buffalo. Loose horses walked in the road. Mountain goats, moose, and ground squirrels didn't seem to fear us.

I was tired but couldn't find a campground or a pullout to boondock. For the next hour we followed a river and then entered a valley between mountain ranges.

Ahead a sign pointed to a campground on Muncho Lake. I certainly wasn't going to be choosy this late even though it looked expensive. I was too tired. I parked behind a line of RV's along the road. We walked over to the office. It was closed. I could not find an after-hours registration. We walked through the campground past dark, quiet RV's and on to the lake.

A group of RV caravaneers sat around a campfire singing. Their leader told the group that the construction of the AlCan around the lake was the most challenging of the entire route. The original route was to follow along the top of the cliffs. This proved to be too hazardous, so with considerable rock excavation the road was relocated close to the lakeshore by benching into the cliffs.

As workers cut into the rocky banks, horses hauled the rock away. Several pieces of large machinery, bulldozers, and tractors plunged into the lake and still are in deep water. The completed road only is a few feet above the level of the lake.

A lingering sunset glowed pink and gold above the western mountains. Reflected colors danced off the lake's ripples. Deep, velvety violet shadows reflected the forest along the far shore.

As the shadows lengthened, the sky glowed a deep aquamarine. Stars twinkled. A full moon rose to be reflected in a long, golden ribbon. The sun was a memory. Midnight. Time for bed. We boon-docked with the other overflow RV'ers.

Chapter 18

Canada

Thursday. June 25. In the morning light we followed the shore of Muncho Lake to a pullout. The deep green and cobalt-blue waters were surreally beautiful. Copper oxide leaching from the mountains into the lake and its extreme depths were responsible for the jewel-like colors. How I wished for canvas and oil paints!

Today we drove through 450 miles of glorious scenery. Time to reflect. Time to dream. I drove with my brain on cruise control. Through Fort Nelson, over mountain passes, along river valleys and through Fort St. John.

We arrived in Dawson Creek, British Columbia. A stone cairn topped with a large sign read "You Are Now Entering World Famous Alaskan Highway." I laughed. We were leaving. Going the wrong way. Another time I'd drive from Mile "O" north. A visitor center, housed in a railcar next to a grain elevator, had a small gift shop, where I picked up two certificates that declared we had "survived" the AlCan.

I learned that this part of the highway actually is a bypass. The original highway passed through downtown one block away. I walked over to take photos of the historic Mile "O" monument. Noted on this monument was the distance to Fairbanks—1,523 miles. That evening we spent the night at a campground called "Swan Lake."

Friday, June 26. As we traveled into the Province of Alberta, broad valleys flattened into high plains. Forests and wilderness gradually showed signs of civilization and cultivation. Agriculture and livestock made use of the fertile land. Villages appeared more frequently and were larger than a service station with groceries, café, and, motel.

Stopping for gas on the outskirts of Edmonton, I asked for directions to the famous West Edmonton Mall. I'm not a "maller"— a mall-walker or window-shopper, but we could not pass up this tourist attraction.

The mall once may have been on the outskirts of the city, but commerce and new subdivisions now hid the mall from easy access. To find a place to park I circled several blocks around the world's largest shopping center. At last I found a lot that was not full. Chris and I entered the mall through a clothing store. Before we reached the far side of the store to enter into the main mall, a signal sounded and a voice announced, "The mall will be closing in 10 minutes."

Strange. The mall closing at 6 p.m. on a Friday night? I asked a clerk whether I had heard right. She replied that only the anchor stores and some of the shops were closing. The amusements and the hundreds of restaurants would be open until midnight. The clerk gave me directions to a parking lot especially set aside for RV's. She handed us a brochure that included a much-needed mall map.

The mall map listed more than 800 stores, restaurants, and services. The mall had water park with a wave pool, a mini golf course, an ice-skating rink, a submarine, dolphins, caverns, theaters and an I-Max, and a spa. A huge, multi-storied amusement park with carnival rides and video games caused Chris's eyes to pop. He wasn't interested in riding the Dungeon Drop, Roller Coaster, the Bumper Cars, or any of the other make-you-sick-to-your-stomach rides, (thank goodness, because he would have wanted me to ride, too). He headed for video games and begged for quarters.

Out of quarters, with all the video aliens disposed of, we followed the map toward the food courts and passed the glassed-in wave pool, a pirate ship, skaters on the ice rink, and many specialty shops.

Every turn revealed a new surprise. A series of fancy, sit-down restaurants led to a spacious food court which was lined on both sides with food choices from Asian to burgers. We walked from one end to the other and then back down the other side before we could decide. Chris wanted pizza; I had sweet-and-sour chicken with fried rice and an egg roll.

Circling back to Galaxyland Amusement Park we stopped so Chris could try some different video games. He used up another pocket full of quarters as he shot aliens, drove racecars, and played games about which I have no clue. I was glad that most of the shops were closed, or we would have been tempted to spend, spend, and spend. The last quarter went into the bottomless slot. The game crashed. Time to go.

Dusk had chased Friday traffic from town. The closest Wal-Mart parking lot was as far as I wanted to travel, so we boon-docked.

Saturday, June 29. From Edmonton I took Highway 2 to Canada 72 toward Drumheller. The landscape looked much like the Midwest, with flowing wheat fields and cattle ranches. Scattered farmsteads, some with well-kept antique farmhouses and some with large, new ranch homes, were surrounded by huge barns and outbuildings. The outskirts of Drumheller was dotted with dinosaur-themed enticements, dinosaur restaurants, and RV parks.

I reserved one of the last sites at Dino RV Park. Our spot for the night secured, we drove to the Royal Tyrell Museum of Paleontology a few miles west of town. The entrance had changed in the 12 years since I had visited here with two-month old Chris in a baby backpack and with eight of my other children. The original parking lot was full, so we proceeded to a new, overflow lot in the back of the buildings. Chris and I walked up a cement ramp and stairs around the outside of the enlarged museum. We went past bright-orange construction mesh and traffic cones.

The museum entrance was as I remember it. A huge, bronze T-rex and a grouping of small Albertosaurus guarded the entrance at the top of a broad stairs. The Tyrell was named after the geologist who discovered the dinosaur beds of southern Alberta. Dinosaur Provincial Park, several miles away, is a rugged badlands where paleontologists still excavate hadrosaur, albertosaur, and other dinosaur fossils. Here at the museum, fossils are studied and put on display.

Inside the extensive exhibits of reconstructed and skeletal prehistoric creatures were arranged and displayed so that they were in naturalistic habitats. We wandered from exhibit to exhibit and marveled at the creatures' size and diversity.

My favorite was a three-foot-long, fossilized fish whose bones remained attached to the supporting rock. Inside the fish's rib cage is the fossil of a smaller fish that had been its last meal. This fish was alive when silt and sand quickly covered it. It was killed before its last meal had been digested.

Only a massive flood could have caused enough silt to bury a living fish of this size. Only the flood of Noah's time could have caused this to happen in central Canada. Also on display were the fossils of other sea creatures discovered in Canada: sharks, turtles, and extinct sea "monsters."

A new area, the Palaeoconseratory, housed in an indoor garden more than 10 species of plants. These plants are related to the ones living in the Alberta area during the age of dinosaurs. They are the ferns, palms, and tropical plants we saw around the hot springs and that we associate with the tropics. Fossil evidence showed that tropical climates existed here before the Ice Age.

Our last stop was the gift shop. All along our route I had been mailing post cards to my grandkids. Now was the time to buy a special something for the little boys. Chris couldn't make up his mind between plastic models or wooden, build-your-own dinos with wooden bones. I was saved by the "closing-in-five minutes" warning. He finally chose a T-rex model and glow-in-the-dark skeletons for my grandsons.

All the sites at the campground, except our reserved site, were occupied. We ate a quick supper before we walked a long block to a grocery store to stock up on groceries and for ice cream. As we exited the store, a strong wind hit us in the face. Wind-blown storm clouds now piled above us. We began to jog as we jostled our shopping bags. Rain fell in a sudden splash. No need to jog now. We already were soaked. As we reached the RV, we raced inside and dripped on the carpet. By the time we had dried off and changed clothes, the sun had broken through the dark clouds. *What would a storm like this have been like in the Badlands? Would it have caused flash-flooding?*

On Sunday morning I daydreamed as I followed the highway through to Calgary and then the highway south. A thud and shaking jolted me awake. Little traffic was on the four-lane highway. I pulled onto the paved shoulder and got out to inspect the tires. The new tire that I had put on in the Yukon was flat.

To my left, across the freeway, I had passed a lonely service station. It appeared to be open, as a few cars were in front. I contemplated walking across the highway but then realized that further ahead I could see an overpass. I remembered driving on one dual in the Yukon, so I decided to drive slowly on one tire, cross over, and back to the station. This seemed to be a better plan than was leaving the RV on the shoulder of the road.

We crept on down the shoulder, over the overpass, and back along the other side to the station. No mechanics worked on Sunday. The clerk recommended a 24-hour tire repair shop in a nearby farm town. She even placed the call for me. Soon the wonderful sight of a tow truck pulling into the station brightened our day. A friendly young man who looked like he'd rather be fishing than working willingly mounted my spare to replace the flat.

The other tire, inside, had a lot of wear. The spare wasn't dependable, either. I followed the tow truck as he turned off the freeway and led me to the tire shop. I felt a shake and flashed my headlights at my guide. He stopped. I stopped behind. We inspected the tires together. Just as I thought: now my spare was going flat, or was this the tire I bought in the Yukon? I was advised that I could drive on with one good tire unless the low tire started to shred. Didn't we just go through this? He gave me directions and then let me go ahead of him so he could guard us with his flashers blinking.

The tire-shop manager and I discussed my options. My spare tire had shredded. My "new" tire was threadbare. I needed to buy at least three tires. Two for the ground and one for a spare. But that would put three good and one very used tire on the duals. Not safe, he said. I took a deep breath and agreed to buy four tires to go on the ground. One used dual would be my spare. The other I'd carry inside as a spare spare and pray that I didn't need either of them.

A couple of hours later we were on our way. Near Lethbridge a sign enticed us off the interstate to Head Smashed-In Buffalo Jump World Heritage Site. Here the buffalo hunters of the Plains Native Americans from ancient times are displayed. An elevator took us to the top of a cliff, where we walked to see at the actual site of a buffalo jump.

Information panels explained how Native American slowly herded buffalo across the nearly level high plain to the west. Piles of rocks provided shelter for the Native Americans and formed a funnel to direct the buffalo. The herd slowly was forced eastward toward the cliff edge, where the buffalo stampeded and fell to their deaths. At the bottom of the cliff, women and children were ready to dispatch injured animals and to skin and butcher the dead. Early explorers discovered piles of bleached bones and stone implements here. This led to the later establishment of the monument.

Fort McCleod was our last stop in Canada. The fort is a reconstructed model of a Northwest Mounted Police post that had been established in 1874. It housed antiques and Chris's favorite rifles, handguns, and cannons. Each summer riders in authentic Northwest Mounted Police uniforms use the tiny, historic town enclosed in the fort for performance precision rides. Unfortunately we missed it.

Chapter 19

Montana and Wyoming

On Monday a traffic jam at the border crossing from Canada into the United States held us up for more than an hour. Eighteen wheelers and truckers passed us on the right while we crept along with cars and other private vehicles. Cement barricades kept us in the slow lane. Construction. I should have guessed. Both lanes became gravel—dusty gravel.

We crept up to the border patrol booth. A sign read "Caution. Did you purchase meat in Canada?" We had not bought any meat while we were in Canada, so we likely could pass through customs without a problem. The border patrol agent checked our passports and the dogs' papers. He asked if I'd purchased meat. Then asked if I'd bought dog food. I had not. I had bought dog food in Alaska. I asked why a problem with dog food existed. Because of the discovery of mad cow disease in Canada, no meat or meat products, including dog food, were being allowed into the United States.

Montana. USA. The same clear, azure sky and golden-yellow fields flowed to the mountains as in Canada. The air felt different, An atmosphere of home. The wind increased as it blew from the west, perpendicular to the north-south highway. I drove under an overpass that temporarily blocked the wind. The RV jerked as the wind hit us again. I hung onto the wheel to hold a straight course. Lose control, and the wind could blow the rig into the left lane.

A thunderous rumbling and shaking sent Sam and Lady to try to get under my seat. Chris yelled, "Another flat?" How could that be? I stopped on the shoulder. I forced the driver's door open against the wind. A gust knocked me into the side of the RV. No traffic. At the rear of the RV the awning cylinder protruded, with the back leg dangling and swinging over the freeway. The blue-and-white awning flew like a partially furled sail above the roof.

I yelled at Chris to get out on the passenger's side. I grabbed the loose leg to try to work it to the back of the RV and out of the freeway. Chris held the leg so I could back up far enough to see whether the air conditioner or vent covers had been damaged.

A green pickup truck pulled up behind me. A straw-hatted cowboy got out and grabbed his hat to throw it back into the cab. "I saw what happened." The driver approached us. "Can I help?" he offered.

"Wonderful. Thank you. I'm at a loss. Thank God there's no traffic."

He retrieved a ladder from a rack on his truck and leaned it against the rear of the RV out of the direct wind. Up he climbed with pliers, screwdriver, and hammer. I hung onto the awning leg to keep it out of the highway. He gathered up the flapping awning. The trucker instructed us to push up on the leg while he guided the cylinder over the air-conditioner and vent covers.

The wind surged to pull the wadded-up awning from his arms as he struggled to stand without being swept off the roof. Clinging to the cylinder for support, he raised it over the air-conditioner and vents while I guided the end of the leg around the back of the RV. Chris kept watch for traffic.

The trucker called out that he couldn't free the fabric. It was ripped from one end and kept wrapping around him. Would it be all right to cut it off? Sure. Why not? I certainly couldn't re-roll it. The cut-free fabric whipped around our heads as Chris and I wrestled it to the ground.

"Look out!" he warned as he unbolted the back leg from the cylinder. I eased it to the ground. Chris loosened the front leg so the man could lower the cylinder and pivot it off of the leg. I held the lowered end. Rescue complete, he inched his way along the roof and backed down the ladder. With his feet on the ground I breathed easier.

"You gonna try to salvage any of this?" he asked. I surveyed the twisted metal and shook my head. The fabric I would keep. The legs and tubing were left on the shoulder.

My roadside angel refused payment. "Just glad to help,

Ma'am," he replied. He waved as he drove away.

The wind rattled the aluminum cover from the awning cylinder. The clattering set my teeth on edge. I planned a stop in Shelby, MT, for an overdue oil change. While I was in the shop, I asked the mechanic if he would take the awning cover off the track. When we were back on the road, no noise disturbed us from the roof as we searched for a campground.

Tuesday our route continued on to Bozeman to visit the Bozeman Dinosaur Museum and the Pioneer Settlement. In the foyer members of an animated triceratops family made sounds. Their eyes moved as their mechanical bodies moved. It rippled their rubber muscles. Other displays echoed the Tyrell.

We entered the pioneer village through a spring garden. The gardener had harvested pumpkins and gourds, which were displayed on the ground. He showed us flax plants used for making linen fabric and medicinal herbs. In the kitchen of the clapboard house volunteers in pioneer dress were cooking in a wood store delicious smelling ham, sweet potatoes, and rhubarb pies. A tour of the root cellar and the outhouse led us back to the parking lot.

I drove Highway 89 to a KOA near the town of Livingston, the closest town to the north entrance of Yellowstone National Park. We arrived early. July is the peak tourist time at Yellowstone. I didn't want to chance not being able to get a campsite. We took advantage of the beautiful pool and laundry facilities in preparation for an early-morning departure into the park.

Wednesday. The historic entrance, a rough-cut, red-brown, stone arch, seemed a monolith out of place standing on a dry plain shrouded in fog. The two-lane highway continued south to cross the border from Montana into Wyoming. We began to climb in a series of switchbacks into a high valley between the Gallatin Range and the Washburn Range.

At the crest of a pass I pulled over into an overlook. Far below the road we had traveled was a tiny, twisting ribbon. As we hiked higher, we looked down on the Mammoth Hot Springs Visitors Center.

Chris pointed out creatures wandering on the lawns between the stone buildings.

"Let's check it out!" he shouted as he scrambled back down the rocky hillside toward the RV. We continued our drive into the quaint old town. A huge bull elk crowned with massive antlers appeared from between two of the stone buildings. It jaywalked and crossed the road directly in front of us. Traffic stopped. Tourists gawked. Vehicular and pedestrian traffic froze to give the magnificent animal his right-of-way and to take photos. Small herds of elk grazed the lawns between the buildings. Some were so confident of their celebrity status that they lay chewing cud. Golden yellow calves cavorted near their mamas and butted their antlerless heads.

Photo op completed, we joined the traffic that crept along bumper to bumper. Over one million visitors arrive during July and August to explore Yellowstone's 2.2 million acres of vastness that is dotted with alpine forests, deep canyons set off by craggy peaks, and cauldrons of hot springs, geysers, and fumaroles.

In this wildlife sanctuary we visitors were in awe over sightings of elk, bison, mule deer, and moose. If we were fortunate and observant, we might see bighorn sheep, black and grizzly bears, pronghorn, mountain lions, and/or coyote. We might get a glimpse of the elusive, reintroduced wolves. Birds were in abundance here. Locating the less-common eagle, pelican, Trumpeter swan, and osprey would take patience and strong binoculars.

Excited to be at this destination I took the western leg of the park's Grand Loop, a figure-eight shaped system of roads that placed visitors within hiking distance of the major attractions. At Mammoth Hot Springs plumes of steam wafted over and across terraced mineral formations. Frozen waterfalls of calcium deposits cascaded over and around ochre, sienna, vermilion, and umber rock ledges.

Parking, we followed a boardwalk through a moonscape of formations that glistened with warm, flowing mineral water. A breeze caught sulfuric smelling steam. The vapor caught us offguard. Holding my nose, I raced Chris out of the fog. He led the way up wooden stairs to elevated platforms where we could see bubbling cauldrons and flowing water that added cinnamon browns and alabaster to stone palette.

Ready to see more, we drove on. Visible through the broken forest were small, intermittent geysers and columns of smoke. We pulled over for a closer look at a steaming, smoking, discolored area of multi-colored rocks. The official Yellowstone Map and Guide explained that the central portion of the park is a 28-by-47-mile basin or caldra. We now were passing through it. What we thought was smoke actually was vented steam called fumaroles. We stopped to investigate several more of these strange phenomenon.

Mud pots, like colored bubble gum, bulged larger and popped as they splattered hot mud. Some mud bubbles grew large and then subsided as they left ridges or rings of mud like frozen, radiating ripples. Others burst with a popping or burping sound. Some sprayed miniature geysers of mud. The randomness of the bubbling kept us watching and guessing which one would pop next. Railed boardwalks and warning signs kept Chris from rushing out, oblivious to the heat, to poke at the burping pots. The sulfur smell and billowing gusts of steam didn't deter him.

We made the obligatory stop at Old Faithful, the famous geyser. At the visitor center a sign read that Old Faithful erupted on an average of every 78 minutes. A manual clock face indicated that the next eruption would be at 12:42 p.m. We had time for lunch.

At a safe distance a cement walkway encircled the geyser's vent. The side closest to the visitor center had benches and paved standing room. We arrived early and chose front row seats. Well before the predicted time of eruption, all the benches were full. The standing-room area was packed with curious visitors. Many people walked around the circumference to get a less-obstructed view from the far side. Watches were consulted.

People murmured. Will it erupt on schedule? I overheard someone say that the geyser sprayed 7,800 gallons of water in a plume 100- to 180-feet into the air. We joined the crowd in a countdown and called off the minutes left.

A collective "ahhh" was heard as the geyser at exactly 12:42 burped up a small spray. A brief rest gave everyone a chance to focus his or her attention and cameras on the vent. Another larger burst of steaming spray riveted everyone's attention. Larger, higher, and longer-lasting eruptions burst continually as they threw a cloud of steam unbelievably high into the bright, blue sky. A gust of wind blew cooled water vapor across the crowd. Chris crowed with delight. It was an experience he never will forget.

All too soon the force of the eruptions began to subside. The crowd became restless as the show ended. As the curious dispersed, we wandered in the direction of the RV. Chris and I each took a dog by the leash and walked them towards the woods that bordered the parking lot. A tall, young man in a park-ranger's uniform walked up to us. He noted our plastic pickup bags. He said that dogs were welcome in the park as long as they were on leash and picked up after.

He added, "Loose dogs will be shot."

I gasped. Yes, he said. Any loose dog is a menace to the protected wildlife. This drastic measure is a park policy.

I thanked him for the warning and was grateful that my dogs never are loose. They are always on a leash or tied out. We kept that warning in mind we returned to the RV and the road south.

The traffic crawled. Brake lights flashed. Our seats in the RV were high enough that we could see over the small sedan in front of us. Ahead of the car rambled a huge bull bison in the center of the road. His huge haunches and rope-like tail swayed back and forth as he led our parade across a two-lane bridge. Approaching cars had stopped at the far end of the bridge to give the monster plenty of maneuvering room.

A bold young man, his ponytail flying, sped his motorcycle around me. He started to pass the sedan. He screeched to a halt. With the bridge blocked by bodacious buffalo buttocks, he geared down.

We burst out laughing. With a quick glance in my direction, he squeezed his bike between the RV and the sedan. Chris and I cracked up watching him try to act nonchalant. Of all the wild animals we had seen, humans undoubtedly are the most unpredictable.

We followed the herdmaster across the bridge. He joined his harem on the shoulder. We continued through the lodge-pole pine forest. The trees thinned out. Black sentinels stood scattered among the telephone-pole pines. The forest was replaced by thousands of burned skeletons of the lodge-pole pines that stood or lay in jumbles on the hills. Both sides of the road evidenced recent forest fires. New, green growth was beginning to reclaim the understory.

Evidence of the devastating 1988 forest fires hardly was noticeable. An occasional sign stated "reforestation" was taking place. Almost 15 years of new growth had covered the burned areas. The regenerated vegetation gave ecologists an opportunity to study the effects of wild fires on the landscape and the wildlife. Today people have greater concern about the impact of the increasing number of visitors on the ecosystem. Although we were visiting in July, one of the highest visitor volume months, the midweek traffic was bearable—except at wildlife sightings. Then all traffic stopped, even in the middle of the road as we ogled bears, a couple of moose, small herds of elk, and grazing bison. We didn't see any of the reintroduced wolves. But we did see many birds I couldn't identify.

Continuing south past Grant Village, the road slowly transported travelers from Yellowstone into the Grand Teton National Park. The ranger station, situated in a small clearing, made one park an extension of the other. Through the forest to my right I began to glimpse a lake. Soon the road followed the eastern shore of huge Lake Jackson.

Across the expanse of shimmering lake to the west, the Teton Range loomed. It was cragged and dusted with perpetual snow. The largest of the three Tetons, Grand Teton, is 13,700 feet. The range rises steeply from the far lakeshore. Blue and white glaciers and rugged pinnacles of granite reflect in the clear, cerulean blue, jewel-like lake. The winds ruffled the surface of the water and temporarily distorted the mirror image of the mountain range. Conifer forests and alpine meadows contributed greens to the Teton's palette: yellow green, bright verdant, dark hunter green. Tiny specks of bright yellow, gold, red, and distant purples evidenced distant fields of blooming wildflowers.

My neck and shoulders were tired from swiveling to take in the scenery. Afraid that I couldn't find a campsite in the parks, I had made a reservation at a RV park in Jackson, WY. I stood in line in the office while other travelers were turned away from the booked camp. I grudgingly paid for a place to park with no hookups. That is the result of supply and demand. We took advantage of the pool before dinner and turning in.

Wednesday. July 4th. From Jackson we made our way to Vernal, Utah, with a stop to gaze at the colors that give Flaming Gorge its name. While we crossed the dam at the southern end of the Flaming Gorge Reservoir, Chris called my attention to a fireboat shooting a geyser of water toward the shore. Helicopters carried containers of water dangling from cables toward pillars of smoke.

The road climbed through dry, rocky forest. We climbed to 8,000 feet and then to 10,000. Gus struggled at 20 mph, floorboarded. A half-dozen descending switchbacks with 25-mph speed limits taxed my brakes. I pulled over to let the brakes cool off and to let cars pass. The descending switchbacks continued. Driving to Alaska was easier on the brakes and transmission.

I rounded an outcropping to be faced with the smoking, smoldering remains of a recent forest fire. I had been following news reports of several Colorado fires that were caused by lightening strikes, but nothing had been said about fires in Utah. No traffic had been in either direction for quite a while. I wondered if the road was closed and feared that somehow I had missed the notice.

Smoke plumes and wispy-gray clouds of smoke set off the charred, standing trees with their stubby, ghostly branches etched against the sky. The spooky scenery enveloped us with foreboding. For miles we saw no sign of animal life or of human habitation—only burned piles of brush, charred trees, and pillars of smoke.

Chris pointed to a single service station that showed no sign of life. A truck appeared circling from the back to park under the station's awning. I slowed to pull off the road and proceeded to the station. No lights were on. The doors were propped open. The building seemed ghostly vacant.

We dared each other to be brave and enter. I wanted to see whether the road was open to Vernal or whether I had to backtrack. Two young men in "gimme" caps, T-shirts, faded jeans, and Western boots leaned on the counter talking to a similarly dressed female clerk. They shared their experiences with us.

Fires had started from lightening strikes on Sunday. An area of several miles had been evacuated for four days and the road closed. The fires had been declared out and the road reopened this morning. The three were checking up on their place of employment. One of the men had lost his home in the fires. Other people had been more fortunate. No reports of lives lost had emerged, although many homes and barns had been destroyed.

Since the electricity still was off, the station had no gasoline or cold drinks. We wished the employees well and continued on toward Vernal. As we left the high elevation, the air became hot and dry. A stop at Dinosaur Gardens gave us a chance to see realistic, full-scale models of the Utahraptor, protoceratops, T-rex, and giant dragonflies with five-foot wing spans. Besides fossils from local fossil beds, the museum had excellent small displays of Native American artifacts.

Dinosaur National Monument, our next stop, extended across the Utah border into Colorado. The road left Utah and re-crossed into Colorado. At the tiny desert town of Dinosaur, a park road wound north through hot, dry, rugged badlands. The road terminated in a surprisingly large, but empty, parking lot. Sidewalks and signs led to a roofed shelter. We could wait here in the shade for a tram to take us to the Dinosaur Quarry Visitor Center.

Dogs were allowed on the tram but not in the center. What a relief! I had been worrying about leaving the dogs in the RV even with the windows open. We went back to get Sam and Lady. Heat shimmered off the pavement in rippling waves. The air was still and stifling.

Two families with young children joined us in the shade of the shelter. Chris and I took the dogs onto the back seats of the tram. We could take turns sitting outside the center with the dogs and exploring inside. The tram ascended through a narrow gorge of dry desert shale and rock. In 1909 apatosaur tailbones had been discovered in these rugged mountains. In 1915 the monument was established on 90 acres at the original quarry site. Today 200,000 acres of high plateaus, canyons, and desert are preserved for paleontologists to explore.

A contemporary, glass, three-story building enclosed a cliff-side quarry packed with fossils. Under the building's roof, the hard, sandstone mountainside bore layer on layer of exposed fossils. Paleontologists no longer removed the fossils as they had been doing when I visited here in 1990. Scientists have excavated more than 2,000 bones since the site was discovered. Each bone has been carefully chiseled out but only if another bone lay underneath. Now the dinosaur graveyard was being left for visitors to view.

A guide repeated what I had heard 12 years earlier. He said that masses of dead dinosaurs had been washed by the currents of a massive flood and piled on top of one another in valleys. Sediment quickly had covered the bodies and caused mountainous fossilization. Many years later uplift tilted the hard-packed strata into a steep angle. Erosion slowly stripped away the rock to expose the fossils of many different species of dinosaurs.

Displays of casts of many of the prehistoric creatures found in the quarry are displayed. These included turtles, crocodiles, and contemporary-looking fishes.

This visit renewed my conviction that dinosaurs had been on Noah's Ark. Baby dinosaurs as well as the young of other large mammals would not have been difficult to supervise. After Noah's Flood had obliterated life and the waters receded, dinosaurs would not have been able adapt to the temperature changes and would have became extinct

The sun slid low behind the western mountains as we returned to the town of Dinosaur. No campgrounds were available, so I continued south toward Grand Junction. Hundreds of ground squirrels sat on their haunches and waved their paws as we passed. Too many had tried to cross the road and now were roadkill. Small herds of pronghorn cavorted on the hillsides in the twilight. Well after dark I pulled off for the night between two 18-wheelers in a rest area off I-20.

Thursday, July 5. My plans to go to Durango and to visit Mesa Verde National Park were thwarted by reports of more forest fires in that area. Eager to return home we took the Interstate toward

Denver. I had not considered that this route took us through the Colorado ski areas until I saw a sign for Vail. The four- and six-lane freeway followed a valley that crossed west to east between rugged mountains. Periodically exits led to up scale villages with mountain retreats nestled into high valleys. Chateaux—winter mansions—dominated the crests. New model SUV's and sedans passed me as if I was in interloper. I dared not stop in this "ritzy" area.

The valley became so narrow and twisting that the divided highway separated into two different levels. Eastbound traffic lanes passed above the westbound lanes. I felt more comfortable driving in the northern mountain wilderness than in this traffic. As we approached Denver, the traffic became more congested, but the highway leveled out. I bypassed Denver and headed south toward Colorado Springs.

A night in Trinidad, Colorado, a climb over Raton Pass, then on to Lubbock, TX, for the night. Overnight in Belton and we almost are home.

The setting sun glinted off my outside mirror as I reluctantly continued east into Houston's urban sprawl. Although home had a magnetic pull, returning meant the end of the adventure of my life-time. I had dared to dream. Now that dream had been accomplished—13,000 miles, three-months' full-timing in an RV, on my own, depending on God alone. I know that even as a senior citizen I had the intelligence and daring to experience freedom—freedom from the mundane, conventional, and other peoples' expectations. My experiences have empowered me and encouraged me to dream anew.

Epilogue

Memories of my Alaska adventure tugged at my heart to return. The summer of 2003 presented a travel challenge of a different nature. Could I combine a trip from Texas to Pennsylvania for a family reunion, 1,400 miles northeast, with a 5,000-mile trip northwest to Alaska?

As long as I was planning for the reunion, I'd pack to return to Alaska, too.

From Pennsylvania we traveled to Niagara Falls, then west along the northern shores of the Great Lakes. Southern Canada is an extension of the rolling hills of the Midwest. Meadows and valleys were bursting with the greens of summer growth. Western mountain ranges magnetically pulled us.

The Alaskan Highway was reminiscent of our return last summer. We watched for familiar landmarks. The Milepost markers made sense now, from south to north. Magnificent vistas caused my heart to soar. A tingling thrill reassured me that I'd made the right decision to return to Alaska.

The sign welcoming us to the LaVerne Griffin Youth Camp in Wasilla was set in a blaze of colorful summer flowers instead of snow. Camp looked much like it did at our departure a year ago. The log-rail fence opened its arms to us. I shivered with joy at our return.

We arrived in time to help prepare for a very special closed camp. Breast-cancer survivors from the Anchorage area would arrive in time for dinner. Mickey assigned me the task of creating table decorations for this small, special group of women. Rummaging through a crafts closet I located small candles but little else that I could use. Lynne and Dale, the new assistant directors, were there to my rescue. Dale cut small birch logs into foot-long lengths. For the candles Lynne and I drilled several indentations into the topside of the logs. With the addition of spruce boughs and lichen, our centerpieces were ready to welcome the campers.

Two women with shaved heads hung a banner on the side of the dining hall. They returned my greetings. The banner read, "Casting for Recovery, Search for a Cure", with the image of a fly fisherman casting his line. The older woman explained the theme. Camp participants would be taught how to fly-cast in the lake for trout and landlocked salmon. They would strengthen arm and chest muscles that mastectomy had weakened. They also would have fun and companionship.

A van arrived. Women wearing wigs, hats, and scarves pulled luggage from the back of the van. Some of the survivors, secure in their recovery, proudly uncovered bald heads. Long-term survivors, leaders for the camp programs, had their heads shaved in compassion for their sisters.

The following afternoon I completed potty patrol (cleaning the bathhouse) and walked outside. Hanging from rope lines tied from tree to tree were a rainbow of fluttering cloths. The colorful rectangles drew me closer.

"These are prayer flags," a bald, young woman stated as she pinned more fabric to the lines.

I fought tears for these women, as I read tributes to friends who had not survived. Poems, drawings, petitions, and thanksgiving expressed the pain, sorrow, and healing of these brave women. The clothesline—a bright expression of hope—would aid healing.

As I performed my chores, I watched from a distance as instructors taught the techniques of casting a fishing line. First they learned to cast without making a bird's nest, then how to hit a target of hula-hoops. The targets became smaller and were placed farther away. Campers took out the paddleboats and canoes. Some braved the icy waters to swim. They became relaxed. They had fun pushing their medical horrors behind them.

Lynne and I changed the table décor to fishing rods and brightly colored paper fish. The women asked to take the fish home as their souvenirs. We readily agreed and cut out more. After evening meals we restocked the tables.

As their skills improved, the fisherwomen progressed to fishing off of the dock and catching trout to freeze and take home. Women who had advanced from novice pulled on rubber waders that had an inflatable flotation (like an inner tube) at the waist. I watched curiously as the two waded into the cold water, settled into their rubber "body-boats", and floated off. They laughed back and forth as they cast, reeled in, and cast again.

On the last evening of camp all of the support staff, including the men, were invited to a fashion show. We stood behind the row of campers and listened to an emcee. To the tune of "Miss America" a woman entered garbed in waders, jacket, fly vest, gloves, and broad-brimmed hat. She carried a fishing rod and an extra-large tackle box. The model walked on an imaginary runway. She posed, turned, and posed again.

In glowing terms the emcee described the model's outfit as the model removed her hat, gloves, and waders. The contents of the tackle box brought a burst of laughter, for she carried a battery-powered hair dryer, hairbrush, nail polish, and makeup.

The model removed her vest. As the music shifted to a "stripper" tune, she played the part and slowly removed a long-sleeved shirt, water shoes, and shorts to reveal a long T-shirt printed with a curvaceous female body wearing black bikini panties and a black, lacy bra.

The crowd hooted and clapped. How wonderful to be able to have fun in the face of suffering! I later learned that the model, age 28, was a three-year survivor. In her previous, before-cancer, life she had been very shy and withdrawn. She, and many of the others, now were outspoken for cancer awareness.

The staff prepared for the next camp. The bathhouse was sanitized, cabins were cleaned, and groceries and supplies were restocked. We had little personal time for a trip to town or to do laundry before our next group, World Changers, arrived.

World Changers are junior- and senior-high school youth from the Lower Forty-Eight who volunteer part of their summer vacations to repair homes. Four-hundred youth and their sponsors arrived in Anchorage to be housed in area churches for orientation. One hundred of the youth and their adult counselors arrived at the camp. Other groups were based in different locations throughout the state.

The teens were a lively group. They arrived in several vans, threw their belongings into their assigned cabins, and scattered to explore the camp before dinner. The staff's daily schedule started the next morning at 4:30 a.m. I was up and at the dining hall by 5 to help prepare breakfast. During the day the kids would be working at home repair and minor construction and deserved a hearty breakfast. They ate at 6 a.m. and by teams were packed into vans by 7.

Each team and adult sponsors were assigned to specific projects. The teams made up of the youngest campers would complete minor home repair and painting. Other teams would re-roof homes, build wheelchair ramps, and make major repairs on the homes of the elderly or needy.

The organizers of World Changers had been in Wasilla and Palmer the previous summer to work with local officials. Projects, qualifications for homeowners, and needs assessments led to donations of materials from local building-supply companies.

I had a great deal of respect for those who volunteered their time in preparation for the arrival of the youth work teams.

Not only did the young people volunteer to do physical labor, but they had paid for the privilege. Each person had to pay for plane fare from home to Alaska.

Every morning the kids left in a whirlwind. We cleaned up the kitchen and dining hall and then the showers and bathhouse. The girls left out their makeup and hair dryers. The boys were worse. They left out dirty clothes and towels. We easily could forgive them when we realized that at home they couldn't be coaxed out of bed for a 6 a.m. breakfast and the promise of manual labor during summer vacation.

Area churches provided noon meals for each team. After cleanup Lynne and I were free until time to prepare dinner. We became inseparable friends as, in their small car, we ran errands for the camp.

We wanted to learn more about the work the kids were doing, so we drove to one of the work sites. We followed directions to a small, isolated cabin in the forest. The plywood cabin was in dire need of a new roof. Kids were replacing decking and hauling shingles. Girls with their long hair in braids joined the bandanna-sweatbanded guys who nailed shingles. Ignoring the heights kids scrambled monkeylike up and down ladders. Other workers painted a sealer/stain on newly replaced windowsills.

The bearded owner proudly supervised the work. Dressed in a plaid flannel shirt and overalls, with well-worn boots and a GI cap over his long, gray ponytail, he introduced himself as a retired Air Force sergeant. Many years ago he and a friend had homesteaded the land. They first built a one-room cabin for a headquarters as they hunted or searched for gold. Over the years a lean-to had been added to enlarge the cabin. His water supply was whatever the sergeant lugged in from a well. Using extension cords he borrowed a little electricity from a neighbor.

Lynne and I took photos of the kids at work. An energetic boy suggested we "go look out back."

We did and discovered a patched, plywood outhouse with a view. The doorway to the outhouse, covered with a heavy canvas curtain, faced away from the cabin. Inside, binoculars hung on the wall within reach. With the curtain pushed back the occupant had incredible view of a marshy lake in the middle of a small, open valley.

To see our reaction a group of giggling boys had followed us. They took turns posing with the binoculars and standing in the outhouse doorway. One of the boys said that the old man saw a lot of moose out there at the lake early in the morning. That very morning the boys had seen a moose. What stories these kids would have to tell on their return home!

In the evening the first teams back to camp rushed to hot showers. The last team in to camp usually had a quick, cold shower. We prepared a hearty dinner for the young people and afterward enjoyed visiting with them. They not only worked, they fished, canoed, or dared to swim. On their final night the staff was asked to join the campers to watch a video that had been made during their week.

As a "thank-you" each of us was presented a copy of the video and a World Changers backpack. Seeing the attitude of selfless giving in these youngsters was the "thank-you" that I will cherish.

The first of August I drove a volunteer couple to Anchorage to catch an airplane to the Lower Forty-Eight. The sun was shining as we passed a time/temperature sign in Wasilla. 7 a.m. and 34 degrees!

At home in Houston, the temperature would reach 100 degrees with 100-percent humidity. How I'm tempted to move to Alaska, but I doubt that in the winter I could adjust to being housebound. The cold and dark quickly would result in cabin fever since I'm too old to learn winter outdoor sports.

On that same day youth from distant, isolated bush villages flew into the Anchorage airport. Some of these kids had first flown in bush planes from their tiny villages to a larger village, then transferred to a small, commercial plane for the trip to Anchorage. I anticipated meeting and serving this group.

As the Native youth arrived by the vanload from Anchorage, I contrasted their quiet behavior with the enthusiasm of the World Changers. To their friends the Natives spoke softly with few words. Their movements were controlled and almost shy. Perhaps this shyness was because of being in such a different environment run by *cheechakos*.

Adult leaders who arrived with the youth from the villages were Mission Service Corps volunteers, pastors, or their wives. One woman shared that she, her husband, and children for several years had lived in their village before they were accepted. Now their church was a social as well as religious center. She had brought eight girls with her. A few of the girls had been to camp before.

Another missionary said that when her family first tried to move into a village, a group of men with guns met them. Her young children were instrumental in their being accepted. The Natives greatly value their children and know that they must pass on oral history, culture, and values before all is lost.

The staff who had been with the Native youth before made the returning campers feel remembered with jokes and anecdotes. New to Native camp, I wondered how I could get to know these shy kids.

The campers' daily routine and our daily chores gave me little time for interaction. I learned not to serve milk. In the villages they rarely had milk except powdered milk for cooking. They liked and ate great quantities of meat but few vegetables or fruit. Fresh produce infrequently reached the villages by plane. The kids enjoyed hamburgers and pizza, though.

The Native youth began to talk more openly to us. Toward the end of the week a day was set aside for shopping in town. Before they left, they sat around the picnic tables in small groups and discussed their intended purchases. Each camper had a list, written or memorized, of the things he or she had been entrusted to purchase for the family: a size-12 jacket for sister, size 9 athletic shoes for brother, a fry pan for mom.

The girls talked of new winter clothes for themselves. The boys would get their ears pierced. Both boys and girls whispered of splurging on colored hair gel or hair dye. Why anyone with such beautiful, thick, blue-black hair would want to color it pink or green . . .? They are typical teens, after all.

Lynne explained that each Alaskan received a yearly dividend check from the gas-pipeline royalties. Far too often the money goes quickly for liquor. As Christianity reached the villages families have reevaluated their lifestyle. The use of sweat lodges that promoted promiscuity and incest were being combated as young women gain confidence in themselves through a belief in Christ. Instead of fleeing to the city many of the young people—previous campers—have gone home and become leaders in their community.

Lynne showed me a lovely, beaded bracelet that she wore constantly. Letia, one of the Native girls, made these bracelets to help pay her way to camp. Lynne introduced me to her young friend. Letia showed me several completed bracelets. They were made without a clasp, like a bangle. None would fit over the width of my hand.

Letia told me to "push" harder. Afraid that I'd break the intricate beadwork, I refused. I asked if she had beads. I thought that if she did not, I'd buy some so she could send a bracelet to me. Without a reply she got up and left. I glanced questioningly at Lynne. She shrugged.

Letia returned with a plastic bag. On the picnic table she set out tubes and baggies of beads and said, "Choose; I'll make."

I picked out turquoise, coral, and gold and from her completed work a pattern. She and her friends went off laughing. At me?

One afternoon I was early for dinner preparation. I heard laughter in the chapel. Across the front several girls practiced lining up while they held something in their hands. Taped music sent the girls into a slow, innovative dance. They gracefully moved forward; each raised a votive-candle cup. They were singing to the music of "Go Light Your World."

Tears streamed down my cheeks. My nose stopped up. My heart sang! *Thank You, Lord, for verifying that this trip was in Your plans for me.* This was the song my daughter sang at my commissioning service—the same song I had heard on the radio after 9/11. God is so good.

Letia sat down beside me at the picnic table. From her bag she withdrew a wide strip of webbed beading. Coral beads zigzagged across a background of turquoise. Yellow hearts filled in the triangles.

I ohhhed and ahhhed. It was lovely. Letia measured the band around my wrist. While she added a few more rows, I ran to get my camera. I treasure the photos of her working on the bracelet as much as I treasure the bracelet itself. She connected the two ends together and finished it on my arm. I've never taken it off.

Lynne and I had struggled to perfect birch-bark basketmaking. For stitching we used purchased raffia instead of traditional reindeer sinew or spruce roots. Digging around spruce trees only had resulted in piles of composted organic stuff, large roots, and broken fingernails. Lynne recalled that Letia's friend, Susanna, might know about making birch-bark baskets.

After dinner, we took our finest, but crude, baskets and went in search of the girls. Giggling stopped when Lynne knocked on the screen door of their cabin.

"Can we come in?" she asked. She was not certain if this intrusion was culturally permissible.

Perhaps because we were revered as elders, the six girls scooted over on their cramped double bunks to make room for us in their tiny cabin.

I praised Letia for my bracelet. Lynne made small talk. The girls sat intently silent. Lynne showed Susanna our attempts at basketmaking. The baskets were passed hand to hand. As she inspected our work, each girl tried to suppress giggles.

Lynne asked Susanna and the other girls if anyone knew how to do it. Susanna responded with a positive nod. The other girls shook their heads, "No."

Lynne questioned Susanna about how she learned.

"Grandmother," was her reply.

"Do you think we can learn?" A muffled giggle.

"Can you help us?" A shrug.

"We have one very important question. How do you find spruce roots? We've tried."

Giggles. Then very seriously as if to a child, Susanna said, "First you find a spruce tree."

Using her hands in a downward motion to indicate the trunk, "Then you follow the roots out."

Her hands continued down the imaginary trunk and out to encompass the soil and roots leading from the trunk. Behind raised hands the other girls hid giggles. They must have thought that we were the most stupid *cheechakos*.

Lynne and I could not contain ourselves any more than the girls could. We all started laughing. The tension had broken. I blundered that we knew how to identify a spruce tree. We'd tried to find the right roots, but they were all tangled up with other roots. How do you know which ones?

"You just know."

We shared hugs around. A warm friendship had begun.

The last evening the staff attended a program presented by the Native youth. In a darkened room with lighted candles in transparent holders the girls gave their performance to "Go Light Your

World." Their graceful movement was like a ballet of angels. Although I was prepared from seeing the rehearsal, my emotions made photography a challenge. Their leader challenged all of us to "light your world" and passed out small flashlights.

I located Kim, the girls' leader, to tell her what their performance had meant to me. She shared that the girls had choreographed the piece themselves. They had perfected several songs and enjoyed performing in church and for socials held in their school's gym. Accepting Christ had made many positive changes in the lives of these girls and in their families.

I asked if I possibly could visit their village.

"You're always welcome," she said. "However, I have to tell you that you have to take two flights—one from Anchorage to Kotzebu and then a bush plane to the village. The cost is around $500."

I gulped. How did the kids afford the cost? Kim replied that they worked at odd jobs and used dividend money. Sometimes churches in the Lower-Forty Eight would sponsor a teen. Besides the cost of the flight, they had the camp fees.

"But that's not all," she warned. "We have to ask visitors to help with expenses. Fresh milk is $10 a gallon. So is gasoline. Don't forget that everything has to be flown in."

I knew that on this trip I could not afford to visit a bush village. If I had the extra money, it would be better spent sponsoring a teen.

Kim showed me some hair pretties (barrettes) that she made from harbor-seal skin and beads. She said that she could not possess the hide since she was not a Native, but she could receive gifts of small, scrap pieces. She also made tiny pairs of mittens and *mukluks* trimmed with beads and fur. Some were earrings. Others were jacket pulls. I bought a spotted seal-hair pretty trimmed with seed beads. Her proceeds will help pay her expenses.

On Labor Day weekend the camp overflowed with youth enjoying fleeting freedom before they returned to school. As they loaded belongings for their return to Anchorage, we volunteers attacked the vacated cabins. Using sanitizer, rags, the vacuum cleaner, and a lot of muscle we winterized the cabins. The bath house was scrubbed down, lost-and-found items collected, and laundry piled by the washers. We gathered in the kitchen to empty the refrigerator and pantry of leftovers that we would use for a potluck supper.

Staff and volunteers gathered around a couple of tables for a leisure meal and a time of reminiscing. Although we joked and teased each other, a sense of sadness at the waning of summer prevailed at dinner.

The final load of dishes was pulled from the dishwasher. Pots and pans were dried and put away. Lynne and I walked the dogs through the golden aspens and turning cottonwoods to the gravel road. Thick stands of fireweed blazed fucshia in the late-afternoon sun. Buds near the tips of the stalks had opened into orchid-like blossoms. Farther down toward the base of the stalks, blossoms had "gone to cotton", or seed. Soft, white fuzz floated on the breeze. It carried seed to burned-over or disturbed ground to be blanketed by snow.

Fireweed "gone to cotton" signaled the end of summer. The first snows already had fallen on the heights of the Chugach Mountains. This first snow, called "termination dust", indicated the termination of summer. Birds were migrating south. Time for us to begin our long trip home.

Alaska's awesome beauty and tiny pockets of eccentric Alaskans have a mysterious magnetism. Memories reinforced by photos will last a lifetime and tug at my heart to return. As I drove over the crest toward Tok, my beaded bracelet slipped down my arm to my wrist. Tiny golden beads, the color of the autumn aspens, formed a pattern of heart-shaped leaves. The zigzag pattern was the coral-fucshia of the fireweed. Turquoise beads reflected the clear, cloudless sky. The endless band of beads that encircled my wrist reminded me of Jeremiah 1:5 as a promise: God knew me before I was born. He will give me the desires of my heart (Ps. 37:4).

I wear the bracelet continually. If I never return to Alaska, I'll cherish memories, photos, and this bracelet. I know the Lord instilled in my heart the desire to make these trips. Who knows but what God's plan for me includes my making, as a volunteer, yet another trip to celebrate another birthday?

Appendix

Alaska Resources

AAA TourBook, Western Canada and Alaska, American Automobile Association, 1000 AAA Drive, Heathrow, FL, 1996.

Anderson, Richard D., *RVing in Alaska: Campgrounds & Services* (Anchorage: Billiken Press, 1998).

Armstrong, Robert H., *Alaska's Birds* (Anchorage: Alaska Northwest Books, 1998).

Armstrong, Robert H., *Alaska's Fish* (Anchorage: Alaska Northwest Books, 1996).

Barrett, Pam, Editor, *Insight Guide: Alaska* (New York: APA Publications, 2001).

Brown, Tricia, *The World-Famous Alaska Highway* (Golden, CO: Fulcrum Publishing, 2000).

Church, Mike & Terri, *Traveler's Guide to Alaska Camping* (Livingston, TX: Rolling Home Press, 2005).

Editors of the Milepost, *The Alaska Wilderness Milepost* (Anchorage: Alaska Northwest Books, 1989).

Elbert, Don, *Fascinating Alaska: Inhale the Essence* (Anchorage: Fascinating Alaska Publishing, 1999).

Ewing, Susan, *The Great Alaska Nature Fact Book* (Anchorage: Alaska Northwest Books, 1996).

Fodor's, *Pacific Northwest & Alaska* (Berkeley, CA: Fodor's Travel Publications, 1997).

Frommer's 2000, *Alaska with Cruises and Wilderness Trips*, (New York: IDG Books Worldwide, 2000).

Hancock, David, *Tlingit, Their Art and Culture* (Blain, WA: Hancock House Publishers, 2003).

Langson, Steve, *The Native People of Alaska* (Anchorage: Greatland Graphics, 1989).

Minshall, Sharlene "Charlie," *RVing North America: Silver, Single & Solo* (Livingston, TX: Gypsy Press, 1995).

Rand, Douglas, *Let's Go Alaska & the Pacific Northwest including Western Canada* (New York: St. Martin's Press, 1999).

Shields, Mary, *Sled Dog Trails* (Fairbanks: Pyrola Publishing, 1984).

Smith, Dave, *Alaska's Mammals* (Anchorage: Alaska Northwest Books, 1999).

Wohlforth, Charles P., *Alaska* (New York: Frommers IDG Books Worldwide, 2000).

Southwest Resources

Austin, Steven A., editor, *Grand Canyon, Monument to Catastrophe* (Santee, CA: Institute for Creation Research, 1994).

Barlow, Bernyce, *Sacred Sites of the West* (St. Paul, MN: Llewellyn Publications, 1997).

Fodor's, *Far West* (New York: Fodor's Modern Guides, 1983).

Parent, Laurence, *Scenic Driving, Texas.* (Helena, MT: Globe Pequot Press, 2005).

Samson, Karl, *Frommer's Comprehensive Travel Guide: Arizona '93-'94* (New York: Prentis Hall Travel, 1992).

Spangler, Sharon, *On Foot in the Grand Canyon: Hiking the Trails of the South Rim* (Boulder, CO: Pruett Publishing Co., 1989).

Spencer, Gwynne, *Places to Go with Children in the Southwest* (San Francisco: Chronicle Books, 1990).

Thybony, Scott, *Official Guide to Hiking the Grand Canyon*, (Canada: Grand Canyon Natural History Association, 2001.)

Vail, Tom, *Grand Canyon: A Different View* (Green Forest, AR, Master Books, 2003).

Zimmerman, Nancy, and Duane, Kit, *The American Southwest* (Fodor's Travel Publications, 1996.)

Traveler's Prayer

Old Gaelic Verse

May the road rise to greet you.
May the wind be always at your back.
May the sun shine warm upon your face.
The rains fall soft upon your fields.
And, until we meet again,
May God hold you in the palm of His hand.

Traveler or Tourist

"Open road travelers are made more than born. They are as different from theme-park tourists as anything you can imagine. Tourists rush; travelers mosey. Tourists look for souvenirs; travelers seek out the souvenir makers. Tourists want to see all the right places; travelers simply go into the country."

—Tom Snyder, Founder, Route 66 Association
Oxnard, CA
from the Introduction to *Route 66: The Mother Road* by Michael Wallis (New York: St. Martin's Press, 1990).

Conversions to Metric

Miles to Kilometers	Kilometers to Miles
1 mi. = 1.6 km	1 km = 0.62 mi.
10 mi. = 16 km	0 km = 6.2 mi.
20 mi. = 32 km	20 km = 12.4 mi.
30 mi. = 48 km	30 km = 18.6 mi.
50 mi. = 80 km	50 km = 31 mi.
100 mi. = 160 km	100 km = 62 mi.

1 quart = 0.95 liter	1 liter = 1.05 quarts	
1 gallon = 3.785 liter	1 liter = .2642 gallon	
10 gal. = 38 liters	10 liters = 2.6 gal.	
20 gal. = 76 liters	20 liters = 5.3 gal.	
	50 liters = 13.5 gal.	
	100 liters = 26.4 gal	

6 US gallons == 5 Canadian gallons

Temperature

Degrees Fahrenheit		Degrees Celsius
212	boiling	100
110		43
100		38
90		32
80		27
70		21
60		16
50		10
40		4
32	freezing	0
20		-7
10		-12
0		-18

Mile "O"—the beginning of the Alaska Highway. Dawson Creek, British Columbia

At left, spring welcomes visitors to the youth camp in Alaska where Carol volunteered. At right, In Fairbanks, AK, Chris points to the distance to Houston—4,682 miles!

Chris and a friend explore Exit Glacier.

Youth with World Changers repair a cabin in Alaska.

Photo Album

At right, Letia completes the beading on Carol's bracelet. Below, Chris with camp manager Anna and her daughter, Alysha, set off gold mining.

How to order more copies of
Grandma's Ultimate Road Trip

and Carol Weishampel's other books
CALL: 1-800-747-0738
FAX: 1-888-252-3022
Email: orders@hannibalbooks.com
Write: Hannibal Books
P.O. Box 461592
Garland, Texas 75046
Visit: *www.hannibalbooks.com*

Number of copies of *Grandma's Ultimate Road Trip* _____

Multiply total number of copies by $14.95 = _____

Number of copies of *Grandma's on the Go*

and *Adopting Darrell* _____

Multiply total number of copies by $9.95 = _____

Total cost of books: $_____

Add $3 for postage and handling for first book,

and add 50-cents for each additional book in the order.

Shipping total $_____

Texas residents add 8.25 % sales tax $_____

Total order $_____

number on check enclosed _____

credit card # _____ exp. date_____

(Visa, MasterCard, Discover, American Express accepted)

Name _____

Address _____

City State, Zip _____

Phone _____

Email _____